Mastering Professional Services

Mastering Professional Services

Thomas E. Lah

Westerville, OH

Copies of this book may be purchased directly from thomaslah.com

Company and product names mentioned herein are the trademarks or registered
trademarks of their respective owners.

Printed in the United States of America

First Printing

ISBN 0-9767184-0-5

Library of Congress Control Number: 2005901861

To Ken Beaudry, who took an early risk.

To Robert Caves, who took the same risk.

To my wife, Carole, who saw no risk.

Thomas E. Lah

July 2005

Contents

Sirens' Songs
and Scylla Fees

The Journey Continues

THE SIRENS' SONG REVISITED

In the summer of 2001, I sat in my study and wrote this introduction to the book *Building Professional Services: The Sirens' Song*:

> May 31st, 2001. Bill Gates grants a live interview. He appears on CNBC's "Squawk Box" to promote Microsoft's latest software release. Two minutes into the interview, host Mark Haines wants to know about Microsoft's service strategy: Isn't Mr. Gates concerned that Microsoft doesn't enjoy the same level of service revenues that Oracle and IBM do? Mr. Gates responds that Microsoft is now offering new consulting services.
>
> A quick search on **www.google.com** using the key words "Professional Services" and "Product" yields hundreds of Web sites for technology product companies also offering professional services. Besides Oracle and IBM, the who's who list includes hardware manufacturers Alcatel, Aspect, Compaq, EMC, HP, Lucent, Nortel, and Sun; software makers PeopleSoft, Sybase, WebCT, Pumatech, and Red Hat. All of these technology companies have heard it. They can't ignore it. The Sirens' song of services.

Several years later, I sit in my study and craft the introduction to this book. In this time, the business headlines have heralded the following:

- Lucent Looks Longingly at Services[1]
- EMC Eyes Storage Consulting Business[2]
- New Siebel CEO Shifts Company Focus from Products to Services[3]

---

1. *Business Week Online,* December 19, 2002.
2. *InfoWorld,* July 7, 2002.
3. *AMR Research,* October 14, 2004.

- HP Combines Services, Enterprise Divisions[4]
- IBM Grabs Consulting Giant for $3.5 Billion[5]
- Novell Sews Up Cambridge Technology Partners[6]
- What Dell Can Sell: Let the Machines Take Care of the Transactions, the Real Growth Is in Professional Services[7]

In the twenty-first century, the Sirens' song of services has risen to a shrill that cannot be ignored. Companies of all sizes and ages and from all industries are exploring their service opportunities. The economic downturn that began in 2001 has done nothing but accelerate the desire to pursue services. Battered product companies in industries such as enterprise storage, database software, and telecommunications equipment have all turned to offering services. In general, the reasons for building service capabilities have remained constant since *The Sirens' Song* was published:

Revenue: Companies continue to seek new revenue streams as sales from traditional product lines have slowed dramatically.

Relationships: Companies want to build deeper, more strategic relationships with their customers. Value-added services are a mechanism that enables more complete account relationships.

Request: Customers continue to whittle the number of vendors they want to deal with. With reduced I/T staffs, corporations do not have the resources to manage multiple vendors providing pieces of a solution. Customers need central contacts that can solve problems. Customers want one throat to choke.

So with the promises of new revenue, deeper customer relationships, and improved customer satisfaction all filling the sails, the product companies race on—before the brisk winds of services.

In reality, the thought of building professional services (PS) has moved beyond the "nice to have" premise for many product companies. Advanced service capabilities have become a required asset in their strategic arsenals. In September of 2004, I hosted a seminar for service executives at the Ohio State University. Attending were service leaders from across the United States. Hitachi Data Systems, Lucent, Computer Associates, Hyperion, EMC, Convergys, and IKON were a few of the companies represented. At the conference,

---

4. *Mercury News,* December 10, 2003.

5. *CNET News.com,* July 30, 2002.

6. *Infoworld,* July 11, 2001.

7. *Always-On Network,* January 21, 2004.

FIGURE I.1 Importance of PS

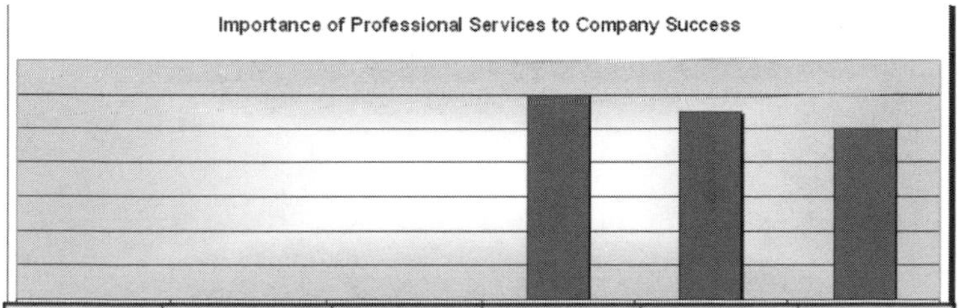

Importance of Professional Services to Company Success

1	2	3	4	5	6
NO IMPACT	SOME IMPACT	GROWING IMPACT	REQUIRED: By Market	REQUIRED: By Business	REQUIRED: By Market & Business
PS makes no difference in our ability to compete or make money.	PS capabilities are nice, but not a business or market requirement.	Importance of PS to market success is growing.	Some level of PS capabilities are required to compete in our marketplace.	PS is becoming a critical part of the business mix (revenues and margins).	PS is a significant business line that defines our value proposition to the marketplace.

I asked the forty-six senior managers how important professional service capabilities had become to the ultimate success of their companies. Figure I.1 summarizes the survey results. As can be seen, offering PS has become a requirement for company success. Although the sample is small, the trend is real. In the last economic downturn, PS revenues and margins became a critical component for many product companies.

How critical have service revenues become? Let's look at some unbelievable industry data. I reviewed the 10K's of eighteen product technology companies from 1999 through 2004: nine hardware companies and nine software companies. I picked a "who's who" list. For the hardware companies, I reviewed:

1. Avaya
2. Cisco
3. EMC Corporation
4. HP
5. IBM
6. Lucent
7. Sun Microsystems
8. Unisys
9. Xerox

For software companies, I reviewed:

1. BEA
2. Business Objects
3. Hyperion
4. Novell
5. Oracle Corporation
6. Progress Software
7. Siebel Systems
8. Symantec Corporation
9. Veritas

For each of these companies, I gathered the following data:

- Total Revenues
- Total Revenues from Services
- Reported Gross Margin Dollars (for the entire company)
- Net Income Dollars
- Percentage of company revenues that come from services
- Gross margin %
- Net Income %

As an example, Table I.1 provides a snapshot of the 1999 data for the nine hardware companies.

With this data from their 10-Ks, I mapped the average percentage of revenues these eighteen companies have received from services starting in 1999 and ending in 2004. Figure I.2 maps the trends for hardware companies. Figure I.3 provides the same trend data for the software companies.

From Figures I.2 and I.3, we can see an ever-increasing percentage of revenues coming from services. I would have loved to include both Dell and Microsoft in these averages, but alas, they currently do not report what percentage of revenues comes from products vs. services. However, with Dell's emphasis on managed services and Microsoft's incubation of Microsoft Consulting Services, I can't imagine these companies would have significantly lowered the calculated averages and veered from the evident trend.

TABLE I.1 Industry Data

Company	Type	1999 Total Revenue		Service Revenue		Gross Margin		Net Income		Service %	Gross Margin %	Profit %
IBM	HDW	$	87,548	$	32,130	$	31,929	$	7,712	37%	36%	9%
HP	HDW	$	42,370	$	6,255	$	12,499	$	3,688	15%	29%	9%
Cisco	HDW	$	12,173	$	1,217	$	7,914	$	2,023	10%	65%	17%
Xerox	HDW	$	19,567	$	3,662	$	8,472	$	1,908	19%	43%	10%
Sun Microsystems	HDW	$	11,806	$	1,641	$	6,136	$	1,520	14%	52%	13%
Lucent	HDW	$	26,993	$	4,589	$	18,615	$	3,786	17%	69%	14%
EMC Corporation	HDW	$	6,715	$	362	$	3,458	$	1,010	5%	51%	15%
Unisys	HDW	$	7,544	$	4,526	$	2,684	$	510	60%	36%	7%
Avaya	HDW	$	8,286	$	1,906	$	3,712	$	282	23%	45%	3%
		$	223,002	$	56,289	$	95,419	$	22,439	22%	47%	11%

FIGURE I.2 Average Percentage of Revenue from Services for 9 Hardware Companies

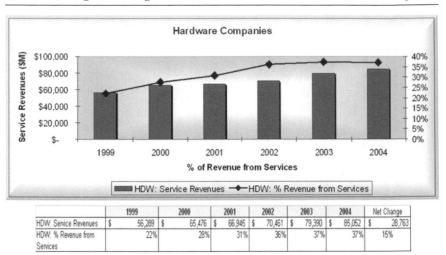

	1999	2000	2001	2002	2003	2004	Net Change
HDW: Service Revenues	$ 56,289	$ 65,476	$ 66,945	$ 70,461	$ 79,390	$ 85,052	$ 28,763
HDW: % Revenue from Services	22%	28%	31%	36%	37%	37%	15%

FIGURE I.3 Average Percentage of Revenue from Services for 9 Software Companies

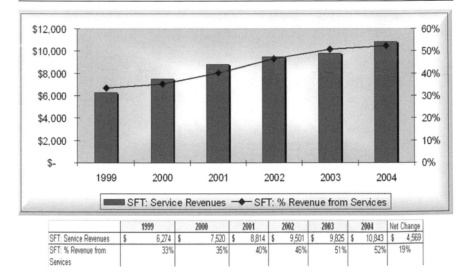

	1999	2000	2001	2002	2003	2004	Net Change
SFT: Service Revenues	$ 6,274	$ 7,520	$ 8,814	$ 9,501	$ 9,825	$ 10,843	$ 4,569
SFT: % Revenue from Services	33%	35%	40%	46%	51%	52%	19%

Now, for the most astounding aspect of the data I collected. When summarizing the data for each year, I tracked overall revenues and service revenues. When summarizing this data, I stumbled on two incredible facts:

1. 98% of revenue growth from 1999–2004 for the nine hardware companies listed can be attributed to services

2. 74% of the revenue growth from 1999–2004 for the nine software companies listed can be attributed to services

Table I.2 documents the summary data that supports these findings. Table I.3 documents the growth mix more dramatically.

Blending the data from these eighteen hardware and software companies together, we can make the following statement:

> Three-fourths of the economic growth these eighteen technology companies experienced from 1999 to 2004 can be attributed to services. ■

TABLE I.3 Economic Growth Mix

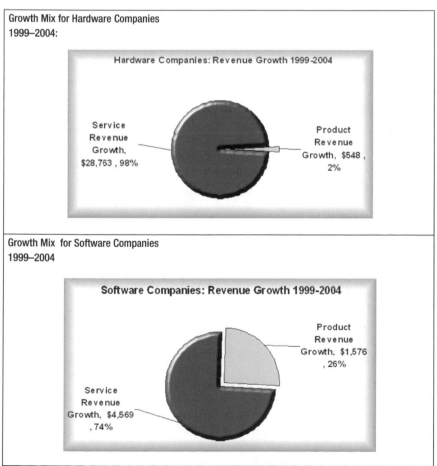

TABLE I.2 Economic Growth Trends

	1999	2000	2001	2002	2003	2004	Net Change	Revenue Growth from Services
HDW: Revenues	$ 223,002	$ 238,246	$ 225,719	$ 212,787	$ 232,618	$ 252,313	$ 29,311	
HDW: Service Revenues	$ 56,289	$ 65,476	$ 66,945	$ 70,461	$ 79,390	$ 85,052	$ 28,763	98%
HDW: % Revenue from Services	22%	28%	31%	36%	37%	37%	15%	
HDW: Gross Margin %	47%	44%	35%	37%	41%	42%	-5%	
HDW: Net Income %	11%	7%	-6%	-12%	1%	8%	-3%	
SFT: Revenues	$ 13,356	$ 16,604	$ 18,366	$ 17,215	$ 17,402	$ 19,501	$ 6,145	
SFT: Service Revenues	$ 6,274	$ 7,520	$ 8,814	$ 9,501	$ 9,825	$ 10,843	$ 4,569	74%
SFT: Gross Margin %	76%	76%	75%	74%	75%	69%	-8%	
SFT: % Revenue from Services	33%	35%	40%	49%	52%	52%	19%	
SFT: Net Income %	-1%	8%	-1%	2%	8%	12%	13%	

This data is incredible. Yes, I realize the service component comprises support services and managed services as well as professional services. If I could report what percentage of the service revenue growth could be attributed to professional services I would. Unfortunately, only twenty-eight of the largest ninety-two technology providers I recently reviewed report actual professional services revenues. This means less than one-third of the largest technology companies are reporting the financial health of their specific service lines.

Are the trends shown in these figures and tables a short-term anomaly? Will the importance of PS revenues and margins fade with the next big high-tech boom? In my opinion—not likely.

IT AND CHANGING SEAS

The way Fortune 2000 companies purchase technology is dramatically different today than it was in the late 1990s. Companies have evolved through three distinct generations of technology-purchasing behavior. Table I.4 documents these changes over time.

When technology was first available, because it was complex and few knew how to make it work, large companies needed help understanding how to implement and leverage it. Technology buyers had to rely on vendors like IBM

TABLE I.4 Three Generations of Technology Purchasing

Generation	Name	Time Period	Success Factors	Predominant Companies
1st	Mainframe	1960s–early 1980s	• Technology leadership • Account management	IBM, Unisys, Wang
2nd	Open systems	Late 1980s – Late 1990s	• Technology innovation • Channel distribution • Product adoption	Sun, Cisco, EMC, Oracle
3rd	Open solutions	2000–2004	• Business impact	IBM, Accenture

and Unisys to manage the entire mess—cradle to grave. To be successful in this first generation, a technology provider needed to demonstrate enough technical leadership to convince the customer it was not severely behind what other vendors could provide. Vendors learned that their real lever was account management and keeping the customer whole. As long as a customer was not grossly dissatisfied, its cost to switch technology vendors was just too high. This was the *mainframe* generation.

By the late 1980s, however, large companies were getting fed up. They were locked into mainframe providers that were charging top dollar for minimal innovation. Thus the *open systems* generation was born. Companies wanted the flexibility to choose multiple vendors, and they wanted rapid technical innovation at ever lower price points. To be successful during this generation, a product vendor needed to demonstrate superior "speeds and feeds." The company also needed to drive rapid adoption of its products because the company with the largest install base became the industry standard. This rapid adoption required that the vendor be adept at working multiple channels. During this second generation, large companies swelled their internal IT staffs to handle the ever-increasing complexity of the IT environment. Yes, technical innovation was occurring at break-neck speeds—but at what cost to the company?

When the economy slowed in 2001, many a company lost its appetite for large technology investments. What was all this hardware and software they had purchased? They were paying *lots* of money for I/T, but what exactly did they get for it? And, oh yeah, they found they really couldn't afford an army of expensive technologists to keep it all strapped together. So the cutting began. The nation's information technology industry lost 403,300 jobs between March of 2001, when the recession began, and April of 2004.[8] IT product sales slowed to a trickle. And once again, Fortune 2000 companies began to rethink how they purchased technology. Although they had shattered the shackles of the mainframe days, now *all* the risk was on them. In this world of open systems they had created, when stuff broke, vendors pointed fingers, stuff stayed broken, and CIOs were changed. In the late 1990s, the average tenure of a CIO was often reported to be eighteen months.

Thus the third generation of technology-purchasing behavior was ushered in. Companies still wanted the flexibility to mix and match vendors; they didn't want to go back to the days of sourcing technology to one vendor. Still, they also didn't want all the risk. They wanted product vendors to step up and share some of the risk. In short, companies now want the best of both worlds:

---

8. "High-Tech Job Market Still Bleak—Report," *Information Week*, September 15, 2004.

FIGURE I.4 Three Generations

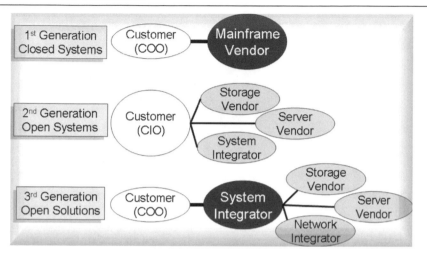

flexibility and security. To achieve this desired state, companies are restricting vendors to a select few, and they are forcing those vendors to deliver complete, viable business solutions. By 2002, customers and vendors alike were well into the *open solutions* generation. The concepts of becoming a "trusted partner" and "solution partner" were no longer "nice to have" attributes for product companies—they are "must haves."

Figure I.4 depicts the transition through the three generations.

Product vendors and buyers are now entering a fourth generation of purchasing behavior. Technology markets are rapidly migrating from *open solutions* to *closed solutions*. In a closed solution environment, buyers' system integrators and product vendors bind together to create a tightly integrated solution ecosystem. This ecosystem is designed to deliver the required business functionality with minimal risk. Not as closed and inflexible as the old mainframe days, but not as open and risky as the open systems days. For traditional product vendors, this fourth generation creates incredible risk. Their product needs to be integrated into these evolving ecosystems. Product feature functionality does not guarantee acceptance. More important, feature functionality does not guarantee the vendor's desired margin! In this fourth generation, service capabilities become even more critical. Figure I.5 illustrates this evolving generation. The product company's professional services capabilities help it integrate its products into the solution ecosystem. Sometimes the services are delivered directly to the customer. Sometimes the services are played into a system integrator that is responsible for the total solution. Without the service capabilities, the product vendor runs the risk of being a replaceable widget.

FIGURE I.5 The Closed Solutions Ecosystem

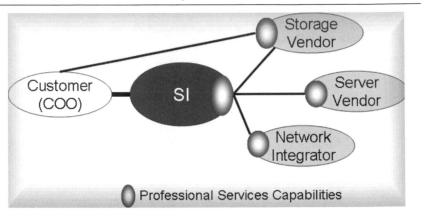

ONE SIMPLE QUESTION

Amid the new realities of technology purchasing, every traditional product company has one fundamental question it must answer regarding corporate strategy:

> Will our company be a "product provider" or a "solution provider"? ■

A *product provider* delivers products to the marketplace and expects others to provide services and solutions around those products. A *solution provider* assumes responsibility for product performance and focuses on delivering a complete solution to the customer.

A product provider focuses on product innovation and is judged by product revenues. The ability to identify new product markets is a critical skill. Finally, a product provider is judged by product revenues. A perfect example of such a company is Cisco Systems. Yes, Cisco has service revenues, but they represent less than 25% of total company revenues. When product revenues are off and service revenues are up, Cisco is criticized by Wall Street analysts. Cisco is relentless in its pursuit of new product markets and brutal in its ability to quickly dominate them (for examples, look at the company's entrance into IP Telephony and SAN switching).

A solution provider not only delivers the core product, but it also builds the software and services required to turn that product into a business solution. The ability to provide a complete solution is the critical skill for solution providers and they will be judged by both their product and service revenues. For example, EMC was not punished by Wall Street when CEO Joseph Tucci announced that only 50% of future revenues would be coming from traditional hardware products. Why? Because he painted it in the context of EMC becoming a successful solution provider. In fact, by the end of 2004, Tucci had become a business-media darling. Just look at some of the headlines he has received:

- Joseph Tucci, EMC—The only company dedicating itself 100 percent to comprehensive networked storage solutions[9]
- CEO Visions: Trends, from Storage to Always-on[10]
- The Vision Thing: EMC's quest for new revenues takes it into the world of consulting[11]
- Managers Who Hit Their Marks[12]

Figure I.6 is a flow chart of a product company's critical strategic decision-making regarding its concentration on solutions or products. After reviewing so many service strategies, I cannot help but wonder how many companies fail to make such a conscious decision. My gut tells me a majority of companies allow the decision to be made for them by the marketplace. Did Lucent or Siebel intentionally morph into solution providers or did ugly market realities drag them there? By deciding if its company is to be a product or a solution provider, a management team dramatically improves its company's chances for success in today's marketplace.

FIGURE I.6 One Critical Question

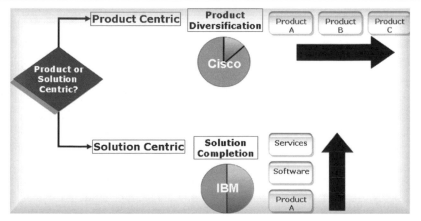

---

9. *Var Business,* September 6, 2002.

10. *Information Week,* January 27, 2003.

11. *Forbes,* October 18, 2004.

12. *Business Week,* January 10, 2005.

PRICE OF ADMISSION, PRICE OF SUCCESS

There are no easy answers when deciding if your company should be a product provider or a solution provider. Multiple variables are in play, including:

- What customers want
- What competitors are doing
- What your company is capable of

In this book, I provide frameworks that can assist a management team through this critical dialogue. Keep in mind, I do not believe every product-centric company should endeavor to become a solution-centric company. In fact, for some product companies, attempting the feat can be the kiss of death.

Regardless of the decision your management team makes, many product-centric companies are being dragged into becoming solution centric. There are two overriding reasons that force the transition:

- Price of admission
- Price of success

Price of Admission

In this fourth generation of how companies purchase technology, product-centric companies are being forced by their customers to provide complete solutions. This customer-driven requirement is forcing product companies to respond by providing more services. At some point, a product company must accept the fact that its target market requires it to be a solution provider. I call this driver "the price of admission." Take a hard look at your target markets and how your competitors are serving customers. Has service become a price of admission? A perfect example of this scenario is how companies buy computer servers. In the early 1990s, companies were looking for beefy servers that could run lots of applications. Scalability and performance were the key drivers. By 2000, however, companies were much more interested in the total cost of ownership, reliability, and serviceability of the servers. This shift in requirements reduced the market share of some server manufacturers such as Silicon Graphics and has prevented some technology leaders such as Apple from succeeding in this market. Being a solution provider has become a cost of admission. Dell understands this completely and is rounding out its service portfolio to compete against HP and IBM.

Price of Success

The price of success is the second key driver that forces traditional product-centric companies to migrate toward solutions. As a product company grows, it needs additional sources of revenue to feed it. This revenue can come from three sources:

- Growth in current product markets
- Growth in new product markets
- Growth in solutions

If a product company has a great product for a growing market, life is great. But what happens when that market matures? The product company must jump into a new product market or grab more revenue from the mature market. A product company can grab more revenue from a mature market by providing more of the solution (software, services, etc.). Look at EMC's diversification into software and services for an example of a company that is providing more of the solution to offset a maturing marketplace. Lucent's hard bet on services is also a result of this scenario.

Should your company move from being product focused to being solution focused? There is no easy answer, but if your customers now require solutions, your market is maturing, and you do not have a new product market to probe, you should at least be exploring the possibility. ∎

ENTERPRISE SOFTWARE: AN EXAMPLE OF SHIFTING SEAS

To explore this point of a changing marketplace, let's drill down on two enterprise software companies: Oracle Systems and Siebel Systems . The traditional business models of enterprise software companies required that their largest revenue stream was from license sales. More important, this was also touted as the highest margin activity the companies could engage in. Hell, it was just the cost of printing a CD! Software license sales for software companies are typically reported to sustain 60–90% gross margins. After the license sale, the software company made great money on lucrative support contracts. Finally, some value-added professional services were thrown in to assure product adoption. Table I.5 documents this using numbers from both Oracle and Siebel in 1999.

TABLE I.5 Enterprise Software Revenue Mix: 1999

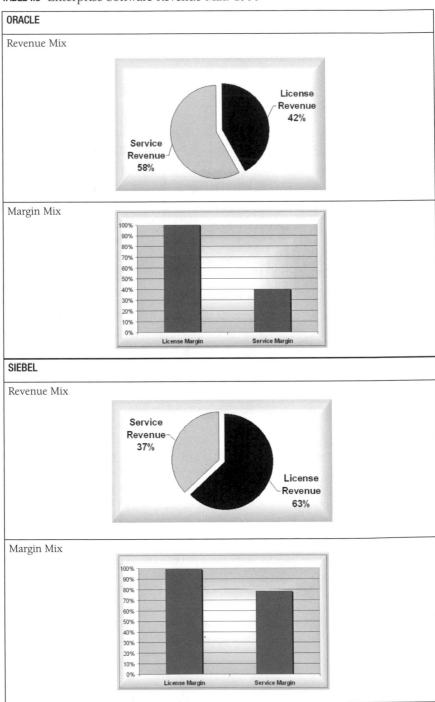

Now jump forward in the purchasing environment. Software license sales have stalled. Support contracts are still very lucrative, but customers are looking for ways to reduce those costs. Where are software companies looking for new sources of revenue and margin? Professional services, of course. The revenue mix has already dramatically shifted for Oracle and Seibel. By 2003, we see a model of thirds. Only a third of the revenue comes from traditional license sales. Two-thirds of the revenue now comes from services. Table I.6 documents this dramatic shift in revenue streams and reinforces the trend introduced earlier in Figure I.2.

This shift in revenue streams has caused incredible angst in the software industry. In 2004, many software companies are still structured and optimized to pursue the old revenue model. This incongruity creates some ugly financial dynamics.

Show Me the Margin

So far, this introduction has documented the significant shift the technology industry has experienced from product-centric business mixes to more solution-centric business mixes. This introduction has also illustrated why this shift is most likely permanent. Now, for the brutal financial reality of this shift.

In 1999, a software company probably had a business mix that looked something like Figure I.7. This mix shows 65% of company revenues coming from high-margin product licenses. Twenty-five percent of revenue came from high-margin support and only 10% of company revenues came from relatively low-margin PS revenues. Blended together, this mix produced a 76% gross-margin business.

Now, forward to 2004, Figure I.8 shows this evolving solution-centric mix. Product revenues have shrunk to 43% of total company revenues. Support

FIGURE I.7 1999 Software Company Business Mix

	Mix	Margin	Contribution	Blended
Product	65%	94%	61%	
Support	25%	53%	13%	
PS	10%	20%	2%	
Consulting	0%	0%	0%	
Outsourcing	0%	0%	0%	
Managed	0%	0%	0%	
	100%			76%

TABLE I.6 Enterprise Software Revenue Mix: 2004

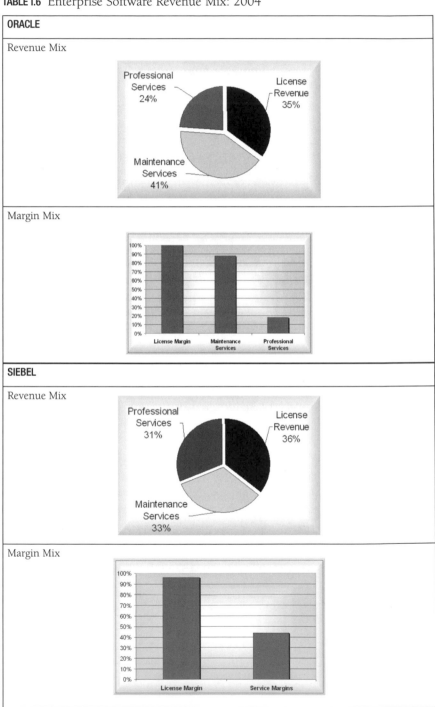

FIGURE I.8 2004 Software Company Business Mix

	Mix	Margin	Contribution	Blended
Product	43%	93%	40%	
Support	39%	65%	25%	
PS	10%	20%	2%	
Consulting	8%	25%	2%	
Outsourcing	0%	15%	0%	
Managed	0%	30%	0%	
	100%			69%

service is the bright spot. Support service revenues have grown and the margins have improved! PS and Consulting revenues are also increasing—but margins are lagging. This new mix throws off significantly less gross-margin dollars. This is potentially bad for the bottom line.

So, where does it go from here? I believe product revenues will continue to become less of the overall business mix. Support margins, which have improved over the past few years, will finally face pressure. To improve the overall company margin, technology companies will need to deliver actual business success—not just lines of code. To meet this objective, the companies will need to excel at value-added services that bring product capabilities to life in the customer's specific environment. Technology companies will need to deliver these value-added services profitably. Table I.7 provides an example of what the future revenue streams may look like for software companies. Figure I.9 documents the contribution margin this type of business mix would generate. As we can see, the continued decline in gross margins continues. Now, how many technology companies are prepared to operate with a company portfolio that only generates 49% in gross margin dollars? How many technology companies are capable of operating their professional services, consulting services, and managed service revenue streams profitably?

Figure I.10 summarizes the overarching "contribution shift" being experienced by technology companies. Instead of contribution coming from high-margin product and support revenue streams, contributions need to come from the lower-margin professional services, consulting services, and managed services. As this shift to the right continues, a successful and sustainable professional services offering becomes ever more important to the overall viability of the product company.

FIGURE I.9 Future Margin Mix

	Mix	Margin	Cont.	
Product	30%	75%	23%	
Support	20%	50%	10%	
PS	20%	25%	5%	
Consulting	10%	35%	4%	
Managed	20%	40%	8%	
	100%			**49%**

Figure I.10 Shifting Contributions

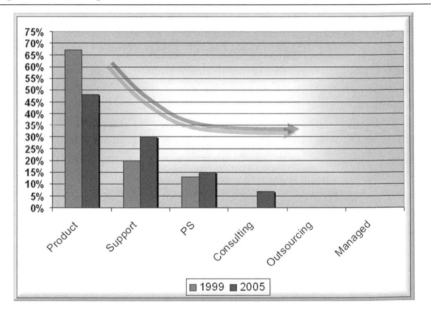

TABLE I.7 Possible Future Revenue Mix for Enterprise Software Companies

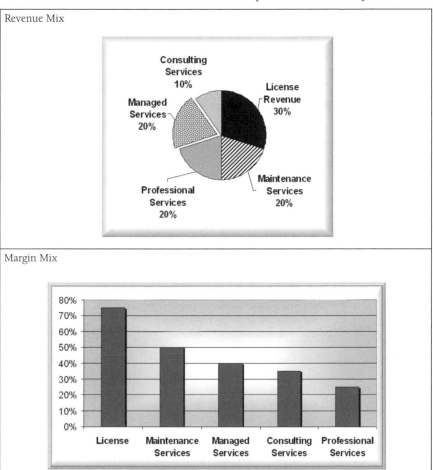

SCYLLA FEES

I have spent this introduction discussing why services have become such an important lever to product-centric companies. I have documented the financial ramifications of this shift in importance. At this point, I hope you are clearly convinced that all management teams should be *consciously* discussing what their professional service strategy should be. It is now time to move on to the details of that strategy discussion. But before I do that, I want to close this introduction with a look at a key theme of this book.

In *Building Professional Services*, I introduced the metaphor of the Sirens' Song of Services. I pointed out how attractive service opportunities (like the beautiful voices of the Sirens in Homer's *Odyssey*) can become perilous endeavors when pursued by product companies (just as the Sirens in actuality were deadly monsters awaiting reckless sailors).

In this book, I will use another challenge faced by Odysseus to help illustrate my thinking. As a reminder, Odysseus is a brave, intelligent Greek king who spends twenty years trying to get home to Ithaca after serving in the Trojan War. Throughout his saga, he encounters many daunting challenges. Every time it appears he is trapped, Odysseus uses his cunning to escape. The story of the Sirens is a perfect example. The Sirens have the most beautiful singing voices. But sailors who respond to the Sirens' voices are driven mad and steer their ships into the boulders. Odysseus is determined to hear what no man has heard and still survive. So, he devises a unique plan. His crew members plug their ears with wax. Odysseus, however, does not plug his ears. Instead, he has himself strapped to the mast of the ship. As they sail past the Sirens, Odysseus hears their song, goes temporarily insane, but cannot harm anyone. Rather ingenious.

The Sirens metaphor serves as a cautionary tale for those building professional services within a product company. The product company must beware of tactics that sound wonderful, but in reality are dangerous. Knowledge, ingenuity, and discipline are the skills that will help the management team avoid the boulders.

We now move beyond challenges where wits alone can be applied to avoid pain. We turn our focus to areas of unavoidable pain. To finally arrive home, the last challenge faced by Odysseus involved a terrible choice between two evils. Odysseus had to pass through a section of the sea that was inhabited by two monsters: Charybdis (pronounced Kuh-rib-dis) and Scylla (pronounced Sil-uh). Charybdis was a massive monster that sucked down water, creating a wide whirlpool that could not be escaped. To try to sail past Charybdis meant certain death. Scylla was a multiheaded beast that picked off sailors as their ship went by. A costly encounter (in terms of headcount), but the ship could survive. In all the previous dangers that faced Odysseus, he had always found a clever way out so when faced with this dilemma, Odysseus's natural approach was to look for the loophole. How could he sail past both creatures without losing any sailors? But the gods assured him there was no clever trick available this time—a price had to be paid. In fact, most sailors avoided the teeth of Scylla for the seemingly safe water of Charybdis's lair—only to be sucked down to their death. Odysseus, this time you must pay the price. And so Odysseus avoided the calm waters of Charybdis and sailed directly by the cliffs that housed Scylla. The maneuver cost six lives—but the ship remained intact and the journey continued.

> I will be focusing on decisions a product-centric management team must face when there are no easy outs—no silver bullets. ■

When creating a viable professional services strategy, a management team must make difficult choices. The team must give up something to achieve a greater endgame. I call these conscious sacrifices "Scylla's Fees." They are unavoidable. For every Scylla Fee I believe an organization must pay there is a *Charybdis Consequence,* the inevitable result of attempting to take the easy way out when facing difficult decisions. This path of least resistance at first appears painless, but the results are ultimately catastrophic.

In today's American style of management, we are all looking for silver bullets. Quick fixes. Impact today. But for some challenges, there are no painless choices. Whether it is the price of admission, the price of success, or simply the price of survival, building a successful services business requires sacrifice.

We may not like that answer—just as Odysseus hated the reality that some of his sailors would be lost. To date, I have not met a product company executive gleeful to see declining product margins. But, as Odysseus realized, the harsh realities of any situation should be squarely faced. Sacrifices should be calculated and strategic. Every item given up should result in a larger, long-term gain. It is an illusion to think a product company can build a successful service business at no cost. Pay Scylla Fees, or say hello to Charybdis.

Thomas E. Lah
June 2005

Chapter | One

Strategy, Structure, Culture

MARGIN KNOTS

Before we explore the concept of developing an effective professional service strategy in complete and gory detail, I want to introduce an overarching framework I use when working with professional service management teams.

When I first meet a professional service management team, the managers are in one of three scenarios. In the first scenario, the team is being asked to build a brand-new professional service organization. In the second scenario, the team is already managing a successful professional service business. In this situation, the management team is seeking to tune existing processes to improve financial performance. In the final scenario, the management team is in charge of a professional services business that is missing financial objectives and struggling. It is this last scenario I am most often called to address. I believe this last scenario is most prevalent in the industry. For how many management teams have a truly blank canvas to start? And how many management teams have consistently met or exceeded their financial objectives for professional services over the past three years? In February of 2004, I was hosting an executive education session on building professional services for leaders from CNT, Emerson, Hitachi Data Systems, Hyperion, SAP, StoragTek, and Xerox. I asked the attendees to rate the current financial performance of their PS function. Figure 1.1 documents the results.Although the sampling size is small I believe the results are indicative of the industry. Many product companies struggle with the financial performance of their PS function.

Regardless of the current state the professional services management teams are facing, there is one common concern they express: How can they improve their margins? Even before they reach the issue of bottom-line profitability, they face this issue of improving gross margins. If there is no margin, there clearly can be no profits.

1

FIGURE 1.1 PS Financial Performance

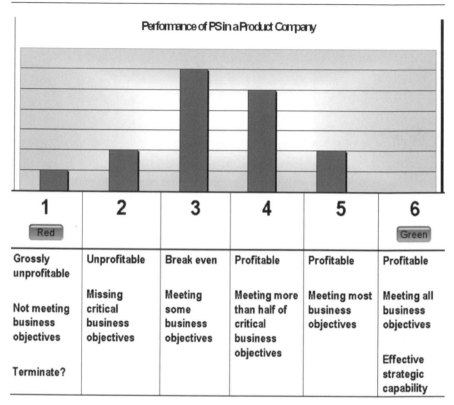

1	2	3	4	5	6
Red					Green
Grossly unprofitable	Unprofitable	Break even	Profitable	Profitable	Profitable
Not meeting business objectives	Missing critical business objectives	Meeting some business objectives	Meeting more than half of critical business objectives	Meeting most business objectives	Meeting all business objectives
Terminate?					Effective strategic capability

To help address this concern over improving gross margin, I like to offer a simple visual aid: a single rope. Take this symbolic rope and stretch it tight. In Figure 1.2, this rope symbolizes the target gross margin a professional services business would like to achieve.

Now, visualize what happens when the rope becomes knotted: It gets shorter. The more knots in the rope, the shorter it becomes. Let's use this knotted rope to represent the actual gross margin the professional service business is achieving. The difference in the two ropes is shown in Figure 1.3.

FIGURE 1.2   Target Gross Margin

Target Margin

FIGURE 1.3   Actual Gross Margin

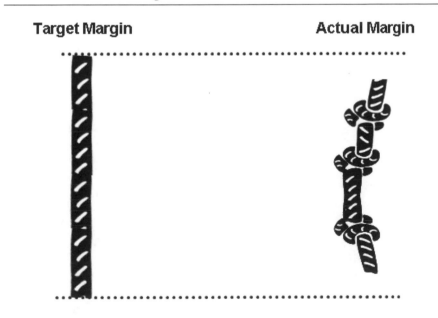

Target Margin   **Actual Margin**

Using this analogy, the astute management team should ask three questions:

1. What is causing these "margin knots"? (What is reducing our gross margin?)
2. Which ones are the biggest? (Which knots are having the greatest adverse affect on the gross margin?)
3. How do we untie them? (How do we fix these issues to improve gross margin?)

The answers to these and other questions drive a prioritized list of what to fix first, based on the effort required to untie the knot and the impact expected when the knot is removed. So far, so good.

So let's focus on the first question asked: What is causing these margin knots? For a professional service organization within a product company, there are three areas in which these knots can be created, reducing overall margin:

- Strategy
- Structure
- Culture

These are shown in Figure 1.4. Let's explore each of these areas in some detail.

FIGURE 1.4   Margin Knot Categories

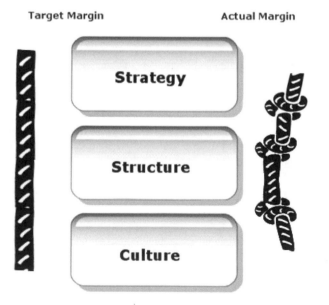

STRATEGY

The first area that can cause strife to a professional services management team is the overall strategy for the business unit. Strategy is a broad term that quickly becomes muddied. Let's try to keep it simple. According to Robert M. Grant in *Contemporary Strategy Analysis*, there are two types of fundamental strategies a management team must deal with:

- Corporate strategy: What markets are we pursuing?
- Business strategy: How will we compete in those target markets?[1]

Corporate strategy is set first. Where can this company make money? From there, the management team moves to business strategy. How do we need to operate to support our corporate strategy? Figure 1.5 diagrams this universal model.

In terms of professional services within a product company, both corporate and business strategies need to be addressed. To define corporate strategy, a management team must answer the following questions:

- What markets do we want PS to pursue?
- What do we want PS to achieve in those target markets?
- What services do those markets need?
- How do those markets like to purchase professional services?

FIGURE 1.5 Corporate and Business Strategy

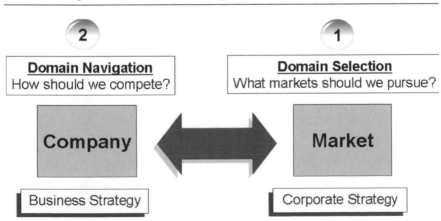

---

1. Robert M. Grant, *Contemporary Strategy Analysis: Concepts, Techniques, Applications* (Cambridge, MA: Blackwell Publishers, 2002), p. 12.

To define business strategy, the management team must answer the following questions:

- What is the financial business model for the business unit?
- What financial objectives make sense?
- How will we differentiate our service offerings?
- What skills and positions will be core to the PS organization?
- What partners will we use?
- How will we scale delivery capability?

These are examples of the types of questions that need to be addressed at a strategic level by the senior management team. It is when these questions are *not* answered that margin knots begin to occur. By having no clear market objectives, PS can become misaligned, abused, or ostracized within a product company. The absence of an achievable financial model causes PS results to seem a continuous disappointment. Finally, an unclear vision on what services should be developed negatively impacts both alignment and financial performance.

STRUCTURE

The second area that impacts the gross margin of a PS business is structure. Here, we focus on the "how." How are you executing the business of professional services at your company? This reflects organizational effectiveness. There are multiple models on organizational effectiveness from folks like Gartner and McKinsey. Most models include the following parameters that need to be managed:

- Organizational structure (design)
- Business processes
- Employee skills
- Metrics
- Compensation policy

Figure 1.6 shows a model I use when assessing the maturity of PS organizations. I rate the different boxes red, yellow, or green, based on maturity. As I have told many product company executives: *"If you make the call on Friday to become solution-centric, on Monday all of these structural issues will not be taken care of. It takes time, energy, and money to move these ratings from red to yellow to green."*

FIGURE 1.6 Organizational Effectiveness

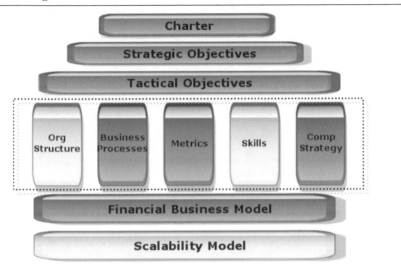

When product companies underinvest or, more likely, don't invest at all in these structural components of the PS business, margin is impacted. And often, the knots are large.

CULTURE

The final broad area that creates margin knots for PS is culture. At this time, we are referring to the intangible "why." Why doesn't consulting seem to work exactly the same at a product company as it does in independent consulting companies? Why is it such heavy lifting? We are now into the discipline of "human physics" where there are never easy or concise answers. However, there are several issues that are clearly identifiable in this area.

First of all, never forget that you are immersed in a product-centric culture. This culture is optimized to design, develop, and sell tangible products. Services and the unique culture that comes with services are struggling to get recognition.

Second, the existing value system of the company will most likely not be kind to a new or struggling PS business. In *The Innovator's Dilemma*, Clayton M. Christensen does a fantastic job of documenting how a company culture can inhibit success in new markets.

> The values of an organization are the criteria by which decisions about priorities are made.

The values of successful firms tend to evolve in a predictable fashion in at least two dimensions. The first relates to acceptable gross margins. As companies add features and functionality to their products and services in order to capture more attractive customers in premium tiers of their markets, they often add overhead cost. As a result, gross margins that at one point were quite attractive, at a later point seem unattractive.[2]

This aversion that Christensen identifies is directly applicable to a fledgling professional service business that is experiencing poor gross margins and represents minimal revenue to the company.

In *Who Says Elephants Can't Dance?* Louis Gerstner comments on the reality that strategy and structure alone will not create desired change:

> Execution is all about translating strategies into action programs and measuring results. It's detailed, it's complicated, and it requires a deep understanding of where the institution is today and how far away it is from where it needs to go. Proper execution involves building measurable targets and holding people accountable for them.

> But, most of all, it usually requires that the organization do something different, value something more than it has in the past, acquire skills it doesn't have, and move more quickly and effectively in day-to-day relationships with customers, suppliers, and distributors. All of this spells change, and companies don't like to change because individuals don't like to change.[3]

Finally, how a product company has historically positioned itself in its markets and completed its value proposition to customers has immense impact on how readily PS will be accepted throughout the company. If a company has historically leveraged service partners heavily, the presence of PS is unsettling. If the product company has a long history of touching customers directly, PS can be more readily accepted.

---

2. Reprinted by permission of Harvard Business School Press. From *The Innovator's Dilemma* by Clayton Christensen. Boston, MA, p. 188. Copyright 2000 by the Harvard Business School Publishing Corp.; all rights reserved.

3. Louis V. Gerstner, *Who Says Elephants Can't Dance?* (New York: Harper Business, 2003), p. 231. Reprinted by permission of HarperCollins Publishers.

UNTYING KNOTS

So with broad strokes, we have defined the three areas that can give rise to margin knots. The next logical question is "Which knots are the largest?" In other words, where is margin being impacted most adversely? Is the lack of charter costing us 5% of gross margin, or is it our poorly defined business processes? The answer to this question will vary on a case-by-case basis, just as the actual difficulty encountered when untying each knot will vary from company to company. However, I do believe that predominantly "strategy" creates the largest margin knots for professional services at product companies. I believe this because I have rarely seen a PS strategy that has gone much beyond base financial objectives such as revenue and margin. I do not hear executive teams at product companies having rich and meaningful conversations regarding their service strategy. What do I mean by "rich" conversation? Is the executive management team discussing the issues itemized below?

- What is the charter for PS?
- What financial model makes sense for this business?
- What market objectives are we attempting to achieve by having this function?
- What service portfolio makes sense based on those market objectives?
- How will we position our services?
- What pricing model makes sense?
- What is an effective sales channel strategy for our new service offerings?
- What new core competencies will we need to add?
- What will our scalability strategy be?

And most important: *How will we keep this services strategy aligned with product strategy?*

Even though an incomplete PS strategy often causes the greatest margin knots, untying them does not negate all of your potential problems. Even if a management team crafts the perfect services strategy, the structure of the company may prevent success. A lack of appropriate processes and tools can cripple any endeavor. And even if the structure is enhanced, the existing product-centric culture can stifle the profitable growth of services.

Depressed? Don't be.

Even if you are part of a struggling PS business and you do not have the ability to address all aspects of strategy, structure, and culture, there is great value in this framework. First of all, the list of issues that create margin knots for professional services business units is very real. Time and time again, I see these specific issues derail PS profitability. Secondly, by getting this list on the table and systematically focusing on these issues, gross margin will improve. If a PS management team picks just one weak spot—say, lack of a financial business model—and corrects it, there will be benefits. I know this, because the converse state is debilitating. A lack of a financial business model prevents any business from managing effectively, much less PS.

In many ways, this overarching framework of strategy, structure, and culture is universal. This is by design and it could be used when working to improve any type of business. The uniqueness comes not in the three categories, but in the techniques employed to help PS untie its specific knots. And I find there are many knots PS needs to untie.

To summarize the concept of margin knots:

> *How can you improve the gross margin of your professional services business?*
>
> Look for places your gross margin is being compromised: margin knots.
>
> *Where can you find these knots?*
>
> Look in the broad categories of Strategy, Structure, and Culture.
>
> In those categories, review specific areas such as charter, financial business model, and metrics. When you have identified a knot, focus on it until it is truly untied.

THIS BOOK AND MARGIN KNOTS

This book delves into the topic of professional services *strategy* in depth. This is done intentionally because I believe this topic is complex and causes the largest margin knots for a PS business. The ability to effectively design and articulate a viable services strategy at a product company is almost pure art. If more product companies want to succeed at this endeavor, discipline must be introduced into the process. After all, not many product companies have the time and the money to make multiple mistakes here. I hope the frameworks that follow will untie many of the complex and frustrating margin knots you face.

I addressed many of the margin knots caused by *structure* in *Building Professional Services: The Sirens' Song*. At some point, I need to update the information and release a new edition. However, the concepts in that book still provide a solid foundation for product companies that are maturing their PS infrastructure.

Of course, culture is the mushiest of the three areas that impact PS margin because it implies a company in transition from being product centric to solution centric. What exactly does that mean? I have done some work in this area, but not enough to warrant a book yet. I do hope to publish on this topic in future. For now, I do highly recommend the book *Who Says Elephants Can't Dance?* by Louis Gerstner. He does a wonderful job of discussing how he guided the IBM culture during its transition.

Let our journey into professional services strategy begin!

Chapter Two

Services Strategy Context

The Evolution of Professional Services Strategy

In *BPS*, I observe that if a professional services organization hopes to be successful, it must first define what it considers success to be. Specifically, I call out the following ten parameters that a PS management should set for the business unit:

1. *Mission* of the PS business unit
2. *Strategic objectives* of PS
3. *Guiding principles* when PS interacts internally and externally
4. Financial *business model* for PS
5. Key *levers* to increase PS profitability
6. *Organizational structure* for PS
7. *Metrics* PS uses to track progress
8. *Compensation model* to help motivate successful behaviors
9. *Current objectives* of PS
10. *Unique issues* facing PS within the company

These parameters seem obvious. Surely, most PS organizations should have them in place. But if the last few years have taught me anything about this business, it is that very few PS management teams are establishing these parameters. In fact, I am often challenged on the importance of these questions. Why do we need to specify a target business model? If we hit our quarterly revenue and margin targets, what else matters? And a mission? Blah, blah, blah. Just a bunch of words. Well, the gauntlet has been thrown down. I have no choice but to pick it up. In doing so, I would like to document the first *Scylla Fee* a management team should consider. As I noted in the Introduction, Scylla Fees are non-negotiable payments that must be made if a management team hopes to master the ability to consistently and profitably deliver professional services. Figure 2.1 documents the first Scylla Fee.

FIGURE 2.1 The First Scylla Fee

Scylla Fee	The strategy for the professional services business unit should be formally and explicitly defined.

TYPICAL PROFESSIONAL SERVICES STRATEGY

When a product company discusses its professional service strategy, it often boils down to the following statement: **"Our professional service strategy is to offer new services that increase company revenues, protect our product position, and delight our customers."**

Now, PS management team, go make *that* strategy happen.

Increasing service revenues, increasing product revenues, and improving customer satisfaction are all noble objectives. But that is exactly what they are: objectives.

> Do not confuse objectives for strategy. ■

A viable professional services strategy must consider much more than results. It must consider the key variables that make or break a service strategy. A viable strategy must also account for the relationships between these key variables. In this book, we will explore the process of successfully setting each of these strategy variables. For each variable you ignore, I believe you introduce risk into your PS strategy. Despite this reality, companies continue to ignore or defer these considerations. Why?

EXECUTIVE EXPECTATIONS

The professional service strategy discussion can be particularly difficult in product-centric companies. When executives at product companies get that "services" gleam in their eye, they often have improper expectations about the services business. The general perception is that there is service money on the table, available for the product company's taking. The comments of Pat Russo, the CEO of Lucent Technologies, are indicative of how many product company executives feel:

We are putting more emphasis on our Services business. Even with the tele-com market as challenging as it is, Services remains a near and clear opportunity. Our customers spend about $30 billion a year on the types of services that Lucent can provide—services that they contract for with other companies.[1]

I have often heard the term "heavy revenue" applied to professional services. Executives believe PS revenues drop right to the bottom line—no pause required at R&D, Marketing, or Sales for expenses. If these executives have cut their teeth building product revenue streams, they have limited experience actually capital-izing on service opportunities and building service revenue streams. In fact, their experiences to date with support services will improperly skew their thinking. Support services are targeted at a locked-in install base that often has little choice but to purchase warranty and education services from the product manufacturer. Often these support services grow in lockstep with product sales growth. Now, however, the management team is looking for more from services—*more* value-added service offerings, *more* revenue. *more* margins, *more* account control. When these new objectives start landing on the table, the rules change.

> A management team must understand that building a profitable professional services business, like building any profitable business, requires time, investment, and prioritization. ■

If I had to summarize how many executives at product companies look at the launch of new professional services, I would draw the graph shown in Figure 2.2.

FIGURE 2.2 Executive Expectations

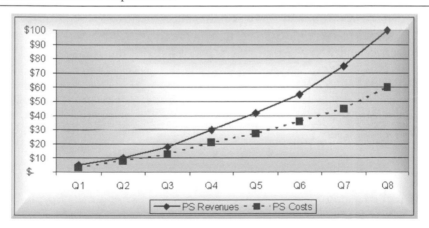

---

1. Lucent 2002 Annual Report, p. 3.

The life cycle that supports this revenue and cost curve is simple:

1. New service opportunities are identified.
2. The service is announced.
3. The service is sold.
4. Staff and partners are identified to deliver the service.

In other words, the company does not make front-end investments to enable the service. It is a "just in time" delivery model where margins get better and better as the service organization tunes the delivery process. Oh, and by the way, the executives are looking for a 40% gross margin from the first day the service is launched.

Executive management needs to understand that building a profitable services business is absolutely no different from building any profitable business. A clear strategy is needed. Investment is needed. The concepts of "time to market" and "time to profitability" are needed just as they are with products. When I speak with executives who want to dive into the professional services business, I tell them: "For each new service you hope to launch, you will need to invest anywhere from $200,000 to $2,000,000."

Unfortunately, this is not what the management team wants to hear. The updated picture the management team needs to have is the one shown in Figure 2.3. Here, the launch of a professional service business is shown realistically. There are expectations that investment will be required to develop services, train delivery staff, and market the service portfolio. Forty-percent gross margins on the service may not be realistic for seven or eight quarters—if ever (more on this later).

This mental adjustment to this reality is hard. The product executives may shake their heads up and down, emphasizing their understanding that time and investment are required. Yet, three quarters later, they pull the plug on new service endeavors because "the return just wasn't there."

For a services strategy to be successful, executive expectations must be set appropriately. If management expectations are unreasonable and ungrounded, all strategy discussions are a waste of precious time. ■

FIGURE 2.3 The Reality of Building PS

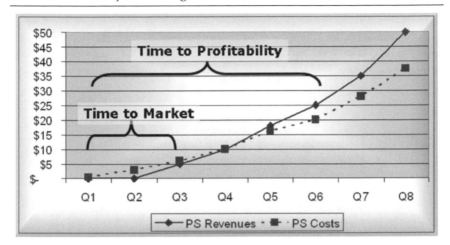

Assume your executive team is open-minded. Assume your management team understands it is building a new business line. Now, let's review the environment in which this services strategy discussion is taking place.

BIRTH OF A SERVICES STRATEGY

Over twenty years ago, Michael Porter wrote the classic book *Competitive Strategy*[2] In this book, he provides a wonderful "five forces" model to help companies understand key variables that should influence strategy decisions. I would like to borrow a diagram from that book's Introduction: *Context in Which Competitive Strategy Is Formulated.* Figure 2.4 presents Porter's diagram with some slight naming modifications. This picture demonstrates the environment that gives birth to a strategy discussion. Simply put, changes to an industry and/or changes to a marketplace force a company to reconsider its strategy. If a new strategy is devised, it must then be implemented throughout the company. As previously discussed, both company structure and company culture may need to be updated to support the new strategy.

2. Michael E. Porter, *Competitive Strategy* (New York: The Free Press, 1980).

FIGURE 2.4 Porter's Strategy Influencers

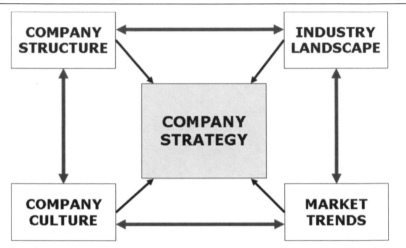

CHANGING INDUSTRIES AND MARKETS

As I outlined in the Introduction, product companies have experienced dramatic changes over the past several years. Customers are requiring complete business solutions, not disparate pieces of technology. Competition has become global and hypercompetitive. Feature differentiation that formerly provided a competitive advantage for a few years now lasts for a few quarters at best. Value-added resellers and system integrators are competing for account control.

The Storage-Hardware Industry: A Microcosm

The enterprise storage industry is a perfect example of these changing dynamics. In 1998, the storage industry was growing exponentially. Product manufacturers such as EMC could barely keep up with the growth requirements. Distributors and value-added resellers multiplied wildly. It was a classic high-tech product tornado. The high-tech bust brought product sales for the industry to a crawl. By 2002, the entire storage industry was scrambling for new sources of revenue.

> In 2002, fewer than 18% of storage resellers received more than 20% of their revenue from services. By the end of 2003, 53% of resellers expected more than 20% of their revenue to come from services.[3] More important, they expected their highest margins to come from services and not products. ■

3. "Storage Resellers: The Front Line of Storage Service," Gartner Group Inc., January 8, 2003.

FIGURE 2.5 Market and Industry Changes

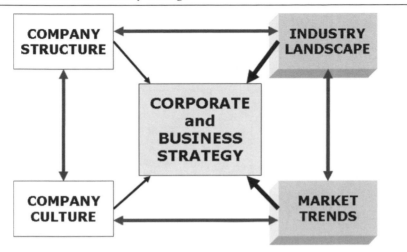

Figure 2.5 highlights how market trends and the consequent industry land-scape forced storage vendors to revamp their business strategy.

The storage industry is but one example of an industry that is being forced to reevaluate company strategy quickly and adjust to dramatic market changes. The question facing executive staff is what to do about all this change.

The Professional Services Strategy Response

To respond effectively to all this change, product companies are realizing that the traditional definition of a product company may no longer be valid. A company that is optimized to design, build, and sell widgets may not be viable in this new environment. The concept of a "solutions company" enters the strategy discussion, and the management team determines that a new, en-hanced, bold services strategy is required for long-term success. So, like the bewildered storage resellers mentioned earlier, product companies are giving birth to a services strategy. Figure 2.6 depicts this momentous event, but it also shows that the services strategy is only a portion of the overall company strategy. The product strategy looms in the background.

FIGURE 2.6 Birth of a Services Strategy

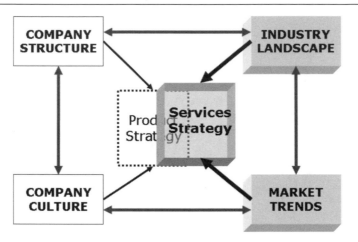

THE SUCCESS OF A SERVICES STRATEGY

Once a service strategy is born, the strategy is much more likely to perish within twelve months than it is to flourish and grow. Let me state that more dramatically:

> At product-centric companies, new service strategies fail more often than they succeed. ■

In 2003, 53% of storage resellers *wanted* to significantly increase service revenues. How many will have actually achieved that objective? Why are they more likely to fail than succeed at this objective? The answer relates back to Chapter 1's discussion on margin knots. When a product company attempts to craft and execute a new services strategy, it can fail in four distinct ways:

1. The new service strategy in itself is not sound or viable.
2. The strategy is viable, but it is not aligned with the product strategy.
3. The strategy is viable and aligned, but the structure of the company is not updated to support the new services strategy.
4. The strategy is good, the structure is modified, but the product-centric culture is not addressed and nullified.

Figure 2.7 documents how a new services strategy must be aligned and driven to succeed.

Building Professional Services focuses on the failure point of *structure*. That book itemizes the organizational structure, processes, and metrics that are

FIGURE 2.7 Success of a Services Strategy

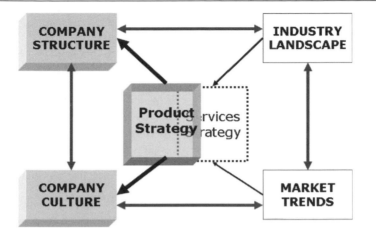

required to support a successful professional services business unit. I believe that book addresses how the structure of a product-centric company must be modified to support a new services strategy.

The failure point of *culture* is also very real. As I discussed in Chapter 1, culture can prevent a company from executing even a perfect strategy. This area of "human physics" is extremely challenging. I hope to address it in future works.

This book is focused squarely on the failure point of strategy. If the new professional services strategy is not viable, all other points are moot. The services strategy must be sound and achievable. But what makes a strategy sound and achievable? A viable services strategy must identify and consider any variables that are critical to success. When defining strategy for a competitive industry, Porter identified five key variables that need to be considered[4]:

1. Who buys the products?
2. Who provides key supplies to make the product?
3. Who produces substitute products?
4. Who are the current competitors?
5. Who could potentially enter the market and compete?

---

4. Adapted with the permission of The Free Press, a Division of Simon & Schuster Adult Publishing Group, from Figure 1-1, p. 4, *Competitive Strategy: Techniques for Analyzing Industries and Competitors* by Michael E. Porter. Copyright 1980, 1998 by The Free Press. All rights reserved.

These five questions only address external conditions. Internal capabilities must also be considered. At the end of the day, a strategy must consider both internal and external factors that influence success. Oh, and the strategy should define what success is!

From Chaos to Control

We are now entering the no-man's-land of strategic planning and strategy modeling. In the classic work *The Rise and Fall of Strategic Planning,* Henry Mintzberg expends hundreds of pages documenting, in painful detail, the consistent failings of strategic planning. When concluding his chapter titled "The Evidence on Planning," he states: *"Conventional planning tends to be a conservative process, sometimes encouraging behavior that undermines both creativity and strategic thinking. It can be inflexible, breeding resistance to major strategic change and discouraging truly novel ideas in favor of extrapolation of the status quo..."*[5]

But even Mintzberg, in all his pessimism, insists that an absence of planning makes no sense. He may be frustrated with the ineffective approach a majority of companies take to planning, but that does not mean it should be avoided. To paraphrase an executive who is quoted in the book, there are only four ways to deal with the future:

1. Ignore it
2. React to it
3. Predict it
4. Control it

By abstaining from any type of strategic planning, a company ignores its environment and relegates itself to reacting to market changes. Personally, I do not believe this approach can create long-term success.

As Mintzberg implies, many (most?) companies are abysmal in their strategic planning efforts. Companies conduct annual financial reviews that are dressed up as strategy plans. I believe a majority of middle and senior managers have had little positive success with strategic modeling, so the process is devalued. Despite this environment, I believe the concept of strategic planning will never go away. Why? Because we are humans and thus are driven to understand our environment. In *Forgotten Truth,* Huston Smith presents a simple diagram that shows how science is always driving to understand the way things are.

---

5. Reprinted with the permission of The Free Press, a Division of Simon and Schuster Adult Publishing Group, from p. 158, *The Rise and Fall of Strategic Planning* by Henry Mintxberg. Copyright 1994 by Henry Mintzberg. All rights reserved.

FIGURE 2.8 From Chaos to Control

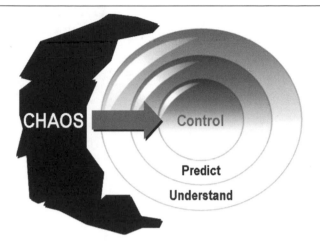

Figure 2.8 presents a modified version of this diagram.[6] This picture correlates perfectly with the four ways managers can respond to the future. Ignoring and reacting leaves a company in the realm of chaos. Effective strategic planning moves a company from observing to controlling (as well as we can in today's fast-changing world). All management teams are inherently driven to better understand their environment and to drive closer and closer to control. An effective strategic planning process is a mechanism to move along that continuum.

THREE SUPPORTING THEORIES

In essence, I create frameworks for a living. Frameworks that are designed to make complex topics more understandable—but not necessarily more simple. Managers often ask me what theory I base my frameworks on. When creating my model for mastering the professional services business, I leaned on three fundamental theories:

1. **Systems Theory**: Systems theory was introduced in the 1940s by the biologist Ludwig von Bertalanffy (*General Systems Theory: Foundations, Development, Applications*, 1968). He emphasized that real systems are open to, and interact with, their environments, and that they can acquire qualitatively new properties through emergence, resulting in continual evolution. Rather than reducing an entity

---

6. From p. 9, *Forgotten Truth: The Primordial Tradition* by Huston Smith, 1976. Reprinted by permission of HarperCollins Publishers, Inc.

(e.g., the human body) to the properties of its parts or elements (e.g., organs or cells), systems theory focuses on the arrangement of and relations between the parts which connect them into a whole (cf., holism).[7]

> A management team must understand the "system" it is managing, not just the pieces. ■

2. **Congruence Theory:** Congruence theory, when applied to planning, argues that a strategy or endeavor can only be successful if it is aligned with the realities of the world. A successful strategy must consider any unique internal and external factors the company is facing.

> A successful business strategy will acknowledge the unique strengths and weaknesses of a company as well as the unique dynamics of the markets served by the company. There are no canned professional services that will work for all companies. ■

3. **Contingency Theory:** Contingency theory is based on the premise that there is no solution which is appropriate for all organizations in all circumstances. Rather, a contingency-based strategy attempts to identify specific aspects of a system that are associated with certain defined variables and determine the appropriate solution.

> Successful professional services strategies adjust to emerging realities and respond appropriately. There is no such thing as autopilot in the world of strategy. ■

These three theories drove my desire to create a model for a services strategy that would successfully define the "system" the management team must manipulate to master the professional services business. The model also had to reflect the harsh reality of building professional services within a product company. Finally, the model had to be flexible enough to allow managers to customize the services strategy to meet their specific needs and markets.

---

7. This definition of Systems Theory is found at *http://pespmc1.vub.ac.be/SYSTHEOR.html*.

THREE TYPES OF STRATEGY

Mintzberg introduces the concept of *emergent strategy* versus *deliberate strategy*.[8] Deliberate strategy is crafted by corporate management, reflecting the "wish list" of executive management. Emergent strategy bubbles up from the field as front-line managers find out what really works and what does not work. Figure 2.9 depicts this reality.

I believe an effective strategy model must consider both deliberate and emergent strategy. Neither can be ignored without consequence.

CREATING BUSINESS SUCCESS: INGREDIENTS VS. RECIPES

In *Building Professional Services,* I use the analogy of recipes vs. ingredients. Some business philosophers provide step-by-step recipes for creating business success. Others simply identify the ingredients required for success—how and when you mix them is up to you. Here, I will first appear to be taking a recipe-style approach. Yes, we will sequentially work through the process of setting a viable services strategy. It may seem as though I am providing you a step-by-step approach to creating your services strategy. However, this is a book of ingredients: I believe there are critical variables (or ingredients) a senior management team must understand if it hopes to create (bake) a viable (edible) services strategy. You may deal with these variables in any order, and you may place different efforts on different variables—but you must address every variable at some point. Otherwise, you are baking mud.

FIGURE 2.9 Three Types of Strategy

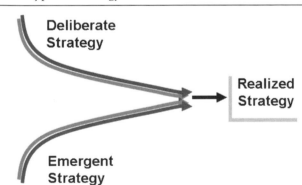

EXECUTIVE SUMMARY

When executive managers of a company sit down to place control around a professional services business that might be in chaos, they want to understand three things:

1. What should we be considering when creating a professional services strategy?
2. What are the key variables in play for a professional services strategy?
3. What are the relationships between these variables?

Unfortunately, many management teams craft their services strategy without asking these critical questions or, if they do, understanding the answers. I hope we can change all that.

Three Pillars
of a Services Strategy

Revenues, Services, and Skills

CHAPTER OBJECTIVE

To introduce a new framework that will assist an executive management team in creating an effective, aligned, and viable professional services business

KEY TOOLS

- Service Business Options Grid
- Three Pillars of a Services Strategy
- Nine Variables of a Services Strategy

THE SERVICES STRATEGY DILEMMA

When a management team sits down to master its professional services strategy, where should they start? What should the managers consider? Figure 3.1 adapts the strategy context diagram from Chapter 2 to demonstrate where the services strategy conversation occurs. Your industry and markets have changed. You need to create a services strategy to respond to these changes. In terms of corporate and business strategy, the model I introduce will help bridge the gap between them. Figure 3.2 shows that a refreshed professional services strategy forces a refresh of corporate and business strategy.

Regardless of where PS strategy lives, how do you ensure that the professional services strategy you create is the right one? How do you ensure it is viable?

FIGURE 3.1 Location of the Professional Services Strategy

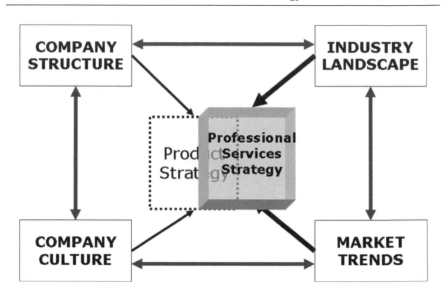

FIGURE 3.2 Three Pillars and Corporate Strategy

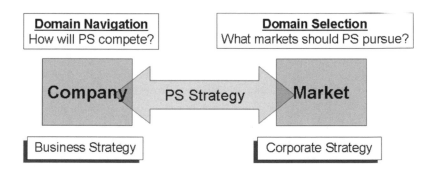

DEFINING SERVICE TYPES

Before I jump into the strategy model, I need to step back and provide a clear definition of the types of services that are involved in professional service strategy. Once a company moves past traditional support services, I believe four types of value-added service offerings can be offered. Table 3.1, provides an overview of these offerings.

TABLE 3.1 Service Types

Offering Type	Description
Consulting Services	Paid for what you know
Professional Services	Paid for what you do
Managed Services	Paid to manage the entire environment
Outsourcing Services	Paid to operate specific parts of the environment

FIGURE 3.3 Services Life Cycle

These service types represent consumption models. Your company has unique expertise that customers can tap into. The way customers "consume" this expertise can vary. Some customers simply want insight (consulting services). Some customers want you to apply your expertise to complete specific objectives (professional services). Other customers don't want to develop an expertise and are looking for your company to provide it (managed services, outsourcing services). Figure 3.3 is another way to view these core service types.

The Service Stack

When we begin to create a professional services strategy, we will discuss building a "service stack." A service stack builds upward from the core products and support services your company offers. In this view, support services are the base of service types on the stack because they are closest to the core products of the company. From that base, we ascend to managed services, professional services, and finally consulting services. Figure 3.4 depicts this progression. *Note that I do not break out education services separately; I include them in the realm of support services, though there are clearly unique challenges to growing and managing education services.* Outsourcing services occurs when a customer requires a combination of support services, consulting services, professional services, and managed services—all bundled together to completely manage a specific business environment.

FIGURE 3.4 Standard Services Stack

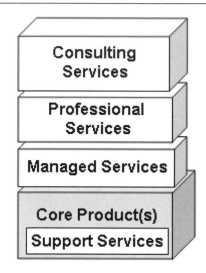

SERVICES BUSINESS OPTIONS GRID

Now that we have created definitions for the basic service types offered by companies, we can begin the process of assessing the service strategy. Of course, most product companies do not start this strategy discussion with a blank slate. Typically, there is a traditional support services business in place. This business can be a cost center or a profit and loss (P&L) center. Either way, it is usually focused on traditional break-fix activities. The management team must now try to determine where to take this business. Should services become an aggressive P&L center that stands on its own (for example, IBM Global Services)? Or should the product company use new consulting services to gain traction in new markets, similar to the sort of subsidized R&D function as described by Geoffrey Moore in *Living on the Fault Line.* Should the company stick to traditional support and education services, or should it include implementation and professional services as part of the mix?

Figure 3.5 summarizes the spectrum of service strategy choices that face the management team. Reflected on the horizontal axis of the grid, a product company must decide how profitable the business should be. Will services be a cost center (somewhere on the left side of the grid) or a profit center (somewhere on the right of the grid)? Reflected on the vertical axis, a product company must decide how complete the service stack will be. Will the company focus on basic support services and managed services (lower on grid) or will the company expand into high-end professional services (higher up the grid)?

FIGURE 3.5 Services Options Grid

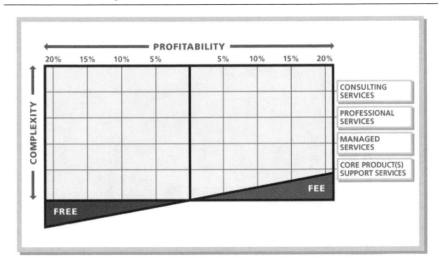

There are sliding scales of profitability and complexity to choose among. The million-dollar question: Where on this grid is the right location for your services business? Figure 3.6 maps three typical strategy zones product companies can target:

1. *Product Centric:* In this zone, the product company offers services that are close to the product (i.e., support and education). Services can be run as a cost center or a profit center.
2. *Product+:* In this zone, the product company begins offering more complex services and, consequently, expects more margin and profitability out of the services business.
3. *Solution Centric:* In this zone, the product company has made two important commitments. First, the company is committed to offering a complete service stack that allows the company to deliver business solutions. Second, the company expects services to generate substantial profits.

THREE PILLARS OF A SERVICES STRATEGY

To determine where you will locate on the services business grid, you must actually consider three distinct areas, which I term pillars.

FIGURE 3.6 Three Strategy Zones

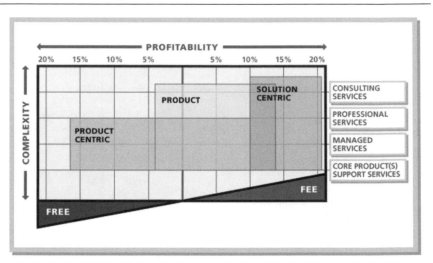

To design a viable services strategy, a management team must consider three distinct pillars:

- Revenue
- Services
- Skills

I define each of these three pillars and the components of each pillar in this chapter, and I demonstrate how the three pillars are related to each other. By the end of the chapter, you will have a unique model for grounding your professional services strategy discussion. ■

REVENUE: THE FIRST PILLAR

More and more, companies are looking at product lines like stocks in a portfolio. Like some stocks, some product lines are low volume but high return. Other stocks are high volume, low return. And still other stocks are an investment in the future. These latter stocks may actually lose money in the short term, but that is acceptable because they represent the potential for future growth. When incubating a services strategy, a management team must consider what type of stock to add to the company portfolio. Therefore, the first question a management team should ask itself when crafting a new services strategy is: *What financial return do we expect from this business?*

Is it a long-term investment or a short-term gainer? When focusing on this pillar, the management team is working to create a realistic financial profile for this new business investment. To effectively define the business objectives of the new services organization, there are three key items the management team should agree upon:

- The *charter* of the new services organization
- The *financial business model* for the new services organization
- The *financial objectives* of the services organization

I discuss in detail techniques to set the charter and business model for the services business unit in the next chapter. When you think of the financial objectives for a services organization, think "broad" or "narrow." Will the company build a narrow services organization that mines existing markets, or will the company attempt to build a broad strategic weapon to help lead to new customers in new markets? The financial model should support whatever the charter is. As an example, a services organization that is narrowly focused on serving the install base will command greater margins and profits and should have a business model that reflects this expectation. A services organization that the company expects to claw into new markets will require greater investment and experience lower margins.

Figure 3.7 shows the first pillar of a services strategy discussion: revenues.

FIGURE 3.7 Revenues Pillar

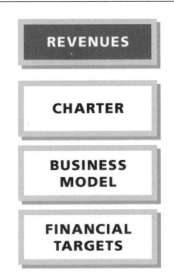

SERVICES: THE SECOND PILLAR

Once a management team agrees on the first pillar, the type of business the company is building, the next pillar of a services strategy—*services*—deals with all of the traditional marketing questions:

- What types of markets are we going after?
- Who will buy our services?
- What services should we offer?
- Are our service offerings aligned with our market objectives?
- How will we position our services?
- How will we price our services?
- What is our sales channel strategy?

In other words, the management team must address the five P's of marketing:

1. Product (i.e., what services are being offered)
2. Price
3. Promotion
4. Placement
5. Positioning

In subsequent chapters, I discuss this dimension in more detail. I provide a model to help product teams determine what services make sense. I also show the critical relationships among market objectives, service offerings, and the sales channel strategy.

While reviewing this dimension, a management team must discuss three key factors:

- What *markets* will the company target with service offerings?
- What *service offerings* make sense for those target markets?
- What *channels* will we use to sell the target services into the target markets?

When discussing this pillar, think in terms of the services stack. Will the stack be tall or short? A tall services stack means the company will be using a rich services portfolio to attack multiple markets. A short services stack correlates to a focused use of services, most likely targeted at the install base. Figure 3.8 depicts the three critical variables of the services pillar.

FIGURE 3.8 Services Pillar

SKILLS: THE THIRD PILLAR

After discussing revenue objectives and the services portfolio, a management team needs to consider the skills pillar. By skills, I mean the competencies required to deliver the new services portfolio. These competencies can include everything from generic skills like project management to the specific technical skills required to design and implement a complex technical solution. When discussing competencies, the management team should identify three key items:

- What are the competencies required to deliver the services that support our market objectives? Of those competencies, which ones will the company consider core competencies to be developed internally?
- Which competencies will be outsourced to *partners?*
- How will we *scale* both core competencies and partnered competencies?

Later, we will take a longer look at how to answer these questions appropriately. At this point, when you think of the skills pillar, think "heavy" or "thin." A heavy skills portfolio means multiple competencies are required to deliver the service portfolio. A thin skills portfolio means few incremental skills are required to make services successful. Figure 3.9 shows this pillar.

FIGURE 3.9 Skills Pillar

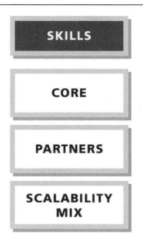

USING THE PILLARS

Figure 3.10 provides a complete view of the three pillars with all nine critical strategy variables shown. Now that I have introduced the three pillars, you might be asking yourself: So what? These are very pretty diagrams, but how do they help a management team craft a services strategy? Once again, we are trying to help a management team design a viable services strategy that meets overall company objectives. To accomplish this goal, I suggested at the conclusion of Chapter 2 that the following questions need to be answered:

- What should the management team consider?
- What are the key strategy variables in play?
- What are the relationships between these variables?

The answers to these questions are found in these three pillars.

What should the executive management team consider when crafting a new services strategy? The management team must discuss three critical areas:

1. The *revenue objectives* of the services organization
2. The *services* the organization will deliver
3. The *skills* required for the services organization to be successful

FIGURE 3.10 Nine Critical Variables

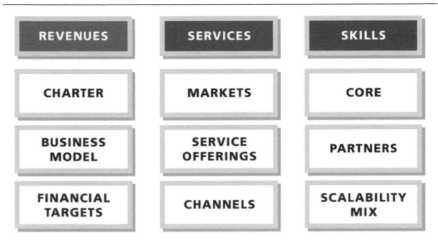

What key variables are in play? Table 3.2 shows the key variables that must be discussed and determined within each dimension.

How do all these variables relate to each other? When crafting a viable services strategy, each pillar should be the same height; one pillar cannot overshadow the others. For example, if the management team increases the financial targets for professional services, then professional services needs a service portfolio that will support these lofty revenue objectives. And of course, professional services will need staff and partners to deliver on those services. To emphasize this point, place a level line across the three pillars. That line represents the target revenue management wants from professional services. Let's say the target is $100 million. This means the product company must identify markets, services, and channels that can support $100M in value-added service revenue. This also means the product company must have staff or partners that can actually deliver $100M of services. Figure 3.11 demonstrates this correlation between pillars. In this example, the product company has not yet identified a service portfolio that will support $100M of revenue. Also, the product company has not yet identified the resources it will use to deliver all of its services.

TABLE 3.2 Strategy Variables in Play

Service Strategy Pillar	Service Strategy Variables	Comments
Revenue	1. Charter	What is the new services organization being chartered to achieve? Enable product sales? Acquire new revenue streams?
	2. Financial Business Model	What is the target business model for this unit? What are the gross margin targets? Sales costs? Operating profits?
	3. Financial Objectives	What are the revenue, profitability, and growth targets for the function?
Services	4. Target Markets	What markets will services target? Install base? New vertical industries?
	5. Service Offerings (pricing, positioning)	What services will be offered? Education, managed, professional, outsourced?
	6. Target Channels	What channels will be used to sell the new service offerings? Direct sales force? VARs? Distributors? Telesales?
Skills	7. Core Competencies	What competencies will the services organization build internally?
	8. Partnered Competencies	What required competencies will the services organization use partners to deliver?
	9. Scalability Model	How will services scale both core and partnered competencies?

FIGURE 3.11 Aligning the Pillars

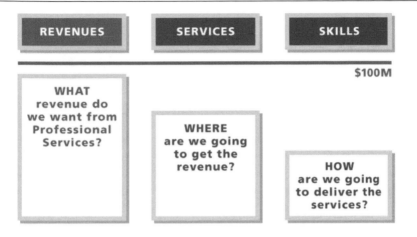

At this point, I can introduce the second Scylla fee of professional service strategy. When first seeing this model, most management teams are inclined to look for "shortcuts."

- *"Hey, let's figure out the services pillar, but wait to set a target business model."*
- *"Do we really need to identify our core competencies and positions?"*
- *"What markets are we pursuing? ALL, of course!"*
- *"If we build good services, the revenues will come. How much time do we really need to spend discussing the markets?"*
- *"We will hire as we go. I don't think there is any more magic to scaling the business."*

Figure 3.12 states the second, non-negotiable aspect of creating a viable professional service strategy. *Every* variable must be discussed. The depth of discussion or degree of clarity achieved may vary. However, every variable that is left for a later date introduces risk into your strategy. Risk, I believe, requires more financial wherewithal than most companies can afford.

FIGURE 3.12 The Second Scylla Fee

Scylla Fee	For a professional services strategy to be viable and sustainable, nine critical variables need to be set.

PILLAR PRIORITIES

Revenues-Led Strategy

When attempting to align the strategy pillars, I showed the most common planning scenario: *What revenues and profits can new service offerings drive for the company?*

Revenue objectives are set and the service management team must determine what services will meet those revenue objectives and how those specific services will be delivered. Strategy discussions are often "revenue led" because the most pressing issue facing the company is meeting profitability objectives. In fact, many strategic planning processes I encounter are actually financial planning processes wishfully dubbed "strategic planning." A service strategy discussion, however, does not always need to begin with revenue objectives.

Services-Led Strategy

In a "services-led" strategy discussion, the management team starts by asking the fundamental question: *"What services do we need to be successful?"*

This means the management team has started the dialogue on the services pillar. The variables the team wants to lock down first are the ones in this pillar. What markets are we targeting? What services do those markets need? How will we make sure these strategic services reach these strategic customers?

Skills-Led Strategy

Finally, the management team can have a "skills-led" strategy discussion. The planning starts here when the team is not looking for dramatically improved revenue objectives or an expanded services portfolio. In fact, management is probably content with the current revenue objectives and service offerings. A "skills-led" discussion is all about execution:

> How do we need to adjust our strategy to make sure we can actually deliver our current service portfolio?
>
> What can we do to improve skills and develop delivery partners?

It does not matter which pillar is the top priority of the management team. What does matter is the alignment of all three pillars. At the end of the strategy discussion, the revenue objectives must align with the service portfolio which must be supported by the right delivery skills.

FROM WHAT TO HOW

The services strategy pillars are used to demonstrate *what variables* need to be considered when crafting a services strategy. The model also clearly demonstrates the relationships that exist among groups of variables.

The next natural question is *how* a management team determines the actual values of these key variables. In other words, how does a management team determine if the services organization should have a charter to enable product sales or a charter to simply deliver profitable services? How do you identify what services should be offered at what prices? And how, please tell me, do you identify the appropriate sales channel strategy? These are all important questions that need answers if the services strategy is to be sound.

In the following chapters, I will work to answer these challenging questions. In these chapters, I discuss in depth each pillar of the service strategy. I will provide specific tactics a management team can use to determine the right settings for each parameter in the company's services strategy. The next chapter begins that journey, starting in the area of revenues, with the daunting variables of charter, business model, and financial targets.

EXECUTIVE SUMMARY

To create a viable professional service strategy, a management team must consider three distinct areas:

Revenues: What revenues and profits are expected from professional services?

Services: Where will the revenue come from?

Skills: How will the company actually deliver the services that have been sold?

To answer these three questions effectively, there are nine critical conversations the management team needs to have. By having all nine conversations, the management team can reduce the risks of pursuing an incomplete professional service strategy. By having all nine conversations, the management team can exponentially improve the odds of success. By ignoring all or some of these conversations, a management team will find it very difficult to create a professional service business it can truly control.

Chapter Four

Mastering Financial Objectives

Beyond Financial Targets

CHAPTER OBJECTIVE

To introduce a set of frameworks that will allow an executive management team to set the financial objectives of a professional services organization

KEY CONCEPTS

- Three Pillars of a Services Strategy
- Services Business Options Grid
- PS Charter Graph
- PS Business Model Table
- The 40/20 Myth
- PS Growth Rates

SETTING FINANCIAL OBJECTIVES

In Chapter 3 I introduced revenues as the first of three pillars that must be considered when defining a viable service strategy. Figure 4.1 highlights the revenues pillar. I start the model here because this is where most managers start the conversation. "Hey, they are asking me to grow 50% next year. Is that practical?" "The PS operating profit is too low—I need to increase it." To respond to these urgent financial pressures, managers focus on budgets based on profit and loss. Although these concerns are important, if you really want to master these financial numbers, do not start the conversation there. This chapter demonstrates why.

43

FIGURE 4.1 The Revenues Pillar

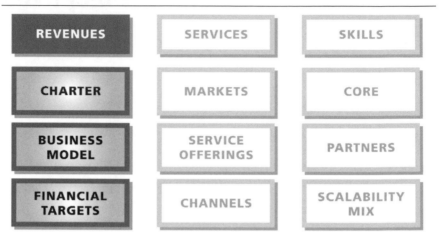

When focusing on financial objectives, the management team must determine what type of services business to build. The best analogy is that of adding a stock to a stock portfolio. What type of stock will be added to the company portfolio with this services business? Will it be a high-return stock? A high-growth stock? Or is it a long-term investment that might actually lose money in the short term? This seems like an obvious place to begin a service strategy discussion. How can you decide what services to add and what to charge for them if no one has established financial expectations for the professional services business as a whole?

The difficulty facing managers at product companies is that they have very little experience setting parameters for a professional services organization. What should be expected from services? Should we expect 60% gross margins and high growth? What do other companies get from their professional services business? With no experience, the management team's business expectations can range wildly and unrealistically.

This chapter is designed to help a management team determine what revenue objectives make sense for the specific professional services business it is managing. We'll focus on three topics:

- The charter of the services organization
- The target business model of the services organization
- The specific financial objectives for the services organization

THE SERVICE BUSINESS OPTIONS GRID (AGAIN)

Think back to that wide open, daunting *service strategy options* grid discussed in Chapter 3. Where on the grid should management aim its dart? By focusing on charter and business model, the management team can assess roughly that location. This location then drives the financial objectives that make sense for your PS business.

Assume that an existing services organization is in place. It operates as a cost center that provides traditional break-fix support services. Currently, if the services business breaks even, management is happy. This starting point is marked by the "Start Here" circle on Figure 4.2.

Moving forward, does the management team expect services to be a profitable business with a rich portfolio (Point A in Figure 4.2), or does management want to add some services to enable product sales and subsidize the business (Point B in Figure 4.2)? Being able to establish where on the grid you want to be is a significant strategic step forward. Setting the charter, business model, and financial objectives lets you take that step. So let's begin by setting a new charter for a services business.

Before we jump into charter, I want to make you aware of one brutal reality that exists relating to the service business options grid:

Distance = Effort ■

If you have an established service business that is currently subsidized (Point B), and you wish to move it over to an aggressive profit center (Point A), there is a great deal of distance to cover on the graph. This distance equates to management energy, investment, cultural change, etc. For this reason, I always recommend that companies run their professional services business as no worse than break-even propositions. This way, if the company does need the PS business to move up and to the right on the grid, the distance to be traversed and the management energy required are not as great.

FIGURE 4.2 Service Strategy Options

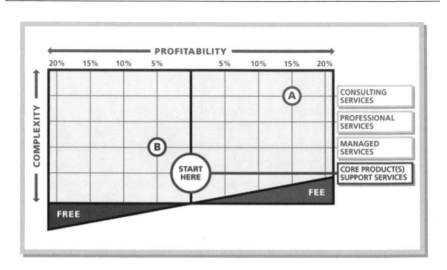

CHARTER

Many managers are familiar with creating "mission statements." When managers are asked to discuss a concept like "mission," they often begin to squirm. Practical managers want simple business missions like "Make money." Wannabe writers craft eloquent missions that involve optimizing the resources of the company for the greater good of the planet. When the creative dust settles, we end up with mushy mission statements that often have little impact on the behavior of the organization. I want to introduce a process that takes the wiggle room out of the mission statement by transforming it into a charter discussion.

> A mission is an assignment. It is a responsibility to perform a specified task. However, a mission statement provides zero insight into how one should go about achieving the assigned mission.
>
> By definition, a charter defines special privilege, immunity, or exemption. A charter grants something. ■

I recommend that the senior management team create a charter for the professional service organization, rather than write a flowery mission statement. Instead of assigning a mission (or multiple missions), I want the senior management team to grant a charter. Big difference: A mission tells you to go make stuff happen but a charter defines what you should and should not do.

To create a succinct and effective charter for a business function, I recommend a simple three-step process:

1. Identify the four *primary* reasons the function exists.
2. Rank these four reasons in their importance to your business.
3. Based on this ranking, summarize the primary charter of the function.

Step 1: Why Professional Services?

I believe that every business function has a set of primary reasons for existing. In essence, a universal list of potential reasons exists for every unique business function. For example, the Information Systems function (IT) at any company primarily exists for these reasons:

- To improve employee productivity through technology
- To improve the customer experience through technology
- To maximize the company's investment in technology
- To create a competitive advantage in the marketplace

Of course, there could be other reasons the IT function exists. The list of primary reasons this function exists is finite, however, not infinite. Furthermore, it is unlikely the IT function is chartered to maintain high employee morale and low turnover. That would be the charter of the Human Resources function. IT would not be responsible for maximizing revenues per customer. IT could support this endeavor, but Sales, Services, or Marketing would be chartered to achieve this objective. My point, again, is that every business function has a finite list of reasons for being in existence.

To accomplish the first step of my charter process, the management team needs to identify the reasons the company would want to have an expanded services business. To expedite this step, I would argue that the four primary reasons a company invests in services are:

- *Revenue:* The company is looking for additional sources of top-line revenue growth.
- *Margin:* The company is looking for higher margin revenue sources in order to offset shrinking product margins in other lines of business.
- *Satisfaction:* The company views services as a vehicle to improve customer satisfaction and protect account relationships.

- *Market Share:* The company would like to use value-added services to expand product sales. Services are used to accelerate the adoption of new products or to carry existing products into new vertical markets.

Once again, there may be other reasons a company invests in professional services, but I have found that in companies both large and small these are typically the primary four reasons.

Step 2: Prioritize Objectives

Now that we have a working list of reasons the service function exists, we need to rank the reasons. The mud that managers fall into here is that they want it all—"Hey, why can't I have a services business that makes lots of high-margin revenue, delights our customers, and leads us into previously untapped markets?" I agree: It doesn't hurt to ask. Also, you might be at a company where your brand equity and market dynamics permit services to meet all of those objectives. But I doubt it. To make this charter conversation meaningful, a management team must force rank the business objectives of the services function. This reality leads us to the third *Scylla Fee* (Figure 4.3) that a management team must pay to master the professional services business.

Recall, I am using the last challenge faced by Odysseus in the *Odyssey* as a reminder that not all challenges have no-loss answers. In his last challenge, Odysseus had to pass through a section of the sea that was inhabited by two monsters: Charybdis (pronounced Kuh-rib-dis) and Scylla (pronounced Sil-uh). Charybdis was a massive monster that sucked down water, creating a

FIGURE 4.3 The Third Scylla Fee

Scylla Fee	The management team must prioritize which of these four objectives are the most important for the professional services organization:
	▶ Increasing professional services revenues
	▶ Improving professional services margin
	▶ Improving customer satisfaction
	▶ Increasing overall company market share

wide whirlpool that could not be escaped. To sail past Charybdis meant certain death. Scylla was a multiheaded beast that picked sailors off their ship as it went by. A costly encounter to be sure, but the ship could survive. In all the previous dangers that faced Odysseus, he had always found a clever way out. When faced with this Catch-22, Odysseus's instinct was to find the loophole. How could he sail past both creatures without losing a man? But the gods assured him there was no escape this time—a price was to be paid. No, Odysseus, this time you must pay the piper. In fact, most sailors avoided the teeth of Scylla for the seemingly safe water of Charybdis's lair—only to be sucked down to their death. But Odysseus avoided the calm waters of Charybdis and sailed directly by the cliffs that housed Scylla. The maneuver cost six sailors' lives, but the ship was intact and the journey continued.

The management team must prioritize the objectives of the services organization. If it doesn't, the services organization may overlook the objective that is most critical to the company.

To make this difficult discussion easier, I recommend a management team look at each potential objective and assign an importance ranking to it. If the objective is mission critical to overall company success, assign the objective a ranking of 2. If the potential objective has no value to the company, assign a 0. If the potential objective has some importance, assign it a 1. Table 4.1 summarizes the ranking values.

Once this is done, the management team should generate a summary table that lists each potential objective in order. Interestingly, the acceptable and defendable answers can vary widely here. A management team may state that incremental revenue and high margins are the critical reasons for expanding services. This answer is perfectly reasonable. On the other hand, a management team may consider improved customer satisfaction the primary reason for having services. Additional revenue is simply a nice bonus of having services, but not the primary reason for carrying the function. Table 4.2 shows a completed ranking table.

TABLE 4.1 Charter Rankings

Ranking Value	Description
0	Objective is not important to the management team or the success of the company
1	Objective is important, but is not mission critical to success
2	Objective is critical to the overall success of the company

TABLE 4.2 Completed Rankings Table

Ranking	Objective Area	Importance Ranking
1	Customer Satisfaction (SAT)	2
2	Market Share	2
3	Revenue	1
4	Margin	1

Step 3: Summarize Charter

The final step is to review the data assembled in steps 1 and 2 to generate a charter for the services function. Before a management team attempts to write out the charter statement, I recommend graphing it. Figure 4.4 takes the data from Table 4.2 and generates a *services charter graph*. This graph conveys why the services function exists in the eyes of senior management. In this example, the management team views services as a sales enabler as opposed to a stand-alone P&L center that drives revenue and margin.

Looking at Figure 4.4, the management team can craft a charter statement that supports this graphic. A charter statement for this particular services function may read as follows:

> The charter of the services organization is to ensure that our existing customers are satisfied with our products and to introduce new customers to the capabilities of our outstanding product portfolio. The services function will be profitable, but never at the expense of the customer experience.

FIGURE 4.4 PS Charter Graph

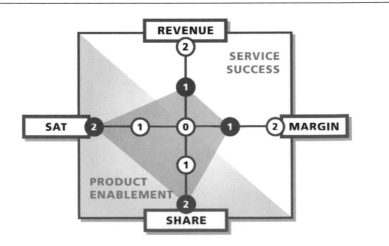

Behold, the Power of Charter

This three-step process to document a concise charter for the services organization is not an academic exercise. This process generates clear business objectives that will guide management behavior. Let me demonstrate.

Let's say your company is launching a new product. One of your existing customers has agreed to migrate to this new product, but the customer is concerned about the pain and costs associated with migration. Your product revenues will be significant if the migration occurs.

During the weekly sales call, the account manager reviews this deal with the district sales director. The district sales director decides that the services organization should become actively engaged by donating a project manager and technical consultant to offset any concerns the customer has with migration.

Subsequently, the regional services manager is asked to allocate a project manager and technical consultant to this account. No, the customer will not be paying for these resources. How should the services manager respond? Using the charter depicted in Figure 4.4, the services manager must consider the fact that the services organization exists to facilitate product sales. So, although a financial impact discussion should probably take place, the services manager should fulfill the request.

What if the executive management team had decided upon a different charter for the services function? What if the charter looked like the one shown in Figure 4.5?

FIGURE 4.5 A Different PS Charter

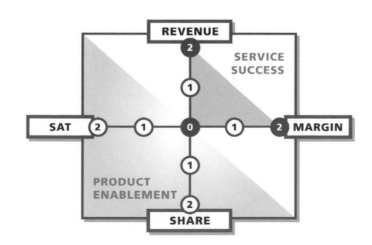

If this were the charter the services manager was operating under, the response would be very different because he is chartered to meet financial objectives first. Greasing the tracks with this customer is not even on the radar screen. If the sales director wants assistance, there should be some cost and margin relief. Otherwise, the services manager needs to apply billable resources to accounts that pay.

You can see that with no charter in place, services managers and sales managers throughout your company will spend too much time arm wrestling over how to interact and engage.

Without a documented charter for the services organization, a product sales force will be unclear about when and how to use the services organization. Without a charter, service managers will be unclear about how to respond to requests for free sales-enabling activities. A clear charter puts a stake in the ground and communicates to the company what business objectives the management team expects the services function to achieve. The charter determines what business model makes sense for the services organization, so we now turn our attention there.

TARGET BUSINESS MODEL

A clear charter is only half the battle when it comes to setting financial objectives for the services function. The executive management team must also discuss and document the financial business model for services. Of course, this business model should be 100% aligned with the charter.

Defining a Business Model

When people think of the term "business model," several elements come into play:

- Target markets
- Target customers
- Product offerings
- Distribution channels
- Margins
- Profits

A sound business model considers all of these items. In essence, a business model reflects and supports the business strategy of the company. The business model demonstrates how a company will manage all of these elements to grow and make money on a sustainable basis.

As a component of a business strategy, a business model defines the costs, investments, and profits required for the business. A successful model allocates the appropriate amount of investment in sales, research, and administration to achieve the corporate strategy, achieve market success, and hit target profitability. The business model should be realistic and *sustainable*.

A business model is *not* simply a financial report. A financial report summarizes anticipated revenues and expenses to show profitability. You could have extremely accurate financial reporting and still have no idea what your target business model should be.

A sample business model is shown in Table 4.3.

TABLE 4.3 Sample Business Model

Category	Common Abbreviation	Definition	Target Percentage of Revenue to Invest
Revenue		Total revenues expected from services by the company	100
Cost of Services Sold	COS	Cost of materials and human resources that are required to deliver the services to customers	75
Gross Margin	GM	Difference between what customers pay for the services and what it costs the company to deliver those services	25
Sales Costs		Total cost of all selling efforts—includes salaries and expense accounts and commissions for sales management, sales people, and sales support	6
General & Administration Costs	G&A	General expenses not captured in COS, sales, marketing, or R&D	5
Research & Development Costs	R&D	Investments made to improve service methodologies and delivery tools	2
Marketing		Investments made to market the service portfolio	2
Operating Profit		Profit generated by services—also known as the operating margin	10
		(Operating profit = Revenue − COGs − Sales Costs − G&A − R&D − Marketing)	

The example financial business model in Table 4.3 shows that the management team believes at least 2% of revenues need to be invested into both marketing and R&D to *sustain* the business. If these investments are not made, future revenues and margins could be compromised.

Example Business Models for Service Organizations

We now have a common understanding of what a target business model is. We also understand how it is different from a financial report.

Before you attempt to document a viable financial business model for your services business, it would probably be helpful to understand what models already exist in the marketplace. Let's begin this review by looking at Accenture Consulting. Accenture is a global consulting firm with over 75,000 employees in 47 countries. Accenture performs the type of high-end technology and business consulting that many product companies wish they could deliver. Table 4.4 shows the financial results for Accenture in 1998 and 2002.

In the far right column, I have reverse engineered a financial business model Accenture could be using. Accenture targets services that will bring in decent gross margins but it needs to invest heavily in sales and marketing to maintain its brand and land large engagements. I make the assumption that some of Accenture's G&A expenditures are actually R&D dollars invested in delivery methodologies.

TABLE 4.4 Accenture Results

	Accenture 1998 (in millions)		Accenture 2002 (in millions)		Sample Business Model
Revenue	$9,511	100%	$13,105	100%	100%
COGs	$5,996	63%	$8,428	64%	63%
GM		37%		36%	37%
Sales & Marketing	$696	7%	$1,566	12%	8%
R&D					2%
G&A	$1,036	11%	$1,616	12%	8%
Operating Income	$1,783	19%	$1,385	11%	19%

A second sample model to review is that of IBM, the poster child of PS at product companies. Table 4.5 shows IBM's results for 1998 and 2003. In 2000, IBM Global Services represented over 35% of total company revenues. What is amazing is how significantly different the IBM services business model is from Accenture's. IBM's services business only brings in an average of 27% in gross margin. After the cost of services, I had to allocate G&A and Sales costs to the services business based on the percentage of total revenues services represented.

Even with the gross assumptions I am making, the sample business model I have reverse engineered in the far right column of Table 4.5 is significantly different from the one Accenture is probably operating under.

Next, consider the point most product companies start from: a support services financial model. A traditional support services business often commands fat margins with minimal investment in sales and marketing. This is due to the fact that support services are a natural attachment to the product sales cycle. Table 4.6 summarizes the target financial business model for a traditional support services business.

TABLE 4.5 IBM Global Services Results

IBM 1998 (in millions)			IBM 2003 (in millions)		Sample Business Model
Service Revenues	$28,916	100%	$42,635	100%	100%
COGs	$21,125	73%	$31,903	75%	73%
GM		27%		25%	26%
Selling, G&A	$3,470	12%	$5,116	12%	12%
R&D					2%
Marketing					4%
Operating Income	$1,959	7%	$4,263	10%	8%[

TABLE 4.6 Support Services Business Model

	Support Services at a Product Company
Service Revenues	100%
COGs	60%
GM	40%
G&A	5%
Selling	5%
R&D	2%
Marketing	2%
Operating Income	26%

So there you have it. Three sample business models for three different service organizations. The variations are wide, with gross margins ranging from 40% to 27% and operating profits ranging from 8% to 26%. What is the right answer for professional services in a product company?

THE 40/20 MYTH

When I first work with organizations regarding their professional services business, the senior management team generally has a common assumption: PS is a fat business. How fat? Executives consistently tell me they are looking for gross margins of around 40% and operating profits of around 20%. What are these expectations based on? It is unclear. I typically ask the following questions and receive the following answers:

- Do you currently achieve 40% gross margins and 20% operating profits with your PS business? *No.*
- Have you ever achieved 40/20 from your PS business? *No.*
- Do you have hard data that other companies are sustaining 40/20 from their PS business? *No.*

Based on these answers, where do the expectations for a 40/20 business come from?

Industry Results

I believe this 40/20 myth is a byproduct of how companies report their service revenues. In preparation for a February 2004 seminar at Ohio State, I reviewed the quarterly financial statements (10-Q's) of thirty publicly traded companies. All but one of them were blending support services revenues with professional service revenues in their public reports. Figure 4.6 documents the gross margin these companies report for "services." Oracle is the one company on the list that explicitly reports the gross margin for its consulting services. As you can see, the gross margin for Oracle's consulting services was significantly lower than the blended numbers reported by the other companies. Interestingly enough, the average gross margin reported on services for these thirty companies was 41.2%. There is the 40 of the 40/20 myth. Unfortunately, 97% of these companies are not reporting the operating profit achieved by their PS business. So it is unclear where the 20 portion of the myth comes from. My assumption is that executives look at the results of independent consulting firms like Accenture, see the high operating profit shown in Table 4.4, and assume that should be the target for their PS business.

Mix Matters

Another insight provided by Figure 4.6 is the impact of service revenue mix. Six of the companies detailed how much top-line revenue was coming from support services vs. professional services. This data supports my premise that a mature service revenue mix with more revenue coming from professional services, managed services, and outsourcing services actually drives down the blended gross margin. To prove the point, Figure 4.7 documents the revenue mix reported in Novell's 10-Q. As shown, the mix is heavily weighted in support services. This helps Novell report an overall service gross margin of a healthy 52%! Unisys, however, has a very mature service revenue mix which includes professional, outsourced, and managed services as shown in Figure 4.8. Support services represents less than 15% of total service revenues. This reality drives down to 21% the blended service gross margins for Unisys. In summary, Professional Services activities appear to drag down total service gross margins. All this data substantiates the premise that PS is typically not a 40/20 business when it is part of a product company. But what does the business model look like?

FIGURE 4.6 Service Results for 30 Companies

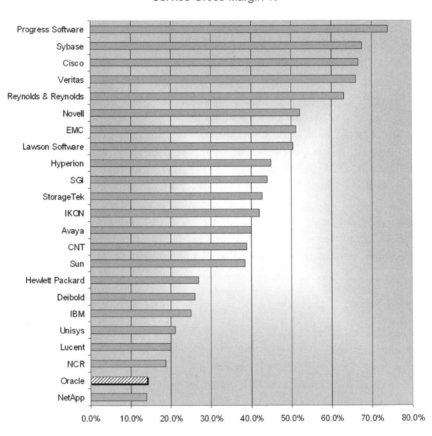

FIGURE 4.7 Novell Service Mix

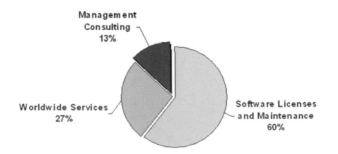

FIGURE 4.8 Unisys Revenue Mix

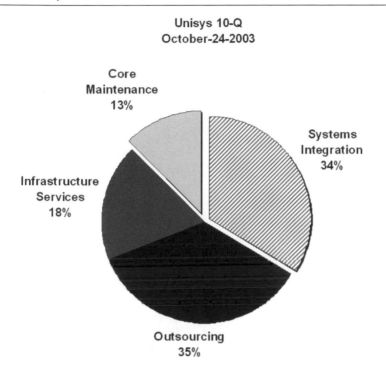

Unisys 10-Q
October-24-2003

Core
Maintenance
13%

Systems
Integration
34%

Infrastructure
Services
18%

Outsourcing
35%

Setting the Boundaries

We have reviewed example business models for service organizations and I have argued that Professional Services in a product company is not the 40/20 business many executives feel it should be. Now, for the million-dollar question. What does a sustainable business model look like for professional services?

First, we should discuss the individual line items of the financial business model. Table 4.7 provides target boundaries for each line item. The table also provides the rationale for the boundaries.

With these boundaries in mind, what overall business model is realistic for the professional services organization at your company? In September of 2004, I asked forty-seven senior service managers that very question. Table 4.8 shows an aggregate of their responses next to a baseline 25/10 model I had provided them.

TABLE 4.7 PS Line Items

Line Item	Recommended Boundaries	Rationale
Gross Margin	15% < Target < 40%	If less than 15%, PS can't sustain itself (no money left to invest).
		Difficult to consistently exceed 40% when asked to pull products or invest in critical company accounts.
G&A	5% < Target < 8%	If less than 5%, required infrastructure for PS is not created and maintained.
		Greater than 8% is a sign critical operational processes are not defined or are not being followed.
Sales	5% < Target < 8%	If less than 5%, service capabilities are not aggressively being sold to customers and channels.
R & D	2% < Target < 5%	If less than 2%, intellectual property is not being documented and leveraged to improve profitability.
Marketing	2% < Target < 5%	If less than 2%, service portfolio is not being positioned to the marketplace. Sales reps are forced to perform general awareness and generate initial demand.
Operating Profit	5% < Target < 12%	Within this range, PS is being asked to carry its own water. However, the organization is not being tasked to sustain unachievable profits.

Table 4.9 provides a range of possible values for the key financial variables that need to be set. This table leads us to the next Scylla Fee (Figure 4.9) that must be paid in order to master professional services.

If the business model does not account for ongoing investments, the PS function will not effectively manage the intellectual capital and people required to generate healthy margins.

In general, if you set your business model with values from the left side of Table 4.9, you risk setting financial objectives that cannot be sustained. For example, having a gross margin target of 50% will be difficult for the services organization to sustain. On the other hand, setting the financial business model with values from the right side of Table 4.9 will make it difficult to keep the services organization alive. If PS brings in low gross margins, no investment is made in sales, marketing, or R&D, and operating profits are nonexistent, senior management may have little patience with the business. Even if services are considered a strategic investment, a business model weighted toward the right will be difficult to maintain. There is not enough investment in the business to help it grow and the anemic return will eventually make it unpalatable.

TABLE 4.8 Seminar Model

	Target PS Business Model	Target PS Business Model (Seminar)
Service Revenues	100.0%	100.0%
COS	75.0%	70.0%
Gross Margin	25.0%	30.0%
G&A	5.0%	5.0%
Selling	6.0%	6.0%
R&D	2.0%	2.0%
Marketing	2.0%	3.0%
Below the line investment	15.0%	16.0%
Operating Income	10.0%	14.0%

FIGURE 4.9 The Fourth Scylla Fee

Scylla Fee	A viable service business model must include ongoing investment for services development, services marketing, and service sales.

TABLE 4.9 PS Business Model Table

	Can't Sustain								Can't Maintain	
GM	55%	50%	45%	40%	35%	30%	25%	20%	15%	10%
G&A	13%	12%	11%	10%	9%	8%	7%	6%	6%	6%
Selling	10%	9%	8%	7%	6%	5%	4%	3%	3%	3%
R&D	8%	7%	6%	5%	4%	3%	2%	2%	0%	0%
Marketing	8%	7%	6%	5%	4%	3%	2%	2%	0%	0%
Operating Income	16%	15%	14%	13%	12%	11%	10%	7%	6%	1%

Using the range table for guidance, the management team should be able to draft a viable target business model for the services organization. The key point here is alignment. The target business model should be aligned with the charter that was created for the professional services organization. Looking at Table 4.9 again, we can see that financial targets from the middle to the left support a service charter that is focused on revenues and margins. However, if a services organization has a charter weighted toward enabling products or satisfying customers, the financial targets from the center to the right will make much more sense.

FINANCIAL OBJECTIVES

Finally! The management team is now in a position to truly address the final parameter to be considered in the revenues pillar. In other words, the management team can now establish the financial objectives for the services organization.

To create realistic financial objectives, the management team should consider the following variables:

- The charter for the services organization
- The target financial business model
- The current service revenue run rate
- The size of the product install base
- The growth rate of product revenues

Using these variables as guides, the management team should be able to create a realistic growth rate for the services organization. The size of the install base and the growth rate of product revenues represent potential sources for future service revenues. The larger these variables are, the higher growth rate management can require from services. As an example, let's assume the services organization is currently a $20 million, break-even cost center. Let's also assume the following:

- There is $500M of product installed with customers.
- New product sales are expected to be $200M next year.

Using these revenue assumptions, the management team can then estimate how much service revenue will actually be captured through these revenue opportunities. For example, the management team can make the following estimates:

- Revenues from existing service offerings will stay steady next year at $20M.
- Using newly developed service offerings, we can go back into the existing product install base and capture 1% of past product sales in new service sales.
- Using newly developed service offerings, we can capture 1% of new product sales in service revenues.

Using these assumptions, the management team can create the growth assumptions shown in Tables 4.10 and 4.11. Table 4.11 sets a $27M revenue target for services in the following year. This number is grounded in some reality because it is based on current run rates and future product growth. The smaller the current services revenues, product install base, product growth rate, and investment in the services business, the smaller the expected growth rate should be.

Having established a grounded growth rate, the management team can take a stab at financial targets for up to three years for the business. Table 4.11 provides an example of the financial objectives for the PS business over the next four quarters. The numbers show how the business can grow 35% to meet the $27M revenue target. These four quarters also show investment to set up continued growth and scalability in years two and three.

TABLE 4.10 Growth Assumptions

	This Year	Capture Rate	Next year
Current PS Business	$20,000,000	N/A	$20,000,000
Install Base	$500,000,000	1%	$5,000,000
Product Sales	$200,000,000	1%	$2,000,000
		Target Revenue	$27,000,000
		Target Growth Rate	35%

TABLE 4.11 First Four Quarters

	Target %	Q1	Q2	Q3	Q4	Year 1	Target Dollars
PS Revenues	100%	$5,000,000	$6,000,000	$7,000,000	$9,000,000	$27,000,000	$ 27,000,000
COGs	70%	$4,000,000	$5,100,000	$5,600,000	$6,750,000	$21,450,000	$ 18,900,000
G&A	8%	$640,000	$640,000	$640,000	$640,000	$2,560,000	$ 2,160,000
Selling	8%	$640,000	$640,000	$640,000	$640,000	$2,560,000	$ 2,160,000
R&D	2%	$160,000	$160,000	$160,000	$160,000	$640,000	$ 540,000
Marketing	2%	$160,000	$160,000	$160,000	$160,000	$640,000	$ 540,000
Operating Income $		($600,000)	($700,000)	($200,000)	$650,000	($850,000)	$ 2,700,000
Operating Income %	10%	-12%	-12%	-3%	7%	-3%	

REALISTIC FINANCIAL OBJECTIVES

I am seeing another common trend in the PS business plans I review. Management teams worldwide are creating the perfect PS business in a workbook. They model what the business will look like over three years. Utilization rates for delivery staff will be high, billing rates will be high, overhead will be low, and growth rates will be exponential. Of course, the business is profitable almost instantaneously. Figure 4.10 documents this optimistic view. How many of these plans are achieved?

To help offset some of this unrealistic optimism, I would suggest a management team think in terms of three years, not three quarters.

> *Year 1: Investment.* Build out some of the infrastructure required to support the service business. Invest in strategic capabilities such as services engineering and services marketing. Expect PS to lose money.
>
> *Year 2: Break Even.* Challenge PS to at least carry its own water as the business matures.
>
> *Year 3: Target Business Model.* Challenge PS to meet its target business model, whatever that may be. By the way, it is probably not 40% gross margins and 20% in operating profits.

FIGURE 4.10 Optimistic PS Business Plan

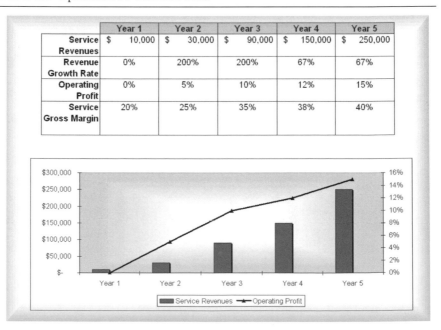

	Year 1	Year 2	Year 3	Year 4	Year 5
Service Revenues	$ 10,000	$ 30,000	$ 90,000	$ 150,000	$ 250,000
Revenue Growth Rate	0%	200%	200%	67%	67%
Operating Profit	0%	5%	10%	12%	15%
Service Gross Margin	20%	25%	35%	38%	40%

FIGURE 4.11 The Fifth Scylla Fee

| Scylla Fee | Because professional services is a human-capital-intensive business, a management team must set realistic growth rates. |

With this saner set of expectations, the business has a chance at viability.

Growth Rates and Camel Humps

Philosophically, management teams typically agree that they should have a three-year horizon. *Emotionally*, they don't like such an extended horizon. They want to "blow this PS thing out. Hey, we're leaving money on the table—we have a huge opportunity here!"

This desire leads to the next Scylla Fee management is often unwilling to admit. Figure 4.11 documents this required payment.

Regardless of how fantastic your particular PS opportunity may be, I believe there are some natural limitations to how fast this human-capital-intensive business can grow. Using human capital takes time and energy. Even if you decide to acquire your way to growth (more on this later), it takes time to assimilate service companies. This kind of business cannot grow exponentially. But how fast can you grow? I asked that very question of a group of senior service managers in the fall of 2004. First, I asked the group what average growth rate could be sustained in the PS organization for three years. Figure 4.12 summarizes the managers' responses. As can be seen, all of the forty-six managers who replied felt that the growth rate they could sustain for three years was 40% or lower.

FIGURE 4.12 Three-Year Growth Rate for PS

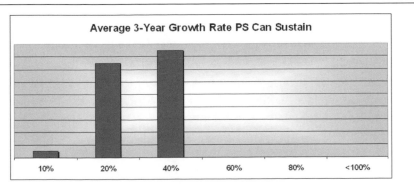

FIGURE 4.13 Maximum Profitable PS Growth Rate

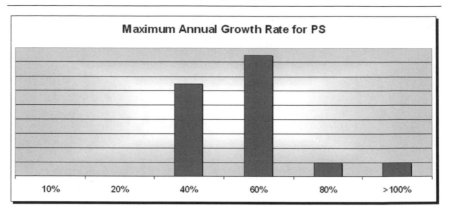

I then asked the group what maximum growth rate they could profitably achieve in a given year. Figure 4.13 documents their responses. As shown, a majority felt PS could not grow profitably at a growth rate greater than 60%.

For more data on achievable growth rates, read the case study later in the chapter on the growth rates experienced by IBM Global Services and Cambridge Technology Partners in the late 1990s.

VALUE OF SETTING ALL THREE REVENUE VARIABLES

In Chapter 3, I outlined nine critical variables a management team must set to enable a professional services strategy to mature. Figure 4.14 shows those variables in a slightly new configuration.

Earlier in this chapter, we were trying to master the process of setting financial objectives for a services organization within a product company. The starting point was the overarching business objective that many product companies now have: Grow the services business. But that objective in and of itself is not enough. It provides little insight and guidance into what a management team really hopes to achieve by expanding the services organization.

To help a product management team crystallize thoughts, I introduced the topics of the services charter and the services business model. These variables should be discussed and established prior to creating specific financial objectives for professional services. If a management team can discuss, agree upon, and document a clear charter for the new services organization, the appropriate business model for the services organization becomes clearer. If a management team can draft a reasonable business model that supports that charter, the financial objectives that make sense become more apparent. If a management team can agree on specific financial objectives that are aligned with the charter and business model, there should be little confusion left. Figure 4.15 documents the ground we covered in this chapter.

FIGURE 4.14 Service Strategy Map

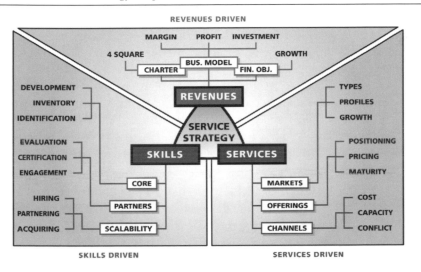

FIGURE 4.15 Variables for Mastering Financial Objectives

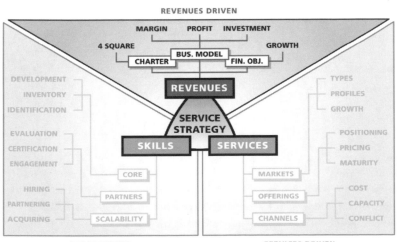

COMPANY CASE STUDIES

This section provides real world examples of how companies have set the variables of charter and business model to improve the life of the professional services organization. This section also reviews real growth data to help baseline what growth rates make sense for a professional service organization.

HITACHI DATA SYSTEMS AND CHARTER

Hitachi Data Systems (HDS) is a leader in providing high available, scalable, and cost effective data storage infrastructure. In 2003, HDS decided to expand its Professional Services business. For many of the reasons previously identified in this book, HDS realized that professional service capabilities were becoming a requirement of the enterprise storage marketplace. To lead the effort, HDS hired a seasoned executive from the outside, Mr. Ken Beaudry. Mr. Beaudry had previous experience building professional service businesses at both established companies and startups.

Coming into HDS, Mr. Beaudry was painfully aware this was not the first attempt HDS had made to expand PS. This time had to be different. To avoid previous missteps, Mr. Beaudry employed several key tactics. For the first time in the company's history, the Global Solutions and Services Group (GSS) was given a seat at the executive committee. Mr. Beaudry reported directly to the President of the company. Also, a three-year financial plan was created that accounted for required investment in the first two years. However, one of the most unique levers Mr. Beaudry used was the PS Charter conversation.

In previous attempts to build this function, the PS charter was not explicitly defined. This lack of charter created conflict between service and product staff. Mr. Beaudry had seen these challenges before. To accelerate management agreement, Mr. Beaudry asked the executive committee what they felt the charter of the PS organization should be. Mr. Beaudry's comment on the process: *"I wanted to make sure the executive team was clear on why we were building professional services at HDS. It was critical we were 100% aligned. If not, history was bound to repeat itself".*

The conversation with the executive staff led to the creation of the charter graph shown in Figure 4.16. Once Mr. Beaudry had agreement on the charter, he quickly crafted a set of ramifications. He wanted the executive committee to understand what this charter meant to both the financial performance and daily behaviors of the PS organization. The ramifications were as follows:

- GSS was created to enable and stimulate growth in the HDS portfolio.
- GSS would not be chasing service revenue for the sake of service revenue.
- GSS would invest resources into strategic account development.
- However, GSS could not afford to give away its services. The function was expected to ultimately reach profitability.

Figure 4.16 GSS Charter

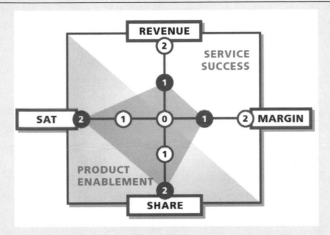

With charter in hand, Mr. Beaudry moved forward with financial targets and organization investments that aligned to that charter. The charter made it clear that Professional Service capabilities were about product enablement. The financial plan put in place for PS reflected this objective of enablement.

Mr. Beaudry reflects on the charter discussion: *"That simple charter graph accelerated many conversations. When people would ask why I was doing A and not B, I would remind them of the charter the executive committee gave me. With no defined charter, many conversations would have become a negotiation. "*

Has a defined charter removed every challenge HDS faces in its efforts to build PS capabilities? Of course not. However, forcing the conversation on the front end does accelerate implementation conversations and decisions that occur later. Why did you take this deal and not that deal? Why do you discount your services so much? Why don't you discount your services more? The rationales behind these decisions are easier to articulate with a clear charter. ■

GENESYS AND BUSINESS MODEL

Genesys, a wholly owned subsidiary of Alcatel, is the #1 provider of contact center software and provides the leading open-standards voice platform. Genesys's mission is to enable companies to deliver superior contact center services. The Genesys software suite captures, routes, reports, and analyzes voice, e-mail, and other communications to ensure that customers are quickly connected to the best available resource—the first time. With more than 3,000 customers in 80 countries including Global 2000 enterprises, government agencies, and many of the world's fastest growing mid-sized businesses, Genesys directs more than 100 million customer interactions every day.

In 2004, Elliot Danziger, the VP of Professional Services at Genesys, was concerned. Every quarter his staff of 140 literally gave a 110% effort—he had the utilization reports to prove it. Yet, PS only sporadically met its financial targets. At executive staff meetings Mr. Danziger would explain how specific customer projects were impacting PS profitability. The issues included:

- Sales representatives reducing the price of PS projects to stay competitive in the deal
- Customers declining to pay for project management assistance—even though the resource was required for successful implementation
- Customers refusing to pay for PS efforts related to product-performance issues.

Of course, customers were critical to the PS success, so the projects had to continue. Mr. Danziger also highlighted the incredible amount of pre-sales support PS provided. Of course, the deals were important, so the pre-sales efforts continued as well.

However, Stacey White, the CFO at Genesys, realized that the unpredictability of PS profitability was not just Mr. Danziger's problem; it was a company problem. *"The unpredictability and low visibility on PS profitability significantly impacted my ability to provide a reliable quarterly P&L forecast for the company to my management team and to corporate HQ in Paris."* In the Spring of 2004, Mrs. White and Mr. Danziger worked together to change the conversation. They opened the topic at the executive level. They asked the executive team to document the PS charter. Once that charter was defined, the PS management team went to work on creating a business model that supported that charter. The development of the PS business model enabled Mrs. White to create a more accurate 2005 budget model for both PS and the company. Figure 4.17 shows the original 2004 financial model PS was budgeted to operate in, the actual 2004 results for PS, and the 2005 financial model PS is now budgeted with following business model work completed. In 2004 there was no formal definition of the below-the-line investments required to sustain the business. With no business model in place, there was little defined investment in the business. With little defined investment, the function was struggling to scale. Also, no one had ever determined how much free sales support activity Genesys could afford PS to do. This gap became apparent in the business modeling process. The 2004 actuals and 2005 business model begin to account for the below-the-line investments in marketing, services engineering, sales, and operations. All of these investments are required to maintain and scale the capability.

When the dust settled after three months of executive management discussion, Mr. Danziger had a charter, a business model, and financial objectives he felt could be achieved. *"Being part of Professional Services in a product company for many years I have seen how shortfalls in PS margin contribution are often attributable to the cost of sales. These hidden costs of sales artificially boost product margins by hiding pre-sales activities, product problem resolution, and deeply discounted PS rates. In reality, these costs are often valid and required to close product deals and maintain customer satisfaction."* ∎

FIGURE 4.17 Genesys PS Business Model Evolution

GENESYS PROFESSIONAL SERVICES	2004 Budget	2004 Actual	2005 Budget
Service Revenues	100%	100%	100%
Gross Margin	34%	28%	32%
Operations	11%	12%	14%
Sales "Enablement"	0%	2%	2%
Services Sales	0%	0%	0%
Services Engineering	0%	1%	2%
Services Marketing	0%	0%	1%
Below the line investment	*11%*	*15%*	*19%*
Operating Income	23%	13%	13%
Corporate Allocations	12%	12%	9%
Operating Profit	11%	1%	4%

IBM, CAMBRIDGE TECHNOLOGY PARTNERS, AND CAMEL HUMPS

To appreciate the value of setting realistic growth expectations, let's look at two companies that aggressively increased their professional service capabilities in the late 1990s: IBM and Cambridge Technology Partners (CTP). Table 4.12 provides an overview of each company.

TABLE 4.12 Growth Rate Data

Company	Years Reviewed	Starting Service Revenues (in millions)	Ending Service Revenues (in millions)	Primary Growth Levers
IBM	1994–1999	$11,346,000	$32,172,000	Organic
CTP	1993–1998	$56,205	$612,041	Organic

Figure 4.18 maps the growth rate each of these companies experienced in their service business over a six-year period. The IBM clock started ticking in 1994, and the CTP clock started ticking in 1993. For just a moment, take yourself back to the late 1990s. In terms of technology-based PS activity, this was the perfect storm. Companies had to verify their computers would work in the year 2000. The internet craze began, and the overall economy was humming. Could any professional services firm hope for better conditions to grow their business?

We gain two insights from the small sampling of data shown in Figure 4.18. First, even in a perfect storm, the highest annual growth rate was 72%—not 200%, not 100%, but 72%. The average growth rate for both companies during these heady times was 41%. The second insight involves the very visible "camel humps" that appear in both growth rate curves. I believe this is the direct result of the energy required to grow a human-capital-intensive business. You can only hire (or acquire) so many new consultants before you must pause and absorb them into the company. Notice the binge of revenue growth (and most likely hiring), followed by the decline in growth.

Now, let's play the optimistic PS business plan shown in Figure 4.10 against the real world. Figure 4.19 maps the anticipated growth rates from an optimistic plan against the real growth data of IBM and CTP. As can be seen, the first three years of a plan often predict growth rates that are far beyond what these two companies have experienced. Of course, if your PS business is $2M and you want to take it to $4M, that is a 100% growth rate that makes sense. However, 90% of the companies I deal with have some run rate PS revenue that they want to aggressively build upon. They are starting out with $15M–$25M and they want to take it to $100M or $250M. Wonderful, but they shouldn't expect to get there by growing 150%–200% a year. ∎

FIGURE 4.18 Growth Rate Graph

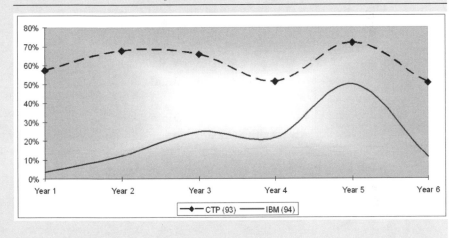

FIGURE 4.19 Desired PS Growth

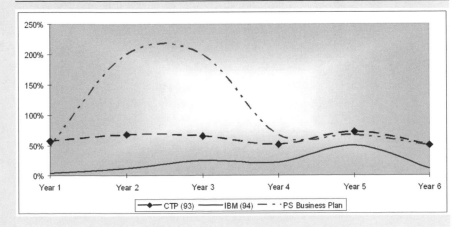

EXECUTIVE SUMMARY

Mastering the ability to set realistic financial objectives for a professional services organization is critical for a product company that wants to successfully grow services. This is often the first place a management team likes to start the PS strategy. Executives want to understand what financial expectations they should have for the professional service business unit. To answer this question, the management team must discuss and set three critical variables:

1. *Charter:* Why is the company investing in professional services capabilities? As a new source of revenue? A mechanism to solidify account position? The rationale should be clearly understood by the entire executive team. And the answer cannot be: *Accomplish it all!.*

2. *Business Model:* What does the steady state business model look like for the professional services organization? The management team must discuss both margin expectations (above-the-line profits) and required expenditures (below-the-line investments).

3. *Financial Objectives:* With a documented charter and business model established, the management team can create financial objectives for the professional service organization that make sense. Since PS is a human-capital-intensive business, the team should not be too aggressive with its growth expectations.

By considering all three variables, the executive team can create a well-defined, realistic set of financial expectations for the professional services business. Of course, we still have not discussed where all this revenue is coming from. Successfully answering that question is the objective of Chapter 5.

Chapter Five

Mastering the Services Portfolio

What to Sell

CHAPTER OBJECTIVE

To introduce a set of frameworks that enable an executive management team to identify a professional services portfolio that is aligned with company objectives

KEY CONCEPTS

- Three Pillars of a Services Strategy
- Five P's of Services Marketing
- Channel Assessment Graph
- Market Mix Graph

FIVE P'S OF MARKETING

Services is the second of the three service strategy pillars introduced in Chapter 3. Figure 5.1 highlights this pillar. When attempting to master this pillar, the management team must determine what type of services the company should be marketing. To answer this primary question, the management team must answer all of the following questions:

- What types of markets are we going after?
- Who will buy our services?
- What services should we offer?
- Are the services aligned to our market objectives?

- What channels will we use to sell our services?
- How will we position our services?
- How will we price our services?

In essence, the management team is working to answer questions around the five P's of marketing:

1. *Product* (or *service*): What products (services) will we sell?
2. *Positioning:* How will the services be positioned in the marketplace and differentiated from similar service offerings?
3. *Price:* How will the service offerings be priced?
4. *Placement:* How will the services be distributed into the marketplace?
5. *People:* What people will buy these service offerings? What are their titles? Their buying criteria?

Attempting to set these marketing parameters can quickly become overwhelming. To simplify the challenge, the marketing discussion can be bounded by the diagram shown in Figure 5.2. This figure shows the three variables critical to mastering the services portfolio:

- Markets
- Service offerings
- Channels

FIGURE 5.1 The Services Pillar

By markets, I mean what target markets will the product company attempt to reach with its service offerings. The install base? A new vertical industry? By service offerings, I mean the specific types of services the company intends to offer. Managed services? Consulting services? Install services? Assessment services? Finally, by channels, I mean the sales channels that will be used to sell the services to the target markets. The five P's of marketing can be superimposed on these three variables to create Figure 5.3.

When working in the services pillar, the most common mistake managers make is at the start of the discussion. Most product companies start by defining "service offerings." "Hey, we have some great ideas for killer services our customers will absolutely love." In fact, the majority of product companies I work with have no trouble defining a long list of service offerings that they believe will be successful in the marketplace. Too few of these companies take the time to clearly define the market for these services. Still fewer ever talk to potential customers in the target market to validate that the service offerings make sense.

FIGURE 5.2 Three Services Variables

FIGURE 5.3 The Five P's of Services Marketing

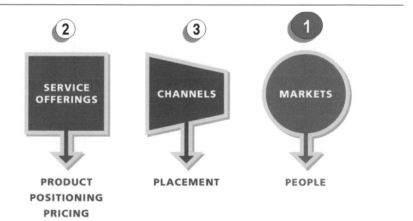

In Appendix B, I provide a framework for services positioning. In Appendix C, I provide a framework for your services pricing strategy. This chapter focuses on the three P's of People you hope to sell to, the Product you will sell to them, and how you will Place the product in front of them. My approach is designed to lead a management team through the marketing discussion in a way that leads to a services portfolio aligned with the company's revenue objectives and grounded in market realities. This is accomplished by having focused conversations in the following order:

1. What markets are the service organization being asked to serve?
2. What services do those markets want and need?
3. What channels will be used to sell services to the markets?

By starting the conversation in the right place, the management team dramatically improves its chances of creating a services portfolio that will succeed in the marketplace.

MARKETS

Before a product company documents its first professional service in a glossy datasheet, I strongly recommend the following question be asked:

> What markets are we attempting to reach with our service offerings? ■

The management team should then focus the discussion by asking:

> Who, specifically, will buy these service offerings? ■

I recommend starting the discussion with the basic target market map shown in Figure 5.4. This map is a modified version of a diagram that appears in the insightful book *The Channel Advantage* by Lawrence G. Friedman and Timothy R. Furey.[1] This market map uses customers and products to define four universal market segments:

> *Install Base:* This represents current customers using company products.
> *New Vertical Market:* This represents new customers the company would like to sell existing products.

---

1. Reprinted from *The Channel Advantage*, Lawrence G. Friedman and Timothy R. Furey, 1999, with permission from Elsevier.

New Product Market: This defines a new product that needs to be launched to existing customers.

Discontinuous Market: The most challenging market of all, this matches markets the company has never sold to before with recently released product.

By starting the conversation with these four categories, a management team can get agreement on which basic markets the services organization should be targeting.

Target Markets and Revenue Objectives

When defining what markets to address, the management team should consider the charter, business model, and revenue objectives of the services organization. Table 5.1 looks at target markets and how they align with revenue objectives. It is important to do this sanity check. If the target markets that are critical to company success will not support the target revenue objectives for services, the revenue objectives should be adjusted downward to stay aligned. For example, a company may be releasing a new product that takes the company into a new high-growth market. To support this launch, the management team would like the service organization to offer new services that will accelerate product adoption by new customers. This is a great way to use service capabilities as a strategic weapon. However, if the services organization is chartered to drive high-margin revenue growth, this request may not align.

FIGURE 5.4 Target Market Map

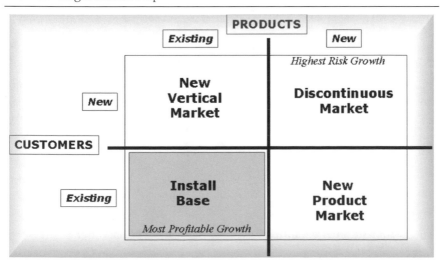

TABLE 5.1 Aligning Markets to Revenue Objectives

Target Market	Description	Risk	Market Growth	Aligned Charters	Aligned Business Model	Aligned Financial Targets
Install	Existing customers Existing products	Low	Flat-Low	Margin SAT	High margin	Slow top-line growth High contribution
			High	Margin SAT revenue	High margin	High top-line growth High contribution
New Product	Existing customers New products	Moderate	Flat-Low	Share SAT	Moderate margin	Slow top-line growth
			High	Share SAT Revenue	Moderate margin	Moderate top-line growth
New Industry	Existing customers New customers	Moderate	Flat-Low	Share SAT	Moderate margin	Slow top-line growth Moderate contribution
			High	Share SAT Revenue	Moderate margin	Moderate top-line growth Moderate contribution
Discontinuous	New products New customers	High	Flat-Low	Share SAT	Low margin	Slow top-line growth Low contribution
			High	Share SAT Revenue	Low margin	Moderate top-line growth Low contribution

The alignment process outlined in Table 5.1 leads us to another Scylla Fee as summarized in Figure 5.5.

FIGURE 5.5 The Sixth Scylla Fee

Scylla Fee	The target markets professional services is being asked to pursue must support the financial expectations set for professional services.

Internal professional services organizations are often asked to lead a product company into new customer markets. This effort comes with a very real cost. If your company has never sold into the health care industry, for example, it will take effort for PS to take you there because your company has no brand recognition, or equity or experience in the industry. For PS to lead you there, it will need to hire consultants that understand health care. Then PS will need to start the arduous process of convincing prospects that your company brings value to the industry. All of this takes time and money. And that time and money will drag down PS profitability. Executives cannot ask PS to aggressively settle new market territories and still show incredible profit. The numbers will not add up.

Getting Specific

Invariably, I see service organizations living in "market darkness." The service managers have limited data regarding the markets they hope to pursue. To further complicate things, the corporate marketing team and the service organization might not even share a common taxonomy when discussing markets. As a management team, are you tracking vertical markets such as health care and banking? Do you track horizontal markets such as IT implementation services or IT outsourcing? Or, do you track market types that are unique to your company, such as "B2B multi-enterprise collaboration infrastructure"? Regardless of what you track, the service organization and the marketing organization need to create a common terminology and market taxonomy. When this happens, the service organization can begin receiving meaningful market data. This potential disconnect between marketing and services creates the seventh Scylla fee outlined in Figure 5.6.

FIGURE 5.6 The Seventh Scylla Fee

Scylla Fee	The Services organization and the Marketing organization must have a common market taxonomy.

Once a management team has invested the time to clearly define what markets the service organization should be targeting, the discussion can turn to service offerings.

SERVICE OFFERINGS

When discussing target markets, I suggested you start with the basic market map shown in Figure 5.4. I make the same recommendation regarding service offerings. When attempting to define what services the company should offer, the management team should start with the generic service stack that was introduced in Chapter 3. The broad types of services are defined in Table 5.2. I broke "Education Services" out of "Professional Services" in the table so it would not get lost. I also added "Staff Augmentation" because many technology companies place specialized service resources on customer sites for a specified time. These engagements do not have itemized deliverables: The customer simply needs the expertise of the onsite consultant available.

A management team can create a first-cut service portfolio by working through the following four steps.

Step 1: Current Services

What services are now offered by the company? How much revenue do they generate? How important does the management team feel these services are?

Step 2: Desired Services

What types of services does the management team believe the company must offer to be successful in the target markets?

TABLE 5.2 Service Types

Service Name	Descripton	Tag Lines	Pricing Attributes	Time Attributes	Proposed Benefits
Support services	Basic break-fix service for products of the company	24/7, Remote administration, Help desk	Fixed percent of product costs or price can be driven by response time necessary.	Annual contracts, over the life of product	Insurance policy for the customer
Education services	Product training	E-learning, Web-learning	Fixed percent of product costs or by the class. Also, as part of the sale, "training units" can be applied to training classes.	Service measured in days of training	Increased employee productivity and employee certification
Staff augmentation	Staff onsite to supplement customer skills		Time and materials	From 4 weeks to years	Allows customer to focus on core competencies
Professional services	Standard and custom services designed to help customer implement the product faster or make the product more efficient	Quick start, System tuning, Turnkey integration	Fixed price for well-defined services, Variable pricing for more complex engagements, Per service requested	1 day 8 months	Time to implement new product reduced, improve effectiveness of products already implemented
Consulting services	Standard and custom services designed to leverage expertise of the product company	Best practices, Assessments	Variable pricing, driven by complexity of deliverables	2 weeks–2 months	ROI, reduced risk, time to implement business solution reduced
Managed services	Standard and custom services from product company, which takes responsibility for specific operational activities	Operational efficiency, Core competencies	Variable pricing, driven by scope of operational responsibility	6 months to years	ROI, staff reduction, staff optimization
Outsourcing services	Staff provided by product company to administer the product for the customer on an ongoing basis	Outsourcing	Fixed rate per head, Fixed cost per time period	Months–years	Reduce costs, allows customer to focus on core competencies

Step 3: Revenue Forecasting

What revenues would the management team initially expect from the desired service portfolio? Table 5.3 provides an example of service revenue forecasting for a set of professional services developed by a hardware/software provider. For each service, the number of engagements is forecast. All service revenue forecasts can be rolled up to create a service revenue-mix grid like that in Table 5.4. This table is used to document which specific services will drive the revenues for the services business.

Step 4: Validation

How does the company convince customers that the recommended services are necessary? How will the revenue projections be validated?

This fourth step in the service definition process suggests another Scylla Fee that must be paid. Figure 5.7 documents this requirement. Managers must make sure the service portfolio being developed is relevant to the marketplace. To date, I have only worked with one product company that did not have a plethora of ideas for new service offerings. Coming up with concepts is the easy part. Making sure they stick in the marketplace is the hard part. Service development lifecycle management is the discipline of profitably creating and releasing services into the marketplace. This is a relatively new discipline and most product companies stink at it. Unfortunately, I will not be covering the discipline of service development in detail; I intend to publish on this topic separately. However, simply documenting and validating a target service revenue mix is a significant step forward for most professional service organizations.

TABLE 5.3 Service Revenue Forecast

Service Type	Service Name	Service Description	Target Market(s)	Target Customer(s)	Average Deal Size	Average Cost	No. of Deals	Target Revenues
Professional Services	Tune IT Install	Installation of Tune IT software	XC200 Install Base	I/T Manager	$ 15,000	$ 10,000	40	$ 600,000
	Software Manager Optimizer	Optimize existing installation of the XZ100 Software Manager	XZ100 Install Base	I/T Manager	$ 20,000	$ 16,000	45	$ 900,000
	X2000 Quick Start	Implementation of X2000 hardware	New customers: X2000	I/T Manager, CIO	$ 10,000	$ 6,000	80	$ 800,000
	X2000 Migration	Migration of customer environment from X1000 to X2000	X1000 Install Base	I/T Manager, CIO	$ 40,000	$ 30,000	65	$ 2,600,000
					$ 85,000		230	$ 4,900,000

TABLE 5.4 Service Revenue-Mix Table

Service Type	Target Revenues	Target Expenses	Target Profits	Expected Margin	Revenue
Education Services	$ 3,000,000	$ 2,400,000	$ 600,000	20%	9%
Staff Augmentation	$ 4,000,000	$ 2,600,000	$1,400,000	35%	12%
Managed Services	$ 5,000,000	$ 3,500,000	$1,500,000	30%	15%
Professional Services	$ 15,000,000	$ 11,250,000	$3,750,000	25%	45%
Consulting Services	$ 2,000,000	$ 1,400,000	$ 600,000	30%	6%
Outsourcing Services	$ 4,000,000	$ 3,400,000	$ 600,000	15%	12%
	$ 33,000,000	$ 24,550,000	$8,450,000	26%	

FIGURE 5.7 The Eighth Scylla Fee

Scylla Fee	Target services must be validated against the actual needs of the target markets.

Forecast Quality

Forecasting the revenue potential of service offerings is a dicey business in product companies. This is the case, in general, because most companies have never been required to do it. Despite this natural handicap, it is amazing to me how loose and undisciplined the service forecasting process is in product companies. To create some clarity, I like to use the concept of forecast quality.

How much confidence does the management team have in the revenue numbers being projected for new or existing service offerings? To answer this, I think a company can refer to four distinct data streams that feed a revenue forecast. These data streams are outlined in Table 5.5.

TABLE 5.5 Forecasting Data Streams

	Name	Description	What it Tells You	Example Sources
1	Market Data	Refers to information and analysis on potential market opportunities. This can include secondary data gathered from existing market studies or primary data from custom market studies conducted specifically for the company.	Projected market sizes, market trends, who the competition is, specific opportunities for your company	Primary sources: commissioned market studies Secondary sources: Gartner Inc., IDC
2	Product Data	Refers to the forecasts for product sales volumes and mix.	The specific markets and customers the company will be focusing on. Potential of attach rate service sales.	Product marketing Field sales
3	Install Data	Refers to detailed information on customers who have purchased products and services from the company. Also includes service sales history.	Volume of existing customers available to be targeted for the new service offerings. What services customers have historically purchased from the company.	Customer database
4	Deal Data	Refers to actual data from past service engagements.	What customers are willing to pay for. What services have been delivered. What skills were required. What customers value.	Project review reports, customer SAT surveys

I call market data and product data "above-the-line" data streams. They are insightful, but can vary greatly in accuracy. Install data and deal data, on the other hand, are based on reality. I term these "below-the-line" data streams. The trends predicted by below-the-line data streams are generally accurate. Combining these data streams, a management team can begin creating a realistic forecast. Figure 5.8 brings all of these concepts together in one diagram. When some (or all) of these supporting data streams are missing, the quality of the service revenue forecast is reduced. Poor quality forecasting can result in money being spent to release services no one really wants.

FIGURE 5.8 Forecast Quality

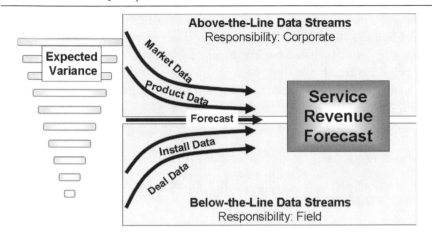

Real Money

Every time a company introduces a new service to the market, real money is spent. Marketing materials are developed, consultants are hired, delivery partners may need to be trained. If the service is complex, the upfront investment can be significant. One of my favorite stories involves one of the first executive meetings I was asked to attend. A billion-dollar hardware company had become excited about offering professional services. The COO chartered a senior director to create a plan showing how the company could launch twenty new service offerings over the next nine months. As the executives reviewed the plan, they asked my opinion. I said, "You realize that each one of these offerings will take anywhere from $100k to $500k to successfully launch." At first, they thought I was exaggerating the costs, but once I itemized the expenditures involved, they realized I had been conservative. Within thirty minutes the list was reduced from twenty to four services that would be piloted and cautiously evaluated. Sometimes, it takes executives a little time to internalize the fact that taking services to market is more than just hiring consultants and throwing them into accounts. Of course, one of the real sticking points is a product company's inability to sell services successfully. The company is hard wired to sell tangible products—not mushy services. This challenge leads us to the next variable that a company must examine when mastering the services portfolio.

CHANNELS

Channels represent the final parameter to be considered in the services pillar. This variable can only be discussed after target markets and target services have been defined. Glance back at Figure 5.2. At this point, we have defined the target markets on the right side and the target services on the left side. The question we have to consider now is what sales channels to use to drive the target services into the target markets.

Channel Options

When selling services, a company has multiple channels to choose from. Figure 5.9 shows six of those options.

1. *Direct:* The existing direct product sales force or an overlay services sales force.
2. *Independent Software Vendor (ISV) or Original Equipment Manufacturer (OEM):* A partner that builds value-added applications on top of your products (ISVs) or embeds your technology in theirs (OEMs).
3. *VAR:* A value-added reseller that takes your product, combines it with others, and solves business problems for a customer.
4. *Distributor:* A partner that simply resells your existing products. No value-added solutions are included.
5. *Telesales:* A   telemarketing organization that is either internal or outsourced.
6. *Internet:* Your company Web site. Internet banner advertisements. Google ads.

FIGURE 5.9 Channel Options

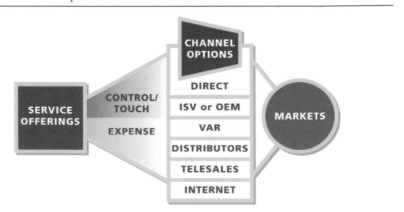

Channel Mix

To determine which specific channels to use in what quantity, a management team can pursue a three-step process.

Step 1: Document Customer Profiles

The company must consider how target customers will prefer to purchase the target services. This can be accomplished by creating a customer profile as shown in Table 5.6. This table maps service offerings to the channels that those services ideally would be sold through. Of course, we are not living in an ideal world.

Step 2: Document Channel Options

Now the company defines channel options that are actually available to the service organization. This can be done by creating a channel options table as shown in Table 5.7. This table documents the costs, current capacity, and "value add" of each channel. The data in this table can be graphed as in Figure 5.10. Once again, for further guidance on the process of assessing channels, refer to *The Channel Advantage* by Friedman and Furey.

Step 3: Align Marketing Mixes

With the service revenue-mix data, the customer profile, and the channel options table in hand, a services marketing manager can map target services to channel options. This effort results in a marketing mix graph like that in

TABLE 5.6 Customer Profile

Target Market	Target Service	Customer Type	Example Title	Buying Criteria	Current Channels	Desired Channels
Install Base	Architecture review	Senior management	CEO, CIO, COO	Minimized risk, ROI	VARs, Distributors	Direct sales
	System consolidation	I/T senior management	I/T director	ROI, Scalability, Feature capabilities	Direct sales, VARs, Distributors	VARs
	Education	I/T management	Data Center manager	Cost, Staff interest	Direct sales, VARs, Distributors	Direct sales
New Product	Migration	Senior management	CEO, CIO, COO	Minimized risk, ROI	VARs, Distributors	Direct sales
	Integration	I/T senior management	I/T director	System stability	Direct sales, VARs, Distributors	VARs

TABLE 5.7 Channel Options

Channel	Number of Services Supported	Cost Per Transaction	Average Deal Size	Expense/ Revenue Ratio	Reps/ Partners	Quota	Channel Capacity	% of Sales
Service Sales Reps	39	$ 800	$ 100,000	0.80%	20	$ 500,000	$ 10,000,000	29%
Product Account Reps	20	$ 500	$ 50,000	1.00%	70	$ 250,000	$ 17,500,000	51%
ISVs	15	$ 500	$ 25,000	2.00%	100	$ 50,000	$ 5,000,000	15%
VARs	0	$ 300	$ 25,000	1.20%	0	$ 500,000	$ -	0%
Distributors	0	$ 200	$ 30,000	0.67%	0	$ 100,000	$ -	0%
Telesales	5	$ 100	$ 5,000	2.00%	10	$ 10,000	$ 100,000	0%
Internet	0	$ 25	$ 5,000	0.50%	1	$ 500,000	$ 500,000	1%
						TOTAL	$ 34,010,000	

FIGURE 5.10 Channel Mix Graph

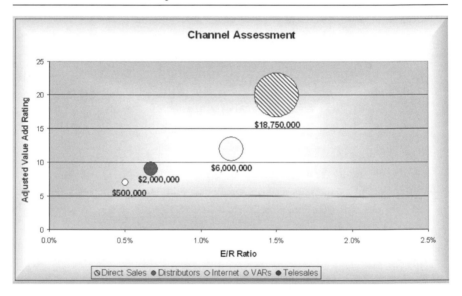

Figure 5.11. This graph directly maps the target revenue for the service organization to the target markets, the target service offerings, and the sales channels. This critical graph definitively answers the question we are addressing when focusing on the second pillar of a services strategy: "Where are we going to get the money?" In the example shown, the company intends to get a majority of its services revenue from the install base. Two new target markets will be pursued. There will be seven core service offerings that drive the $35M business. Finally, the direct sales force will be significantly augmented by VARs to sell the services portfolio.

The exercise of creating the marketing mix table leads us to not one, but two Scylla's Fees that must be paid. Figure 5.12 delineates the first one.

FIGURE 5.11 Marketing Mix Graph

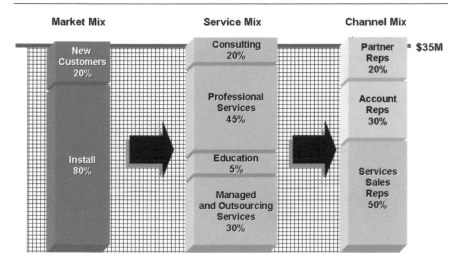

FIGURE 5.12 The Ninth Scylla Fee

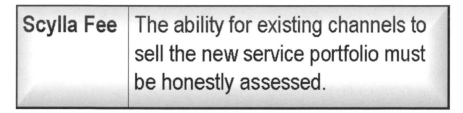

Scylla Fee	The ability for existing channels to sell the new service portfolio must be honestly assessed.

Product companies consistently overestimate the ability of the existing sales force to sell new service offerings. There is always a raging debate over whether this is a skills, training, or service-maturity issue. Do product sales reps fail to sell new services because they do not have the required soft skills to sell intangible services? Or is it because the company has not adequately trained them to sell services? Or, do the service offerings simply suck? In reality, I believe it is a combination of all three factors. The point, though, is that initially the direct sales force will not be a very effective channel for selling services. This failing needs to be offset, either by hiring an overlay sales force or by beefing up other channels or both. If the company does not address this channel shortage, service revenues will be short of expectations.

The second Scylla Fee concerning sales channels is documented in Figure 5.13.

FIGURE 5.13 The Tenth Scylla Fee

| Scylla Fee | Channel Mix must be understood. |

To be brutally honest, I have yet to work with a services organization that could show me a complete marketing mix table. Often, the revenue target for services is assigned to sales reps, but no one has done the work required to create a channel mix that is achievable. In other words, no one has done the homework to determine exactly what services will drive the service revenue targets, how customers want to buy those services, and what capacity *really* exists in the current channels to sell those services. I think there are many reasons for this depressing reality:

- Executives have not asked for this channel mix data.
- The field staff has no ability to forecast revenues for specific service offerings.
- The Services marketing manager is not comfortable assessing channel options.

Whatever the reason, the void exists—and this void creates risk. To date, this risk seems to be acceptable to many service executives. When service revenues start to represent more than 25% of company revenues, however, I doubt CEOs and CFOs will remain comfortable with this void. As always, Scylla must eventually be paid her fee.

VALUE OF IDENTIFYING MARKETS, SERVICES, AND CHANNELS

When we began this chapter, we had set the charter, business model, and financial objectives for the services organization. We knew *what* we wanted the business to achieve financially. However, we had no idea *where* the revenue would come from. By defining the mix of markets, services, and channels, the management team has created a realistic first cut of where the service revenue

FIGURE 5.14 Variables for Mastering the Services Portfolio

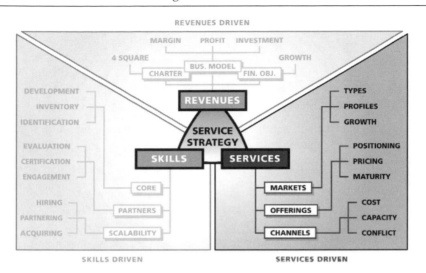

would actually come from. Figure 5.14 documents the areas we've discussed in this chapter, culminating in the creation of the *marketing mix graph*. This graph is an indispensable view into any services business.

Do I believe that executives and service marketing organizations will accurately estimate service revenues and channel capacities the first time through? Hell, no. But by thoroughly discussing and documenting the services pillar, the management team begins to take uncertainty and risk out of the service strategy. It has begun mapping where the money will be coming from. These estimates can be revised and refined as market data and field feedback become available—as with all marketing numbers, the revenue projection process is iterative. Also, by putting a stake in the ground, the management team provides much needed guidance to the field. What services are mission critical to the long-term success of the company? The ones identified in this service strategy planning process.

COMPANY CASE STUDIES

PROGRESS SOFTWARE AND TARGET MARKETS

Progress Software Corporation (PSC) supplies software to simplify and accelerate the development, deployment, integration, and management of business applications.

Users of information technology today demand software applications that are responsive, comprehensive, reliable, and cost-effective. PSC products address their needs by:

- boosting application developer productivity, reducing time to application deployment, and accelerating the realization of business benefits,
- enabling highly distributed deployment of responsive applications across internal networks, the Internet, disconnected users, and
- simplifying the connectivity and integration of applications and data across the enterprise and between enterprises.

Their goal is to maximize the benefits of information automation while minimizing its total cost of ownership.

The mission of PSC is to deliver superior software products and services that empower their partners and customers to dramatically improve their development, deployment, integration, and management of quality applications worldwide.

Progress Software Corporation delivers products and services through its operating units that include:

The **Progress OpenEdge** product line offers a complete platform for developing and deploying business applications. Through its standards-based, Service Oriented Architecture, OpenEdge allows the development of business applications that can be deployed and managed over a wide range of computing platforms and across the Internet. OpenEdge offers a unified environment, including development tools, application servers, flexible integration options, its market-leading embedded Progress database, and systems management tools.

Sonic Software is the inventor and leading provider of the Enterprise Service Bus (ESB), the standards-based foundation for building a Service Oriented Architecture, or SOA. Sonic products provide reliable, manageable, and cost-effective distributed infrastructure to integrate applications and orchestrate business processes across the extended enterprise.

ObjectStore's data management, access, and synchronization products for the real-time enterprise help businesses handle streaming event data such as RFID or stock tickers, accelerate the performance of existing relational databases, and support occasionally connected users requiring real-time access to enterprise applications.

DataDirect Technologies is the leading provider of components for connecting software to data. Products from DataDirect use industry-standard interfaces such as ODBC, JDBC, and, ADO.NET to ensure consistent behavior and performance across diverse environments such as J2EE, .NET, Web, and client/server. DataDirect also offers an XML development tool, Stylus Studio, and it has been instrumental in the development of the XQuery standard for querying and processing XML data.

The computer software industry is intensely competitive. Progress Software experiences significant competition from a variety of sources with respect to all its products. Progress believes that the breadth and integration of its product offerings have become increasingly important competitive advantages. Other factors affecting competition in the markets served by Progress include product performance in complex applications, application portability, vendor experience, ease of integration, price, training, and support.

Progress Professional Services (Progress PS) Strategic Planning

In the spring of 2003, Progress Software was creating a multiyear strategic plan for its professional services business. A Progress Professional Services Leadership Team headed up this planning initiative. They documented the following five-phase process:

Phase 1—Scenario Identification: By reviewing past experience, researching industry experience, and interviewing senior management, Progress would identify several potential scenarios for the future of the professional services business.

Phase 2—Impact Analysis: Potential scenarios would be reviewed, evaluated, and prioritized. Recommendations on what scenarios to pursue would be made to executive staff.

Phase 3—Roadmap Creation: The professional services management team would create a business roadmap that documents how Progress would move from current state to the target scenarios decided upon in Phase 2.

Phase 4—Financial Planning: The financial requirements to support the roadmap would be determined. The 2004 annual budgets would be set based on the requirements defined in the roadmap.

Phase 5—Continuing Improvement: Progress Software would implement a metrics and monitoring program to track roadmap progress.

All senior managers within the company were interviewed for input on the process and the Progress PS strategy.

Progress PS Markets

As Progress Software went through the planning process, the global Progress PS management team navigated the nine variables of a professional services strategy. The team started the strategy discussions in the Services Pillar. The services management team wanted to first understand what services the company required from its organizations. Then, the team would create a business model and financial objectives to support that services portfolio. In Chapter 3, I named this a "services-led PS strategy."

When starting in the services pillar, the Progress PS management team first defined the target markets they provided services to. By having this discussion, the team quickly realized there were four very different markets they were responsible for servicing:

1. *Elite and Premier Application Partners (APs).* These are large application partners that resell significant amounts of the Progress product line. These APs require in-depth technical support to optimize their applications on the Progress platform.

2. *Large End Users.* These are large Progress product users that are serviced directly by Progress with technical support, professional services, etc.

3. *Preferred and Member Application Partners.* Smaller application partners that resell Progress products.

4. *Smaller End Users.* Smaller users that occasionally request assistance directly from Progress.

Figure 5.15 documents these four distinct markets. As the management team started to better define these distinct markets, they realized how different the services requirements of each market were. The management team also realized how different each market's financial models were. Understanding these differences, Progress PS was able to work with executive management to gain agreement on the appropriate service strategy for each segment. The services team was then able to engineer the appropriate financial model to support these agreements.

FIGURE 5.15 Target Markets Served by Progress Professional Services

	APs	End-Users
Leverage PSC Community *(Business Driven)*	[I] **Improve competitive position**	[II] **Gain business advantage**
Effective and Efficient *(Technology Driven)*	*Extend life of the application* [III]	*Optimize value of Progress applications* [IV]

Mr. Edward Sugrue was Vice President of Professional Services during this strategy planning process. He makes the following comments on the lessons learned:

> Before clearly defining the needs of our unique markets, Progress Professional Services was trying to be all things to all people. From the services perspective, we approached Partners and End Users with the same financial metrics. In the end, that is not what the business needed from us. Our President, David Ireland, wanted Progress PS to enable partners as cost effectively as possible and to augment customers' requirements when they requested. We needed to align our business to address these different objectives.

Clearly defined target markets changed the conversation for Mr. Sugrue and his team. Jeanice Koronowski, the current leader of Progress Software's professional service organization, observed: *"Our financial objectives were not aligned to our market objectives. This misalignment was making it difficult for Progress PS to succeed. Now, as a function, we can articulate and defend our business model to executive management."*

CONVERGYS AND SERVICE MIX

Convergys Corporation (NYSE: CVG) is a global leader in integrated billing, employee care, and customer care services provided through outsourcing or licensing. Convergys focuses on developing long-term strategic relationships with clients in employee- and customer-intensive industries including communications, technology, financial services, and consumer goods. Convergys has two reporting segments: (1) the Customer Management Group (CMG), which provides outsourced marketing, customer support services, accounts receivable management, and employee care services; and (2) the Information Management Group (IMG), which provides Business Support Systems (BSS) and Customer Relationship Management (CRM) software and services. This is a review of how Convergys's IMG business unit worked to develop a strategic value-added services mix to complement its existing traditional outsourcing and license-oriented business model.

Historically, Convergys had utilized services to enable the sale of its products and outsourcing capabilities. The services provided included training, testing, implementation, and customization related to the deployment of its products. However, this product-centric focus was limiting Convergys's ability to provide broader solutions for the clients it served:

- Convergys was often limited to being a technology provider within the broader solution sold by other service vendors.
- Because of the focus on providing an outsourcing or licensed product offer, Convergys was missing out on a critical opportunity to build stronger client partnerships through consulting. Convergys realized that the path to enhancing these partnerships required a consultative approach that helped clients identify and solve their broader business problems.
- Convergys recognized it needed more on-site presence with current clients.

To address these challenges, Convergys expanded its point of entry into clients by broadening its services portfolio to include more professional and consulting services. Figure 5.16 documents the service stack Convergys built in order to become a more consultative company.

FIGURE 5.16 Convergys IMG Services Portfolio

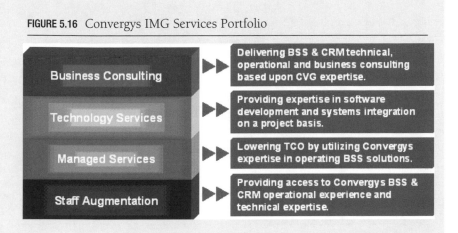

To accelerate the development of this new service initiative, Convergys dedicated a proven senior executive, Randy Mysliviec, to launch a global professional services business unit. Mysliviec had to assemble a new management team and begin crafting an appropriate go-to-market strategy for services. One of the first questions facing the team related to the services portfolio: What service offerings should Convergys develop and deploy to improve its competitive position? As Mysliviec recalled: *"We had a list of over forty ideas for new consulting and technology services. Obviously, we couldn't develop and deploy all those services ideas at once."*

To prioritize the service-offering queue, Mysliviec established a services engineering team led by Greg O'Brien. The team employed a set of five criteria to qualify each service idea:

1. Revenue (direct, full solution)
2. Repeatability (consistent need across multiple accounts)
3. Capability (Convergys strengths)
4. Competition (competitive differentiation)
5. Market readiness (effort required to make offering available)

The team also communicated the service development process it would employ. This helped set expectations of how Convergys would take new offerings to market. Figure 5.17 documents its approach.

FIGURE 5.17 Convergys's IMG Service Development Process

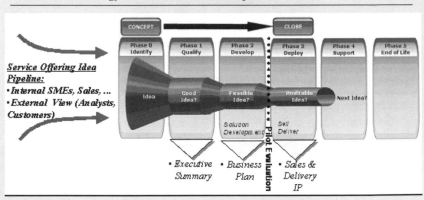

By employing a disciplined approach, the services engineering team was able to segment offerings into three distinct tiers, with Tier 1 representing offerings that should be deployed immediately. There were fewer than ten offerings identified as Tier 1. Each of these offerings was successfully developed and deployed in the first year.

O'Brien had this to say about the process: *"By creating specific criteria and a clear process, we were able to align around a tight set of service offerings. These became the initial core of our new services portfolio. We had the confidence these offerings were aligned with our client's needs and Convergys's strategic objectives."*

LUCENT AND SALES CHANNELS

With over 32,000 employees, Lucent Technologies offers the leading global communications service providers, governmental agencies, and leading Fortune 2000 companies a comprehensive portfolio of products, services, and solutions through three primary operating units: Integrated Network Solutions (INS) for sales to wireline service providers, Mobility Solutions for mobile service providers, and Lucent Worldwide Services (LWS) as the underlying professional services organization.

Lucent combines the rich history and heritage of the famed Bell Labs expertise with its 12,000 employee strong global service group dedicated to solving today's most complex networking challenges. From deploying multivendor solutions based on industry-leading technology in optical, packet and circuit switching, spread-spectrum CDMA, and network operations software to providing leading-edge consultative design and optimizations services, Lucent is positioned as the knowledge behind the network.

Building Professional Services

Due to the dramatic downturn in telecom spending that began in 2001, Lucent Technologies logged over ten consecutive losing quarters. A key piece of Lucent's recovery plan was (and is) to capture incremental service revenues while growing the existing revenue base. CEO Patricia Russo stated, *"Even with the telecom market as challenging as it is, our customers spend about $30 billion a year on services contracted out or that they do themselves. Our competitors are scaling back on services, but we are expanding."*

To accelerate this building process, in 2003 Lucent hired Mr. John Meyer, a former senior executive from EDS, to head up the 11,000-person global services division known as LWS. Mr. Meyer quickly moved to expand Lucent's services portfolio. Specifically, Mr. Meyer saw an opportunity in enterprise services. He brought on board Mr. Ron Rendeiro to spearhead Lucent's re-emergance into the North American Enterprise market. Mr. Rendeiro and Mr. Meyer believed that the following benefits could be achieved if Lucent could gain traction in the enterprise services marketplace:

- Enable Lucent to achieve sustainable, profitable revenue growth in 2005 and beyond—improve shareholder value!
- Diversify Lucent's customer base into adjacent industry verticals—to accelerate Lucent's revenue growth and diversify the company's current risk profile
- Help Lucent's Service Provider customers be more successful serving their own Enterprise customers through a partnership model
- Capture profitable services and solutions revenue that was not being addressed by current SP channels (Managed Services, Strategic Business Consulting, etc.)
- Take advantage of overall Lucent brand awareness to establish mainstream Services acceptance outside of the service provider community
- Greatly enhance Lucent's credibility as a "vendor neutral" services provider
- Drive acceptance of Lucent solutions directly to the end-user organization, thereby improving sales through all channels

However, one of the greatest challenges to successfully entering and then capturing this market was not in just creating new service offerings, but in selling them!

Three-Pronged Attack

It is well known that Lucent has a long heritage as a product company. This means the sales channels at Lucent historically have been optimized to drive product sales. Complex service sales were left to partners such as AT&T and Verizon. However, the executives realized that if Lucent was to gain any real momentum in services, the historical sales channel structure would need to adapt. To address this need, Lucent aggressively moved in the following ways:

- *Dedicated Service Sales Force:* Lucent invested and created a specialized sales force dedicated to selling services globally. This new sales force was chartered to work with in-place Lucent product account managers in existing accounts to better position services. These new services sales reps were also chartered to find new accounts Lucent could sell services into.

- *New Alliance Partners:* Lucent identified new alliance partners such as Enterasys, EMC, and Sun. These partners had products and services that complemented Lucent's updated service portfolio.

- *Refreshed System Integration Relationships:* With its new service capabilities, Lucent needed to revisit existing partnerships with system integrators and created relationships that allowed Lucent to successfully sell its new services to new markets.

By addressing all three areas, Lucent had a plan to increase sales channel capacity. These new levers were deemed critical to Lucent's successfully driving significant service revenues. Figure 5.18 is a Lucent company diagram that documents this multichannel approach. As Mr. Rendeiro stated:

> Lucent must now reach our customer's customers and gain their acceptance of Lucent as a provider of best in class solutions. This requires a much different sales channel strategy for the company. We need to improve our market reach while not creating a competitive model against our Service Provider customers. If we don't find a way to reach these new prospective clients, we will not accomplish our goals.

FIGURE 5.18 Lucent Sales Channel Strategy for Enterprise Services

As with everything, this multipronged approach is not without challenges. Lucent must now manage a whole new level of channel complexity. Previously, Lucent had two primary channels: the direct sales force moving Lucent products and a reseller model reselling Lucent products. With the plan underway, Lucent must now manage the potential overlap between the multiple channels that are now selling products and services. Despite this new level of complexity, the massive Fortune 200 networking communications manufacturer is seeing progress in its ability to reach Fortune 2000 companies and ultimately sell services and solutions. After 18 months into this effort, Mr. Rendeiro has some reasons to be optimistic:

> Two years ago, the largest nonservice provider services deal Lucent had ever landed was under $4,000,000. Today, we are bidding and winning complex deals that are over $150,000,000 in service content. We still have a way to go, but our multipronged approach is showing progress and one that should pay off in the near future. If we would have stayed the course, our future would have been more linear and predictable, but now, we have traction and leverage into a unique and new market that will serve to fuel Lucent's growth in the years to come.

■

EXECUTIVE SUMMARY

By exploring the services pillar, an executive team can thoroughly answer the ever-pending question: "Where is the money coming from?" To create a sustainable PS strategy, a management team should have a clear understanding of what will drive PS revenues. To achieve this understanding, the team must define the following variables:

1. *Markets:* What markets will the PS business be asked to pursue? Existing install base? New vertical industries? The farther PS is asked to stray from the existing markets of the company, the more investment will be required.

2. *Service Offerings:* Now that we understand what markets PS is pursuing, what services does PS need to offer these markets? Consulting? Managed? Outsourcing? Which specific services are required by critical customers or partners in these markets?

3. *Channels:* Finally, with the target markets and target services defined, the company must make sure there is a sales channel to reach the target customers.

By assigning real dollar values to the target mixes in all three areas, the executive team can create a *market-mix graph.* This picture shows if there are any deficiencies in opportunity or sales reach. By making sure there is enough well-defined opportunity to support the revenue objectives of PS, the chance for success is increased. By making sure the company can capture that sales opportunity, the chance for success is increased again!

HOME STRETCH

The revenue objectives have been put on the table. The services that will drive those revenues have been identified. All this is good. But the strategy is not complete, not yet viable. Why? Because we have no idea how the company will actually deliver on the service portfolio we have defined. Professional services is a human-capital-intensive business. Also, it requires employees with high-end soft and hard skills. These attributes make PS extremely difficult to scale. In fact, matching delivery capabilities to service demands is the foremost challenge on the mind of every service manager out there—regardless of their specific role in the organization. So, let's complete this service strategy and make it viable by mastering the ability to scale a professional services organization. Let's move to the final pillar: skills.

Chapter | Six

Mastering Scalability

How Are We Going to Deliver?

CHAPTER OBJECTIVE

To introduce a set of frameworks that enable a management team to identify the core skills required to deliver the service portfolio of the company and establish strategies to scale service delivery capabilities

KEY CONCEPTS

- PS Function Map
- PS Position Map
- Skills Table
- Scalability Mix Graph
- The Hour Glass Model

CORE COMPETENCY CONFUSION

In Chapter 4, I defined the process of creating financial objectives that make sense for the professional services organization. In Chapter 5, I defined an approach to identify where all those service revenues would come from. Now, we must master the process of scaling our service delivery capabilities. Because if we don't deliver the services, we don't get paid!

Skills is the third and final service strategy pillar. Figure 6.1 highlights this pillar. When focusing on this dimension, the management team must determine how the company will actually deliver the service portfolio. Joseph Walton, when he ran EMC's $600 million service organization, had a simple mantra for his management team: "Global, Scalable, Consistent." This mantra strikes at the heart of the skills pillar. To master a professional services business, a management team must be able to deliver its service offerings consistently, anywhere in the world, and sometimes on very short notice.

To begin getting a handle on scaling skills, a management team must start by understanding what competencies are core to the company and the service organization. "Core competencies" has become a very fashionable phrase. *"We need to refocus on our core competencies!"* OK, but exactly what do you mean by "core competencies"? Unfortunately, the concept of core competencies has become overused and underimplemented. In this chapter, we will work through a model to clearly define core competencies and to describe how they drive partnership and sourcing decisions. So let us begin clearing the mud.

PS FUNCTION MAP

In *Building Professional Services*, I define five distinct functions that compose a mature services organization. Table 6.1 provides an overview of these five functions. For more detailed information on each function, please refer to the original text.

FIGURE 6.1 The Skills Pillar

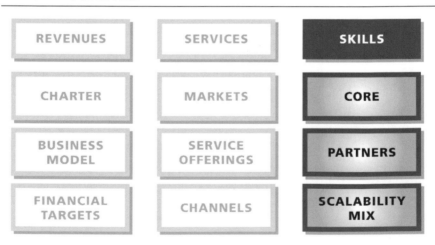

REVENUES	SERVICES	**SKILLS**
CHARTER	MARKETS	**CORE**
BUSINESS MODEL	SERVICE OFFERINGS	**PARTNERS**
FINANCIAL TARGETS	CHANNELS	**SCALABILITY MIX**

TABLE 6.1 Five Functions of PS

Function	Overview
Service Sales	There is an ocean of opportunity awaiting your new services organization. However, someone needs to navigate these waters, search out the most hospitable locations, and help you establish yourself in those locations. This part of your organization needs to be truly expert in positioning and selling complex services. Otherwise, they will lead you into rough waters or bring you to shore on forbidding terrain. This is why you need a distinct service-sales element in your organization that can identify and close service opportunities.
Services Delivery	Once your services organization has identified territory that can be settled, you need to execute. You need a services-delivery element in your organization that assigns resources, manages their implementation, and collects the money when you are done. These are the folks that actually settle the new territories and build the deliverables that will generate revenue.
Services Engineering	As you settle more and more terrain, you should experience efficiencies. Revenue, references, and repeatability are the key to profitability. The notion of repeatability requires that you capture your intellectual property from each engagement, evaluate it, and determine how you can leverage it in future customer engagements. In this way, you do not need to create new blueprints every time you need to build a new structure. To achieve this leverage, you need a services-engineering team dedicated to managing this critical function.
Services Marketing	And, of course, every business needs to position and promote its services. You need an organization that will wave your flag— an organization that will let the world know how much you have accomplished, how much territory you now inhabit. This is your services-marketing department. They will be focused on differentiating your service offerings and evangelizing them.
Services Operations	Finally, there are other general operational activities that need to be managed for the benefit of all the organization's departments. These include tasks such as the documentation of standard business procedures and the management of core infrastructure. The services-operations team is the group that manages any infrastructure that cuts across all departments or is mission critical to manage the business.

FIGURE 6.2 PS Function Map

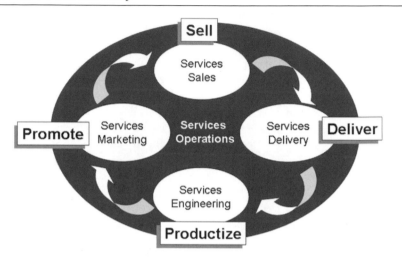

These five functions are shown in Figure 6.2. As I have discussed before, each one of these five functions is critical to the long-term success of the service function. If a company decides to ignore or commit less than full resources to one of these functions, profitability and growth of the services function will eventually suffer.

This PS Function Map enables us to incubate the conversation regarding core competencies. Each one of these functions requires that specific positions be filled. By identifying these positions, we can get a sense of the scope of our core competencies.

PS POSITION MAP

Every business function has a hierarchy of positions (despite our never-ending desire to flatten organizations). To keep the discussion simple, we will define four basic position levels:

Staff: Front-line employees carrying out the day-to-day activities of the department.

Senior Staff: Employees that have specialized expertise or more experience than the front-line employees.

Managers: Front-line managers, department directors, etc.

Senior Managers: Top managers of the organization. General managers or managers who have profit and loss responsibility.

These four levels are shown in Figure 6.3. Of course, some organizations may have more than four levels of responsibility. Your company may have junior staff, staff, senior staff, and executive staff before ever entering the management level. Regardless of how deep or flat your organizational hierarchy is, there most likely is a hierarchy of ever-increasing responsibility as you move toward the top.

Now we can take the five required service functions previously defined and map them onto the organizational levels, as shown in Figure 6.4. This map shows that each function will have multiple levels of positions, some or all of which need to be filled. I have segmented the services delivery function into sections of "business skills" and "technical skills" because many service organizations have both business and technical tracks for employee advancement. The business track includes such positions as "analyst" and "project manager," which require business skills more than technical skills. The technical track includes such positions as "technical consultant," "software developer," and "solution architect."

Finally, we can define example positions for each function and level to create a *position map* as shown in Figure 6.5. This position map defines eighteen distinct position responsibilities that the senior management team needs to fill.

FIGURE 6.3 Four Position Levels

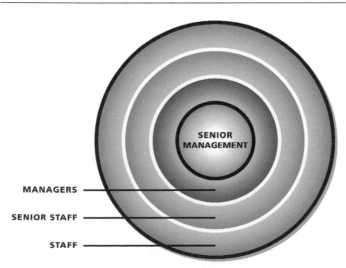

FIGURE 6.4 Functions and Levels

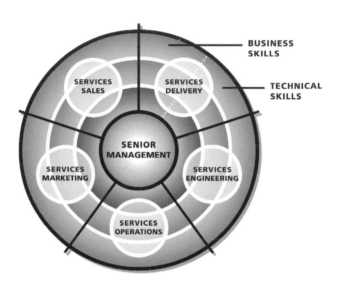

FIGURE 6.5 Position Map

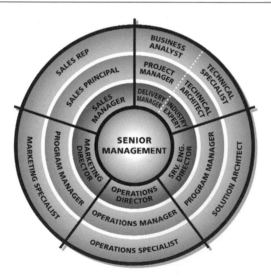

SKILLS TABLE

Each position documented in a position map requires a specific set of hard and soft skills. Documenting required skills for each position can be done by completing a skills table (or resource profile, as it is sometimes called). As an example, Figure 6.6 demonstrates a skills table for the position of delivery manager.

The skill requirements of some positions will vary widely from company to company. For example, a technical architect at a storage infrastructure company would require very different technical knowledge from a technical architect at a software company. As you work your way toward the center of the position map, soft skills become more critical and hard skills become less company specific.

As a side note, an increasing number of tools are available to help you create accurate skills tables. There are also plenty of firms that can help a management team create one. Despite this availability of devices and experts, many professional service organizations limp along without documented skills inventories. Accurately assessing your available skills is essential in scaling a human-capital-intensive business. In the professional services business, your people are your product. The more you understand about their specific skills and the organization's needs, the better you can match demand to resources. This understanding leads to the next Scylla Fee, shown in Figure 6.7.

When a management team has developed an organizational position map that is supported by a skills table, the team is ready to discuss core competencies.

SCOPING THE CORE

With a position map in hand, you can now have an informed conversation regarding what skills are required for your service strategy to succeed and match these to those available in the organization's skills map. The management team can survey the position map and tag the positions the company should develop internally. Positions are flagged as core for one of the following reasons:

- The position is critical to succeeding with customers.
- The hard skills required by the position are unique to the company.
- The soft skills required by the position are difficult to find.
- The effective execution of the position is how the company differentiates itself.

FIGURE 6.6 Sample Skills Table

Position	Hard Skills		
	Education	Certifications	Experience
Delivery Manager	B.S.	PMI Preferred	8 years in consulting industry
	MBA Preferred		2 years managing staff
			Project sizes: > $1M

	Soft Skills		
	Competencies	Sub competencies	Descriptors
1	Expertise	Business Ops	Understands the operational environment of the customer
			Can assess the business challenges of customer
		Industry	Comprehends industry dynamics and identifies business opportunities
		Technical	Understands general technology concepts and terminology
			Can apply technology and services to business challenges
2	Delivery Management	Scope Management	Organized: Tracks multiple engagements and multiple priorities
			Keeps the customer satisfied
			Keeps the customer informed
		Project P&L	Analyzes project P&L data.
		Project Success	Effective change order management
3	Interpersonal Skills	Self-confidence	Accepts recommendations from project managers and implements them
			Accepts constructive criticism
		Communication	Demonstrates articulate verbal communication with peers, executives, and clients
		Personal Growth	Desire to grow and improve skill set.

FIGURE 6.7 The Eleventh Scylla Fee

Scylla Fee	To profitably scale a professional service business, you must understand the skills required to deliver the target service portfolio.

Using these criteria, positions are flagged as core. Figure 6.8 shows the position map with twelve positions flagged as core. Table 6.2 summarizes the information.

FIGURE 6.8 Core Position Map

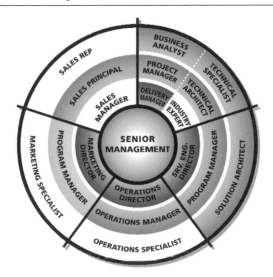

TABLE 6.2 Core Position Table

Position	Department	CORE
PS Senior Manager(s)	Senior Management	YES
Services Operations Director	Service Operations	YES
Operations Manager	Service Operations	YES
Operations Analyst	Service Operations	
Services Marketing Director	Services Marketing	YES
Marketing Program Manager	Services Marketing	
Marketing Specialist	Services Marketing	
Services Engineering Director	Services Engineering	YES
Services Engineering Program Manager	Services Engineering	YES
Services Engineering Solution Architect	Services Engineering	YES
Services Delivery Manager	Services Delivery	YES
Delivery Project Manager	Services Deliver	YES
Business Analyst	Services Delivery	YES
Industry Expert	Services Delivery	
Technical Architect	Services Delivery	YES
Technical Specialist	Services Delivery	
Sales Director	Services Sales	
Services Sales Principal	Services Sales	YES
Sales Rep	Services Sales	

PARTNERING

Once core positions are flagged, the management team must decide how to source noncore positions. In an ideal world, they would not be sourced by direct hires.

Internal Partnering

One option for sourcing noncore positions is to leverage existing departments and resources within the company. Certain areas naturally suggest internal partnering:

- *Sales Management:* Why should the service organization implement an entirely redundant staff of sales executives? Yes, the service sales reps are needed, but they can roll up under the same sales management structure.
- *Marketing Communications:* Marketing communications is not a core competency for a professional services organization. The company should leverage internal and external resources already in place.
- *Business Analysis:* Business and financial analysts that already understand how the systems work within your company probably exist within the corporate finance area. Map their expertise to someone who understands how PS finances work.

Figure 6.9 shows our position map with new markings to indicate where internal resources will be used. Table 6.3 summarizes this updated sourcing data. This particular sourcing strategy has the services organization utilizing resources from product sales, product marketing, finance, support services, and product engineering, In sales, the services organization expects the existing product sales management team to supervise the service sales reps. In marketing, the services organization does not want to duplicate marketing analysis and marketing communication capabilities already in place. With finance, the operations team expects to receive general business analysis support. The traditional support services organization will be asked to provide a certain number of billable hours each quarter to assist in the delivery of specific services.[1] Finally, the services engineering department would enlist company product engineers to assist in the developing the architecture of new complex solutions.

---

1. This can be a touchy negotiation process between professional services and support services. However, this is quite a cost-effective scaling strategy assuming senior managers don't get bogged down in discussions on internal transfer rates and revenue recognition!

FIGURE 6.9 Internal Partnering Position Map

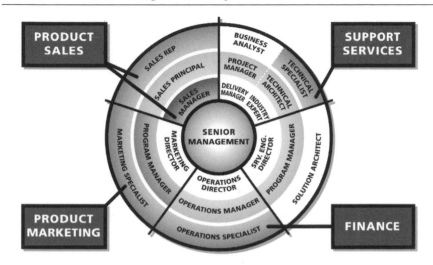

TABLE 6.3 Position Table with Internal Partnering

Position	Department	CORE	Internal Partner
PS Senior Manager(s)	Senior Management	YES	
Services Operations Director	Service Operations	YES	
Operations Manager	Service Operations	YES	
Operations Analyst	Service Operations		YES
Services Marketing Director	Services Marketing	YES	
Marketing Program Manager	Services Marketing		YES
Marketing Specialist	Services Marketing		YES
Services Engineering Director	Services Engineering	YES	
Services Engineering Program Manager	Services Engineering	YES	
Services Engineer Solution Architect	Services Engineering	YES	
Services Delivery Manager	Services Delivery	YES	
Delivery Project Manager	Services Delivery	YES	
Business Analyst	Services Delivery	YES	
Industry Expert	Services Delivery		
Technical Architect	Services Delivery	YES	
Technical Specialist	Services Delivery		YES
Sales Director	Services Sales		YES
Services Sales Principal	Services Sales	YES	
Sales Rep	Services Sales		YES

FIGURE 6.10 External Partnering Position Map

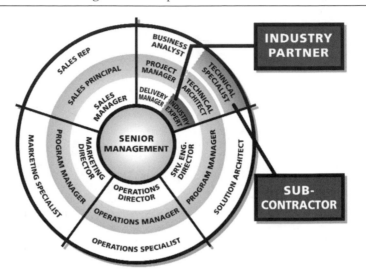

External Partnering

Once internal partnering options have been exhausted, the management team must cover any remaining position requirements with outside resources. The most natural area for external partnering is services delivery. Partners and subcontractors can be used to augment the organization's delivery staff. Figure 6.10 shows that industry experts and technical consultants are sourced with partners. Table 6.4 provides the final summary of the sourcing strategy.

At this point, every position required to sell, deliver, market, and manage professional services has been accounted for. The management team can now begin making intelligent decisions regarding partnering and scalability strategies. Without this map, how does a company determine what service partners are needed? The partners with the largest client list? The partners with the "right" relationships? The partners most willing to resell your products? But what if a potential partner has a large client list, strong executive relationships, is willing to resell your products, but offers the exact same service capabilities you do? How do you get that partnership to blossom while you spend real company dollars to establish your competitive service capabilities? A documented position map is the first step to successful service partnership.

TABLE 6.4 Position Table with External Partnering

Position	Department	CORE	Internal Partner	External Partner
PS Senior Manager(s)	Senior Management	YES		
Services Operations Director	Service Operations	YES		
Operations Manager	Service Operations	YES		
Operations Analyst	Service Operations		YES	
Services Marketing Director	Services Marketing	YES		
Marketing Program Manager	Services Marketing		YES	
Marketing Specialist	Services Marketing		YES	
Services Engineering Director	Services Engineering	YES		
Services Engineering Program Manager	Services Engineering	YES		
Services Engineer Solution Architect	Services Engineering	YES		
Services Delivery Manager	Services Delivery	YES		
Delivery Project Manager	Services Delivery	YES		
Business Analyst	Services Delivery	YES		
Industry Expert	Services Delivery			YES
Technical Architect	Services Delivery	YES		
Technical Specialist	Services Delivery		YES	YES
Sales Director	Services Sales		YES	
Service Sales Principal	Services Sales	YES		
Sales Rep	Services Sales		YES	

SCALABILITY MIX

In Chapter 4, I discussed the unrealistic growth rates that executives often place on the professional services organization. In summary, I do not believe 100% annual growth is sustainable. Having said this, a professional services organization does have a number of levers that can be used to scale the business.

First of all, there is *organic growth*. Sales, delivery, and management staff can be hired directly. The strength of this approach is that the organization should be able to identify and hire staff that directly meets the current needs of the organization. The weakness of this approach is that it takes time to bring resources into the organization this way.

Secondly, a PS organization can *partner* in the areas that have been defined as noncore. Partners can sell and deliver aspects of the service portfolio. Volume makes this approach attractive: Generally, there are plenty of willing partners happy to share in your service opportunities. Control is the concern with this approach. Once partners are involved in your accounts, they may not want to leave. If your partners are better at solving your customers' needs than you are, *your* customers may become *their* customers.

A third option is to *acquire* existing service firms. Management teams at product-centric companies are drawn to this option like moths to a flame. Why are we wasting all of this time building PS? Why don't we just buy an existing PS business? Once again, I must reiterate those famous words of caution from the old TV series "Lost in Space": "DANGER WILL ROBINSON, DANGER!" The history of product-centric companies acquiring large service companies is a sad one. Novell and Cambridge Technology Partners is one of the more recent examples. In his book *Who Says Elephants Can't Dance?*, Lou Gerstner had this to say on the topic of using large acquisitions to accelerate service capabilities at a product company:

> We had to bet that we could build recruitment, training, compensation, and HR processes to bring in 1,000 or more people a month—even though we'd never attempted anything remotely close to that. In fact, in the mid- to late 1990s, when services was consistently growing we knew we could do even better if we had more people. But we capped our hiring simply because we thought we'd overextend our ability to hire and train qualified people.

> Finally, we had to learn how to be disciplined—how to negotiate profitable contracts, price our skills, assess risk, and walk away from bad contracts and bad deals.

> For all these reasons, I've said repeatedly that this is the kind of capability you can't simply acquire (though our competitors keep trying). The bet you're really making is on your own commitment to invest both the years and the capital, then build the experience and discipline it takes to succeed.[2]

This topic of scaling services through acquisition deserves a book of its own to explore thoroughly the issues involved. For the purposes of services strategy,

---

2. Pp. 133-34 from *Who Says Elephants Can't Dance? Inside IBM's Historic Turnaround* by Louis V. Gerstner. Copyright 2002 by Louis V. Gerstner, Jr. Reprinted by permission of HarperCollins Publishers, Inc.

simply bear in mind that acquisition is no silver bullet and should be viewed as a piece of a larger scalability strategy.

Finally, I would like to introduce one more scalability option. In between acquisition and partnering, there is a new hybrid option that is emerging. Large firms like Accenture refer to this option as "transformational outsourcing." I refer to it as *incubation*. In this option, a product-centric company leases services management expertise from a services firm. At the end of the lease, the product company has the option to buy the expertise, continue to lease the expertise, or terminate the relationship. The attraction of this option is that it allows the product company to have more direct control than traditional partnering does. Also, you can scale almost as fast as you are willing to spend money. However, I have obviously simplified the intricacies of such a business relationship. How such deals are financially crafted can be complicated. Both the leaser and the company leasing want to protect themselves. Also, what happens to the intellectual property created during the relationship—specially if the companies part ways?

Pulling all the scalability strategies together, a company can create a realistic *scalability mix*. This is the mix of organic, partnering, acquiring, and incubation the company intends to use to achieve services revenue objectives. Figure 6.11 documents how one company intends to scale PS capabilities over the next three years. Once again, we are in the skills pillar of the services strategy. We are trying to answer the question, "How will we pick the money off the table and actually deliver our services?" If your company can draw a scalability mix as shown in Figure 6.11, I believe you are close to answering this question.

FIGURE 6.11 Sample Scalability Mix

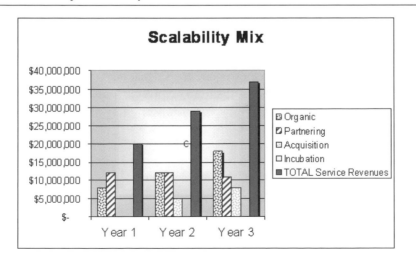

SMEES AND THE HOURGLASS MODEL

I cannot leave the topic of scalability without commenting on the changing dynamics regarding PS staff.

The professional service organizations I work with are not law firms or accounting firms but service organizations that deliver complex technology-centered (CTC) services. In other words, complicated technology is at the center of the service offering. This creates a difficult burden on CTC service providers. They are looking for competent delivery staff that have the following profile:

- Strong technical knowledge of the company's core product offerings (hard skills)
- Good understanding of the customer's operational and business environment
- Strong interpersonal, consultative skills (soft skills)

Typically, it is difficult to find delivery staff that truly possess all of these skills in adequate amounts. Such employees are often dubbed "subject matter experts" (SMEEs). These SMEEs become the lifeblood of the CTC services business. SMEEs are the consultants the customer love to see because they bring real value add.

The problem with SMEEs is that there aren't enough of them. When you shake the recruiting tree, twenty don't fall out. Get used to this shortage—it will be getting worse in the next ten years.

To help offset the SMEE shortage, a professional services organization must think about managing an hourglass. Figure 6.12 introduces this model. At the top of the hourglass are front-end sales resources that sniff out new deals and verify initial deal qualifications. Is the customer serious? Is a budget established? At the bottom of the hourglass are junior-level delivery staff or subcontractors that are qualified to deliver components of the complex technical solution. In the middle of the hourglass are the subject matter experts. The trick is to shield these hard-to-find SMEEs from involvement in every sales call and every project status meeting. In other words, keep the SMEEs away from the edges of the hourglass. Figure 6.13 shows how sales-channel partners and delivery subcontractors are used to expand both the top and bottom of the hourglass. This expansion is all about creating leverage for the expertise locked in the bodies of the SMEEs. Figure 6.14 is a detailed breakdown of how geographic based sales staff partner with subject matter experts to manage service opportunities.

I believe a common mistake being made within many product companies is their general approach to building the PS business. The product company attempts to build out practices by hiring senior partners who then add junior staff beneath them. This is the classic PS pyramid model David Maister wrote so eloquently about in *Managing the Professional Services Firm*. However, this is not the type of PS organization a typical technology company needs to implement because it does not work. *The leverage point is no longer senior partners who sell but subject matter experts who design.*

FIGURE 6.12 The Hourglass

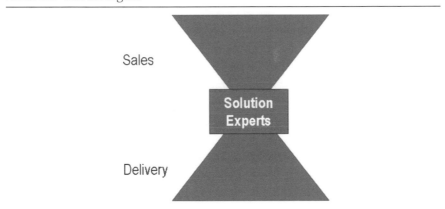

FIGURE 6.13 Expanding the Hourglass

FIGURE 6.14 Managing Opportunity

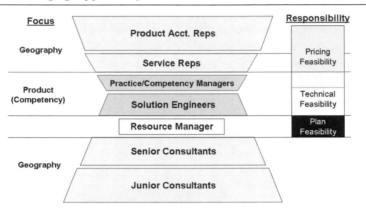

At the beginning of this chapter, I wanted to answer a simple question: "How will we deliver all these services?" Figure 6.15 depicts all of the ground that must be covered before that question can be answered confidently. In theory, the services management team should be most comfortable addressing the variables in this pillar. In a sense, these are the fundamentals of managing a profitable services business. These discussions are much more familiar to PS managers than the ones outlined in previous chapters such as "setting a business model" or "setting target markets." Still, services organizations limp along with poorly defined scalability strategies. Hire a little here, partner a little there—and acquire someone if the forecast really gets optimistic. This approach, unfortunately, is a far cry from mastering the scalability of a professional services business.

FIGURE 6.15 Service Pillar Variables

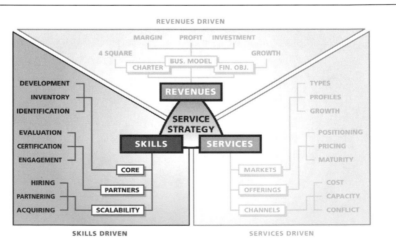

COMPANY CASE STUDIES

EMC and Scalability Strategies

In September of 2002, I had the opportunity to work with managers from EMC to present a case study on EMC's strategies to scale service capabilities. EMC had just announced a relationship with Accenture to create a new EMC business unit focused on storage consulting services. John Madden, a Practice Director at Summit Strategies, wrote the following when the partnership was announced in July of 2002:

> EMC's troubles during the past year have been well documented. Faced with a sour economy, declining hardware sales and increased pressure from traditional systems vendors peddling their own storage offerings, EMC has focused on three areas that it sees as key to its future: software, partnerships and services. The company already has taken major steps in the first two areas and, true to its new vision, recently made a major services-related announcement.

> This month, the company announced a five-year agreement with Accenture, a longtime partner, to create a new business within EMC, called Information Solutions Consulting (ISC). This is not a joint venture per se. EMC and Accenture, under a business-transformation outsourcing agreement between the two, will both provide resources to ISC, but it will remain an EMC business, under EMC's corporate structure and governance. The company positions ISC as an extension to its existing professional-services unit, which EMC has been attempting to build up in the past year. EMC, the storage-market leader, will leverage its storage expertise, while Accenture will provide consulting expertise and its experience in working with global clients. Interestingly, the agreement does not bar the companies from entering into new partnership agreements, but each is prohibited from entering into an agreement that would create a similar entity.

> ISC will initially offer four services in its portfolio:

> 1. Storage infrastructure strategy will align long-term business goals with IT to provide quantifiable reductions in total cost of ownership;

> 2. Storage management optimization will focus on storage-management solutions, and provide tools, policies, best practices and procedures on how IT managers can manage their storage environments;

3. Information storage consolidation will focus on the design of a storage infrastructure to leverage current storage investments and prepare to meet future data needs; and

4. Business continuity planning will provide business-continuity strategy, including disaster-recovery planning.

The new organization will have a total of about 200 dedicated employees, with new "client directors" in ISC to scope potential sales opportunities among customers. The client directors will work with the EMC sales organization and the sales team from the professional-services unit as primary channels, with Accenture and other EMC channel partners as secondary sales channels. According to EMC officials, services are already a part of the sales compensation model for the EMC sales force, so that team has an incentive to promote new business for ISC. Although ISC will at first offer services in the four areas listed above, it plans to expand the roster, based on customer needs.

The Accenture arrangement is a unique method for EMC to complete the triad for its new way of doing business. EMC had already demonstrated that it is serious about selling software, through initiatives such as AutoIS and WideSky, and about reaching out to new partners, through new relationships with vendors such as Dell Computer. EMC needed to demonstrate a similar commitment to its services business. With storage services a major focus for all of the major systems vendors, ISC will allow EMC to remain competitive and provide the types of consulting that customers are looking for.[3]

In essence, EMC was executing an incubation strategy to accelerate its consulting capabilities. How does this new lever scalability option work? Some folks are not impressed. One year after the partnership had been created, *Storage Magazine* reported the following:

> Ever wonder whatever became of EMC's ISC, the "vendor neutral" storage consulting service the company launched with Accenture last summer? Word on the street is that it's a dud—at least when it comes to recommending non-EMC hardware.

---

3. John Madden, "EMC and Accenture Team Up on Storage Services," *www.summit-strategies.com*, 2002.

Not so, says EMC's Rich Martin, Senior Marketing Manager for the ISC. "Since its inception, ISC has seen strong market response. Presently the practice has over 250 consultants in North America and Europe, and has delivered over 300 engagements. Most engagements have made a significant impact on their client's storage strategy, resulting in measurable reduced cost, improved service level performance, and improved information protection."

That could be true. According to Frank Brick, chairman and CEO of Arsenal Digital Solutions—a provider of storage management services to managed hosting companies—Arsenal employees have run across ISC consultants "in large environments, especially as they move from direct-attached storage (DAS) to SAN environments on a vendor-specific platform."

Meanwhile, Richard Scannell, vice president of corporate development at GlassHouse Technologies, flat out "has yet to come across the partnership. It could be that I'm not at the most senior level, or it could be that the deal isn't real on the street."[4]

Regardless of how the industry perceives the success of the partnership, EMC had very specific reasons to pursue it. Service capabilities were becoming critical to EMC's success in the marketplace. EMC management had realistically assessed the various options of scaling high-end, product-agnostic consulting services. From the case study EMC delivered on this topic, Table 6.5 summarizes how EMC viewed the strengths and weaknesses of each scalability option. From this table, it is clear why EMC was willing to test the option out with Accenture.

TABLE 6.5 Scalability Options

Success Criteria	BUILD	BUY	PARTNER	INCUBATE
1. TIMING	RED	GREEN	GREEN	GREEN
2. CUSTOMER RELATIONSHIP	GREEN	GREEN	RED	GREEN
3. TECHNICAL FIT	GREEN	RED	YELLOW	GREEN
4. SCALABILITY	RED	GREEN	GREEN	GREEN
5. GEOGRAPHIC FIT	GREEN	RED	YELLOW	GREEN
6. CHANNEL CONFLICT	RED	RED	YELLOW	YELLOW
7. HISTORICAL SUCCESS	RED	RED	RED	TBD

4. "EMC/Accenture Partnership Bears Few Fruit," *Storage Magazine,* May 2003.

At the same time the ISC was being created, EMC was aggressively pursuing other levers to deliver different aspects of the services portfolio. Organic growth, targeted acquisition, and certified partner delivery were all levers EMC exercised. Several years later, we can see that EMC has clearly met its objectives to grow services as a part of overall company revenues. Figure 6.16 tracks the percentage of company revenues that come from services and the profitability of those service dollars. I think the critical observation for other management teams is EMC's willingness and aggressiveness in pursuing multiple scalability levers. Compare this incredible growth in services with the service revenue growth of Lucent Technologies and Hewlett Packard. Both of these technology firms have communicated a desire to aggressively grow service revenues. However, both firms appear stalled in their efforts to actually drive service revenues forward as a percentage of total company revenues. Service revenue growth for these companies is documented in Figures 6.17 and 6.18.

FIGURE 6.16 EMC Service Revenues

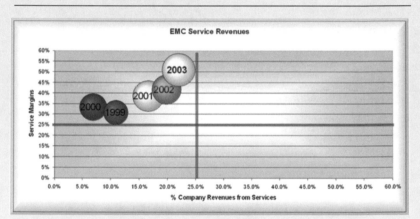

FIGURE 6.17 Lucent Service Revenues

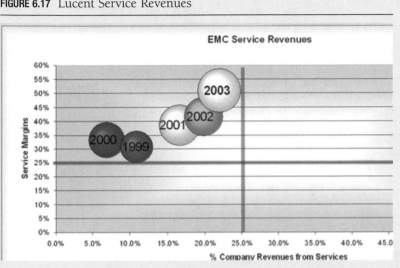

EMC Service Revenues

FIGURE 6.18 HP Service Revenues

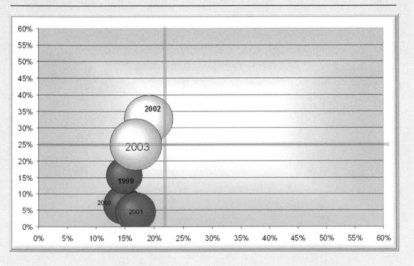

CISCO AND PARTNER ENABLEMENT

If you look at the revenue mix of Cisco Systems, you can see that Cisco is a product-centric company. Over 80% of the company's $20B+ in revenue is product based. The company wants to maintain this mix and its current margin structure. The challenge for the company is to preserve this mix while moving into new markets such as voice, security, storage, and virtualization. Cisco has coined the term Intelligent Information Network (IIN) to describe these adjacent and evolutionary markets. IDC uses the term Dynamic IT. As the company steps up to this challenge, Cisco must manage the scalability of service capabilities both in terms of coverage across the company's customer base and complexity across technologies. Cisco's customers range from large service providers and Fortune 50 enterprises to small- and medium-sized businesses. These customers have a wide variety of service needs, and Cisco's broadening IIN product line calls for a wide variety of services to ensure successful deployment and operation in a customer network. To help meet these service needs, partners are key to the company's strategy. Cisco has implemented a disciplined service enablement strategy around its partner ecosystem.

Historically, a core competency of Cisco's has been the development of skilled personnel in its partner community who can offer the planning, design, and implementation services around its core routing and switching product lines. The CCIE program was a significant success factor in helping develop a set of partners with staff capable of delivering services around Cisco's core offerings. Delivery partners were qualified based on the organization's number of CCIEs and their skill levels.

TWO CHALLENGES

As Cisco expands into new but related technologies within the context of the IIN, the company is facing and stepping up to two new challenges.

Challenge 1: Partner Enablement

The first challenge is finding and/or enabling partners around the lifecycle services needs of these new IIN technologies. The second challenge is helping ensure that not only are the partners enabled on the new technologies but also that they understand the business model or models that can help them become more profitable in the delivery of these lifecycle services.

In stepping up to the first challenge, Cisco introduced its Lifecycle Services framework to partners in 2004. This framework identifies the minimum services required for successful customer deployment and operation around each of Cisco's technologies. Partner certifications and specializations are built around a partner's capabilities in delivering these services around specific technologies. With the Lifecycle Services framework, Cisco is looking for a win-win-win. The customer wins by experiencing accelerated success in deploying and operating new Cisco technology within its network and doing so in a consistent fashion. The partner wins by having a clear engagement model defined between Cisco and itself together with a clear process to get either very specialized or to broaden within Cisco's product lines or both. Cisco benefits by accelerating the marketplace absorption of its new technologies while still preserving the margin structure of its current business model.

Partners are "enabled" around Lifecycle Services via:

- A Services Practice Agreement
- A Lifecycle Services Enablement Workshop

Cisco encourages its partners to build Practice Areas around the company's technologies. The Workshop helps partners measure their Practice Areas' alignment and consistency with the experience Cisco wants for the end customer.

Challenge 2: Implementing Business Models

Cisco has also stepped up to the second challenge to help partners understand and implement the business models that lead to viable services businesses. A partner may be technically competent in lifecycle services, but struggle in an effort to manage a profitable service business. To address this reality, Cisco made a rather interesting investment. Cisco created a team of service management experts and a program called Partner Business Consulting (PBC). The PBC team works with Cisco delivery partners and assesses the health of the partners' services businesses. Specifically, the team reviews its delivery partners':

- Organizational Structure
- PS Process Maturity

- Skills Management
- Partner Management
- Service Metrics

In each area, partners are provided scorecards and action plans. Liz Lawson, the executive in charge of both the Lifecycle framework and PBC programs, says about PBC, "Our objective is to educate our partners on what is required to create a mature, sustainable service business." Since its inception, the Cisco PBC has engaged with delivery partners nominated by Cisco's regional partner managers. "A delivery partner has to be nominated, and then the partner has to dedicate resources to the process," explains Lawson.

In essence, Cisco has identified partner enablement of both lifecycle services and partner business models as a core competency of the company's success. Cisco has applied resources to this competency and developed industry-leading techniques to enable partners to better manage a services business. Cisco Systems has taken the concept of "channel friendly" to a whole new level.

■

EXECUTIVE SUMMARY

Professional Services is a human-capital-intensive business. If you want to scale this business, you need to scale human capital. In any enterprise, the process of bringing on employees is time consuming and costly. For product companies, the challenge is exacerbated because they are trying to scale staff that typically have very specialized skills. To approach these challenges haphazardly is suicidal. A management team must *manage* this process. In so doing, the team must wisely choose how to scale the business. To achieve this, there are three critical variables the management team should consider:

1. *Core:* What positions in the professional service organization will be considered core to the company?
2. *Partners:* Based on the positions that are core to the company, what partners should be engaged by the professional services organization to assist in sales and delivery of the service portfolio? Some partnership resources may come from other organizations internal to the company.
3. *Scalability mix:* What mix of hiring, partnering, and acquiring will the company use?

In the twentieth century, product companies developed the ability to produce capital goods and scale their production capabilities to obscene levels. Companies that could scale cost effectively, *won.* In the twenty-first century, companies must apply the same level of discipline and enthusiasm to scaling specialized human resources. Companies that do learn to scale service capabilities effectively *will win.*

Chapter Seven

Strategy Evaluation

Are We on Track?

CHAPTER OBJECTIVE

To introduce a set of frameworks a management team can use to evaluate the maturity and viability of the company's professional service strategy

KEY CONCEPTS

- Service Strategy Map
- Strategy Variable Alignment
- Strategy Variable Maturity
- Strategy Variable Stress Ratings
- Strategy Data Maturity

SERVICE STRATEGY MAP

Our ultimate goal is to master our professional services business. We want to understand, predict, and control this business. To achieve that objective, we need to create a strategy that is viable and sustainable.

I have introduced three pillars of a service strategy: revenues, services, and skills. Within each pillar, I reviewed three critical variables a management team must discuss and then establish. If these nine variables are not reviewed, the service strategy is not mature and potentially not viable. Figure 7.1 documents the main strategy variables we covered.

FIGURE 7.1 Nine Variables Again

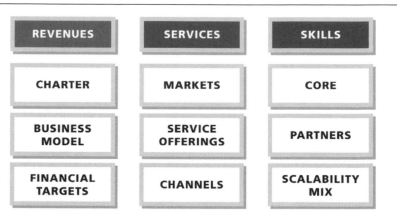

As we reviewed the pillars and their variables, we actually touched on several supporting variables. These are conversations a management team must have to make intelligent decisions about the core variables, and service strategy conversations become quite complicated. Figure 7.2 expands Figure 7.1 and documents all of the areas we have covered so far. In Chapter 3, I stated that strategy conversations are often driven by revenue, services, or skills. That theme is illustrated in Figure 7.2.

FIGURE 7.2 Service Strategy Map

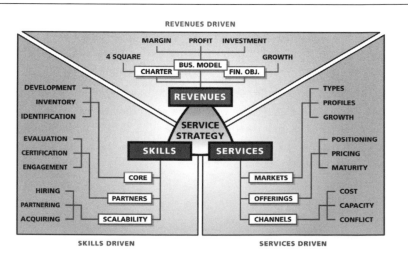

As Figure 7.2 clearly demonstrates, the complexity of professional services strategy within a product company can quickly get to be overwhelming. In a sense, so many subtle variables are in play that it is easy for the management team to lose the way. Are we on track? Are we creating a services strategy that makes sense? That is executable? To counter this anxiety, I would like to suggest both qualitative and quantitative approaches a management team can use in assessing the health of the service strategy.

QUALITATIVE STRATEGY ASSESSMENTS

First, I would like to start with two qualitative assessment techniques that require subjective judgements by the management team. Even if judgements are slightly mistaken, the frameworks push the dialogue in the right direction.

Strategy Variable Alignment

In this approach, the management team reviews the nine main variables to determine if they support each other and the general business strategy of the company. To complete this evaluation, I refer you back to the three service strategy zones I introduced in Chapter 3 and that are depicted here in Figure 7.3.

FIGURE 7.3 Three Zones of Service Strategy

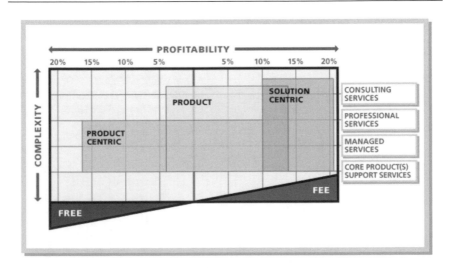

As the management team works through the services strategy variables, how each individual aligns to the overall objective the company has for the professional services business should be assessed. If the company wants to move into the product- or solution-centric zones, do the variable settings support this move? Figure 7.4 shows a simple framework management can use to test variable alignment. For each of the nine variables, the management team should plot where on the *free-to-fee* spectrum the variable is set. For example, is the charter graph the team created for professional services about customer satisfaction or about driving services revenue? And is this charter aligned with where the company needs PS to be?

Although this assessment approach is based on subjective judgement, it enables the management team to quickly determine if there are any significant disconnects in the strategy. The assessment shown in Figure 7.4 documents where a management team believes each of the nine strategy variables currently sits on the spectrum of free-to-fee. For instance, the current sales channels strategy is far to the left, which is very much aligned with Professional Services being an investment center that is not very focused on selling lots of services for profit. Overall, the following discrepancies are highlighted by the assessment shown in Figure 7.4:

FIGURE 7.4 Variable Alignment Chart

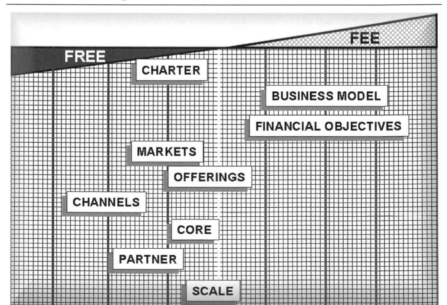

- PS has a charter of product enablement and customer satisfaction, yet the business model and financial objectives are very aggressive.
- PS focuses on the install base as the primary market and creates offerings to support the install base. Once again, this limited scope will not support the aggressive financial objective established for the business unit.
- The only sales channel PS intends to use is the existing product sales force. This sales channel has historically done a terrible job of selling services.

Strategy Variable Maturity

A second qualitative technique for assessing the service strategy is for the management team to review its understanding of each variable. In this approach, the management team assesses how well it can control each variable individually. Figure 7.5 illustrates the progression from chaos to control I introduced in Chapter 2. Table 7.1 documents how the management team can use four basic levels of understanding to assess each variable.

FIGURE 7.5 From Chaos to Control

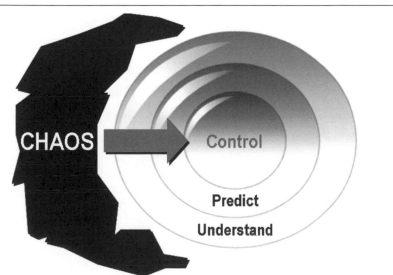

TABLE 7.1 Levels of Understanding

Level of Understanding	Description	Numeric Rating
Chaos	Management team did not even know the variable needed to be managed.	0
Understanding	Management team has identified the variable as important. Management team has begun discussing how it should be set.	1
Predictability	Management team has decided initially how the variable should be set. The company is starting to track relevant data. Management team understands how the variable impacts the overall business.	2
Control	Management team thoroughly understands the variable. The management team has relevant data associated with the variable. Variable can be adjusted to meet changing business requirements.	3

Using this rating system, the management team reviews each of the nine variables and assigns a numeric rating from 0 to 3. For example, if the management team has never discussed the charter of the professional service organization, rate that variable with a 0. If the management team has started to discuss the PS charter but has no clear agreement, rate it 1. If the charter has been set for the first time, rate it 2. If the charter has been set for a while and the management team is comfortable with making adjustments as required, rate it a 3. Using this approach for each variable, the management team can create a spider graph, shown in Figure 7.6, that documents how mature the service strategy is. The shaded area maps an example rating.

The line on the spider graph demonstrates where I find the typical initial maturity of professional strategy discussions:

- Financial objectives are locked and loaded.
- A service portfolio is in place.
- Some discussions on target markets have occurred.
- Some service sales reps have been hired.

FIGURE 7.6 Strategy Maturity Graph

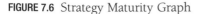

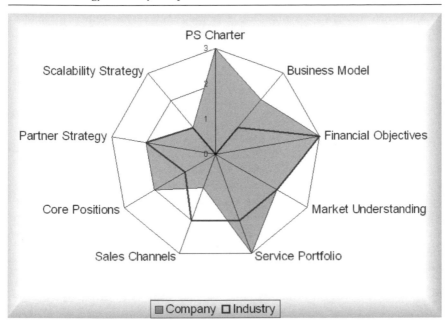

However

- The PS charter has never been discussed.
- The PS business model is not defined.
- The sales channel mix is not adequate to meet revenue objectives.
- The positions core to the PS organization have not been flagged.
- A clear scalability mix has not been defined.

QUANTITATIVE STRATEGY ASSESSMENTS

I realize that many senior managers are not comfortable with fuzzy, qualitative assessments. *"Hey, we need to take the wiggle room out of the discussion!" "We need to look at some unbiased, hard data!"* OK, OK. For those data diehards, here are two quantitative frameworks for assessing the health and maturity of the service strategy.

Strategy Stress Rating

The first quantitative assessment involves reviewing each variable and assigning a numeric stress rating. The objective of this approach is to determine how aggressive your services strategy is. In this assessment, you rate objectives you have set in each of the three pillars. Table 7.2 provides a baseline example of the ratings that could be applied to objectives in the revenues pillar.

Using the type of data shown in Table 7.2, a management team can compare the current services strategy to a proposed services strategy. The management team must understand how aggressive (or stressful) the proposed strategy will be for the organization. This is shown graphically in Figure 7.7. If a proposed services strategy creates significant stress in a pillar, the stress rating shoots out to that edge of the triangle. If a strategy creates significant stress to all three pillars, the management team must question the viability of the strategy. I will never forget the first service executive I showed this model. We were reviewing the struggles of his services business over the past three years. When I plugged his targets into this model, all three dimensions pegged out. In other words, his company had a strategy that was aggressive in all three areas: financial performance improvement, portfolio expansion, and skills development. *"Now I know why I have felt so* ———- *for the past three years!"* he said to me.

TABLE 7.2 Stress Rating Table

Pillar	Variable	Objective	Stress Rating
Revenues	Target revenue growth rate for PS	Grow revenue by 0–15%	1
		Grow revenue by 16–40%	2
		Grow revenue by +40%	3
	Target gross margin for PS business unit	Gross margin 0–20%	1
		Gross margin 21–25%	2
		Gross margin +25%	3
	Operating profit improvement	Improve operating profit by 0– 2%	1
		Improve by 3%–5%	2
		Improve by +6%	3

FIGURE 7.7 Strategy Stress Rating Graph

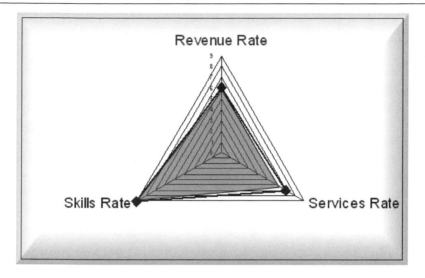

Framework Maturity Rating

The second quantitative assessment involves simple yes or no answers. I have provided several key frameworks that help document the professional services strategy of your company. In this assessment, I ask the management team to inventory which critical frameworks it has documented. Table 7.3 lists the six frameworks that are critical to understanding and mastering the professional services business. If your management team can accurately produce a framework, give yourself a 1. If not, give yourself a 0. Using this approach, you can tabulate a rating from 0 to 6. If your services business frameworks total 0–2, you should be concerned.

TABLE 7.3 Strategy Frameworks

Pillar	Framework	Related Variables	Text Reference
Revenues	PS charter graph	Charter	Ch 4, Figure 4.4
	PS business model	Business model	Ch 4, Table 4.7
	PS financial objectives	Financial objectives	Ch 4, Table 4.11
Services	Marketing mix graph	Markets, services, channels	Ch 5, Figure 5.9
Skills	Position map	Core, partners	Ch 6, Figure 6.5
	Scalability mix graph	Scalability mix graph	Ch 6, Figure 6.11

EXECUTIVE SUMMARY

This book is dedicated to the process of creating a viable, sustainable, and ultimately successful professional services organization. Often, in the heat of the process, management teams lose sight of how much progress they are (or are not) making. This chapter provides four quick-and-dirty tools management teams can use to assess the maturity of their strategy discussions. Reviewing the relevant alignment of the strategy variables provides a qualitative assessment of the strategy. Another qualitative assessment involves determining the maturity of the management team's understanding of each strategy variable. More quantitative assessments such as stress ratings and framework availability are also helpful. The management team that performs all four assessments on its service strategy will clearly understand how much heavy lifting is left to be done.

Chapter Eight

Metrics that Matter

Preventing Business Blind Spots

CHAPTER OBJECTIVE

To introduce a methodology to enable a management team to identify and implement a metrics portfolio that provides meaningful insight into their services business

KEY TOOLS

- Metric Perspectives
- Metric Perspectives Graph

MASTERING AND MEASURING

My son Michael has earned a black belt in Tae Kwon Do. Having this belt signifies he has mastered a specific set of physical skills. To acquire those skills, he had to spend years working through a series of tests. If he hadn't passed the tests, he would not have earned the belt. If the tests were not in place, the belt would be meaningless. In other words, the measurement enables the recognition of accomplishment. For someone to be considered a master at something a mechanism must be in place to assess that honor. If there is no tangible evidence of mastery, then the title has little meaning.

This rule applies to mastering professional services too. If you have no tangible evidence of your progress in managing your professional services business, it is difficult to claim you are mastering the business. Of course, the most prominent metrics of success are revenue and profitability. Unfortunately, these metrics are severely limited in their ability to truly assess whether your company is mastering the professional services business. Just because my son can break a wooden board with his foot does not make him a black belt—he must demonstrate multiple skills to earn that distinction. Just because

143

you made money last quarter in PS does not mean you are mastering your business. This chapter introduces a framework for measuring true mastery of the professional services function.

THE PROBLEM WITH METRICS

"You can't manage what you don't measure." Everyone has heard this statement at least once in his or her management career. But then again, "the numbers don't tell you everything." And of course, there are "lies, damn lies, and statistics." To top it off, we are awash in an age of "information overload."

This is the problem with metrics in business. On one hand, almost all managers know they should have some form of measurement for their business. On the other hand, managers and employees alike approach metrics with caution and skepticism.   Managers are already bombarded with reams of business data they don't use. They are reluctant to pile on more. Is it really required?

When it comes to the professional services business, managers will agree on a short list of metrics that are "must haves." Yes, we need to understand the utilization rate of our consultants. Revenue and bookings are obviously critical to track. Then what? Load costs? Project margins? Employee turnover rate? Let the debate begin. Table 8.1 details ten metrics for a professional services organization. Each one of these metrics provides specific business insight. Despite the obvious value of these metrics, I have yet to meet with a PS organization that had all ten of these metrics at their fingertips. I am learning that metrics are a "premium" activity for most service organizations: "Yes, it would be nice to have all this data and insight, but we don't have the staff, time, or systems to generate lots of metrics."

Elizabeth Davis is the CEO of QuickArrow, a provider of professional service automation (PSA) solutions. I asked Ms. Davis why more professional service organizations do not have decent metrics at their disposal. *"We find that many professional service organizations are still spending countless hours processing spreadsheet data with the belief that this approach meets their business needs. However, this labor-intensive, error-prone method does not produce up-to-the-minute, accurate metrics. Also, the data is often dispersed throughout the organization—so no one has a consolidated view of their entire services operation."* Why don't PS organizations take the plunge and automate their environment? *"They don't think they have the time or money required to truly automate their business. Of course, they are not calculating the opportunity cost of not having the real-time data required to streamline and optimize their business either."*

I hear you. Resources are tight. You do not want to add metrics (or PSA software) for the sake of having one more number to review. You want to add metrics that bring true strategic insight and help you improve the state of your business. You want to add metrics that matter. How do you do this? Here are six key concepts that will enable a management team to craft an effective metrics strategy:

- Metric perspectives
- Metric perspectives graph
- Metric zones
- Blind spots
- Prioritization filters
- Phased implementation

Using these six concepts, a management team can define and implement an effective set of metrics for strategically managing a services business.

TABLE 8.1 Ten PS Metrics

Metric	Definition
Backlog	The total value of contract commitments yet to be executed. Total Backlog = Previous Fiscal Year's Commitments + Latest Fiscal Year's Sales – Latest Fiscal Year's Revenue.
Bill Rate	Average billable rate achieved by class of consultant.
Gross Margin (%)	The gross profit generated per dollar of service delivered. Gross Margin = Total Services revenue – Cost of services delivered (COS), traditionally called "cost of goods sold" (COGS).
Hit Ratio	The competitive success rate of the company in the markets it chooses to compete in. Does not include single-sourced bids.
Load Costs	Total business costs that are not directly related to the cost of delivering services.
Profit per Project	The profit generated by a specific project. Project Profits = Total Project Revenue – COS – Sales Costs.
Rate Realization	The amount of revenue actually earned as a percentage of potential revenue represented by list prices.
Sales Costs	The total costs for the selling efforts of each line of business. Total Sales Costs include salaries, expense accounts, and commissions for sales management, salespeople, and sales support.
Total Services Revenue	Measurement of the different types of revenue; should be listed separately by Consulting, Solutions, and Third-Party pass-through.
Utilization Rate	Measures the organization's ability to maximize its billable resources.

METRIC PERSPECTIVES

In their well-received book *The Balanced Scorecard*, David P. Norton and Robert S. Kaplan introduce the concept that common performance measurement approaches relying on financial accounting measures are becoming obsolete. Norton and Kaplan are convinced that metrics which simply focus on financial performance "hinder an organization's ability to create future economic value." Furthermore, they state that "the success of organizations cannot be motivated or measured by financial metrics alone." The authors engineer a balanced scorecard that has four distinct data categories companies should track:

1. *Financial:* ROI, revenue growth, revenue, mix
2. *Customer:* Customer satisfaction, account share
3. *Internal:* Quality control, time-to-market
4. *Learning and Growth:* Employee satisfaction, training, skills development

Broadening the areas companies should track is a significant step in the right direction. However, creating additional categories does not help a management team determine which specific metrics it should focus on. To begin addressing this challenge, I want to define the concept of metric perspective.

Every metric provides a certain perspective on your business. There are at least five metric perspectives you should consider:

1. *Functional perspective:* What business function (sales, delivery, etc.) does this metric help evaluate?
2. *Business objective perspective:* Almost every internal company initiative has one of two objectives: improve operational efficiency or create future value. Does the metric track improvements in operational efficiency or assess the return on strategic investment?
3. *Timeframe perspective:* Just like economic data, is the metric a leading or lagging indicator of how the business is performing? Does the metric indicate that you already have a real problem, or does the metric warn that soon you will have a problem if the current trends continue?
4. *Scope perspective:* Does the metric measure the performance of specific individuals, or specific projects, or the entire business unit?
5. *Stakeholder perspective:* Does this metric provide insight into how your external stakeholders (customers, partners, etc.) view you?

TABLE 8.2 Metrics Perspectives

Metric	Function Perspective					Timeframe Perspective		Economic Perspective		Scope Perspective			Stakeholder Perspective	
	Service Sales	Delivery	Service Mkting	Service Engin.	Service Oper	Leading	Lagging	Efficiency	Value	Staff	Project	Business	Internal	External
Backlog		Y			Y	Y			Y			Y	Y	
Bill Rate	Y	Y					Y		Y	Y	Y	Y	Y	
Gross Margin (%)	Y	Y	Y	Y	Y		Y		Y			Y	Y	
Hit Ratio	Y		Y			Y			Y	Y	Y	Y	Y	
Load Costs					Y		Y	Y				Y	Y	
Profit per Project		Y		Y			Y	Y			Y	Y	Y	
Rate Realization	Y	Y					Y		Y	Y	Y	Y	Y	
Sales Costs	Y					Y		Y				Y	Y	
Total Services Revenue	Y	Y	Y	Y			Y		Y			Y	Y	
Utilization Rate	Y	Y	Y		Y		Y	Y		Y	Y	Y	Y	

In Table 8.2, these perspectives are applied to the ten metrics previously introduced. The table shows which perspectives are satisfied by each metric. For example, *backlog* is a leading indicator. If backlog drops below a certain threshold, the business could be moving in the wrong direction even though revenue targets have been met for the quarter.

METRIC PERSPECTIVES GRAPH

Using the concept of metric perspective, we can create a balanced metrics portfolio that enables us to *minimize any perspective blind spots*. For example, you would not want to pick ten metrics to guide your management of your services business only to realize that not one of them is a leading indicator of how your business is doing.

Figure 8.1 introduces the metrics perspective graph. This graph enables you to map a set of metrics to determine if you have any obvious perspective blind spots. There are four distinct zones to which metrics can be mapped:

ZONE 0: *Lagging, Economic Value.* Metrics in Zone 0 represent how your business has actually performed. The metrics are those ultimately used to evaluate a management team, including total services revenues and profitability.

ZONE 1: *Lagging, Efficiency.* Metrics in Zone 1 indicate a serious and immediate problem in the way you are running the PS business. If operational efficiencies are not improved, revenues and profits will suffer.

ZONE 2: *Leading, Efficiency.* Metrics in Zone 2 provide early warning that you may have efficiency issues. Poor performance on these metrics does not mean revenue and profits (Zone 0) will be immediately impacted. However, these metrics are a pointer to areas that, if not addressed, could impact future financial performance.

ZONE 3: *Leading, Economic Value.* Metrics in Zone 3 provide insight into how the business *will* do in the future. Are you creating economic value that will generate future revenues and profits, or are you whittling down intellectual and human capital to pay today's bills?

We'll discuss these zones in detail later in the chapter, but first we need to map scope and stakeholder perspective onto the graph. Figure 8.2 adds these two perspectives. We have added three rings that represent the scope of the metric. Metrics that only measure the overall business are placed in the outer ring. Metrics that assess the health of projects are placed in the middle ring. Metrics that can evaluate down to the staff level are placed close to the center of the graph.

Stakeholder perspective will be shown by the color used when placing the metric on the graph. Metrics colored in RED have an internal perspective—the metric is important to you and your superiors. Metrics colored in GREEN have an external perspective—your customers or partners care about your performance in this area.

Great, we now have this pretty graph. We need to put it into action.

FIGURE 8.1 Metrics Perspective Graph Introduction

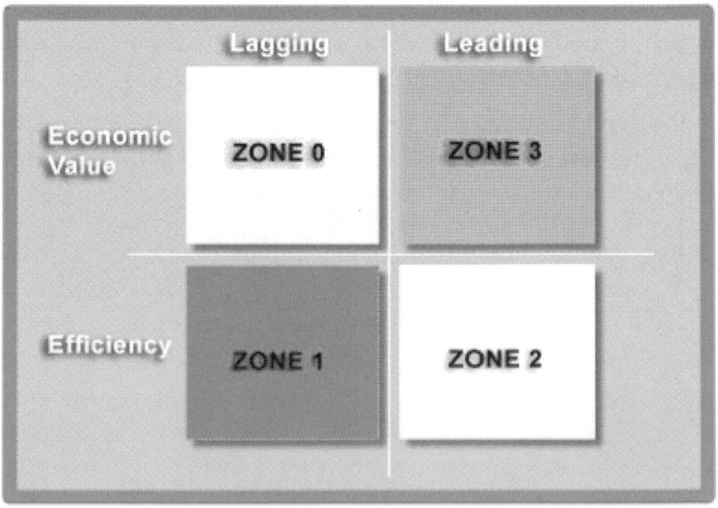

FIGURE 8.2 Metrics Perspective Graph Ready for Use

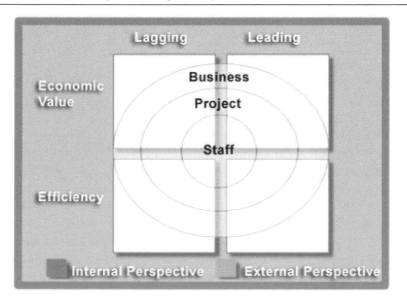

USING THE METRICS PERSPECTIVE GRAPH

Let's try out the graph by mapping an industry standard metric that almost every services business considers: utilization. As a metric, *consultant utilization* provides the following perspectives for your service business:

Functional perspective: Utilization evaluates the service delivery function.

Economic perspective: Utilization evaluates the efficiency of your services organization.

Timeframe perspective: Utilization is lagging metric. When utilization goes down, you have a problem *now*. After the low-utilization report comes in, you can't recapture those lost billable hours. Like airplane seats and hotel rooms, consulting capacity cannot be inventoried.

Scope perspective: Utilization evaluates the performance of individual employees. This data can be used to evaluate the health of projects and eventually the overall business. In other words, utilization is a metric that can provide insight on all levels of your PS business.

Stakeholder perspective: Utilization is an internal viewpoint. Your customers and partners are not concerned about your utilization rates.

With this perspective information, Figure 8.3 maps utilization onto the metrics perspective graph.

The good news about utilization is that it covers the lower quadrant of the graph nicely. It is a metric that hits the center bull's-eye of "staff." This means the metric can provide insight on individual employees, specific projects, or the overall business. However, if utilization is the only metric you use to measure your services business, you will have several blind spots:

Functional blind spots: Not specifically evaluating sales, marketing, or services engineering.

Economic blind spots: Not evaluating the return on investments you are making into the business. Not understanding the economic potential of your service portfolio. Yes, you are fully utilized today, but what about six months from now?

Timeframe blind spots: No leading indicators that will warn you if the business is heading south.

Stakeholder blind spots: No indication how customers and partners feel about the services you are delivering.

Only using one metric provides a simple example to demonstrate how blind spots can exist. Now, let's map the top ten metrics we called out in Table 8.1. We use a two-letter code for each metric in Table 8.3.

FIGURE 8.3 Mapping Utilization

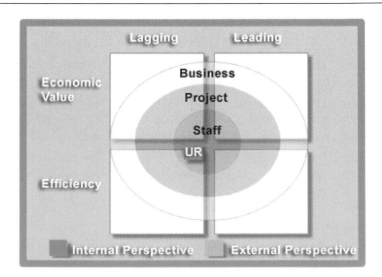

TABLE 8.3 Metric Reference Codes

Metric	Code
Backlog	BL
Bill Rate	BR
Gross Margin (%)	GM
Hit Ratio	HR
Load Costs	LC
Profit per Project	PP
Rate Realization	RR
Sales Costs	SC
Total Services Revenue	TR
Utilization Rate	UR

Figure 8.4 maps these metrics onto the perspective graph. Remember, the closer to the center the metric lands, the greater potential scope it offers. Being close to the bull's-eye is a good thing.

FIGURE 8.4 Ten Service Metrics Placed on Graph

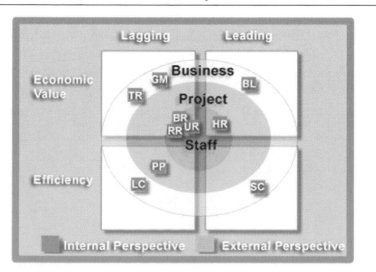

A majority of the PS organizations I have worked with do not have all ten of these metrics at their fingertips, but even if they did, there would still be weak spots:

1. There is not a single metric that provides an external perspective. How do customers view the business? How do critical partners feel about your skills and ability to deliver? None of these ten metrics provide insight on how the external world views your business.

2. Off these metrics, 70% are lagging. They provide little insight on the direction the service business is moving: positive or negative. Yes, you made money this quarter, but are you headed in the right direction? Hit rates, sales costs, and backlog do provide leading information—so you are not totally blind. However, you have no leading indicators on the health of the services portfolio or the skills of your staff.

3. None of these metrics evaluate the health of individual projects. Project profitability tells you after the fact how it went. Are your projects on track now? Are you getting better at managing your projects?

The power of this graph should now be apparent. By considering the concept of metric perspectives, you can develop an understanding of which metrics provide what insights. Mapping these perspectives onto a picture makes the assessment more intuitive. If you mapped the metrics you currently use to manage your PS business onto this graph, what would the picture look like? I am guessing you'd see the following:

- Very few (if any) leading metrics.
- Limited insight on the cost and effectiveness of your service sales activities. Yes, you might track revenues and bookings, but what about hit rates, sales costs per rep, or sales cost per project type.
- Very little insight into overall operational efficiency. Are we getting faster, better, less costly in the way we deliver our service portfolio?
- No metrics evaluate the activities of services development and marketing.

These blind spots should be addressed. Once again, I am not advocating you track thirty PS metrics, but you should track ten to twelve metrics in order to minimize the types of blind spots I have listed above.

Now that we have reviewed the framework, let's look more closely at the zones I introduced earlier.

ZONE 0 METRICS

Zone 0 metrics provide lagging information about the economic health of the professional services business. In other words, metrics in this zone tell you how you how much money you just made—not how much you *will* make. Also, this zone does not provide insight into the operational efficiency of your organization. Despite these deficiencies, the metrics in Zone 0 are critical to the continued employment of the management team.

If targets in this Zone 0 are too often missed, *the management team will eventually be replaced.* That's why this zone is always a focal point of interest.

Specifically, what metrics do I place in this critical zone that impacts employment longevity? I believe there are ten metrics located in Zone 0. Table 8.4 defines them.

ZONE 0 PRIORITIES

In the first column of Table 8.4, I have established the priority level for each of the metrics.

> *Priority 1:* Total service revenues, operating profit, and gross margin. These are the metrics that *every* service organization tracks. When these three go soft, executives need answers.
>
> *Priority 2:* Bill rate, rate realization, and labor multiplier. These metrics are next most likely to be tracked by management. They provide immediate insight into how profitable you will be for the quarter.
>
> *Priority 3:* Revenue per practice, profit per practice, solution revenue, and solution margin. These are Zone 0 metrics that many service organizations do not take the time to calculate. Nevertheless, they provide immediate insight into the profitability of specific service lines and predict where profitability problems may exist.

TABLE 8.4 Zone 0 Metrics

	Metric	Description
1	**Total Services Revenue**	Measurement of the different types of revenue; should be listed separately by Consulting, Solutions, and Third-Party pass-through.
1	**Operating Profit**	The profit generated by operations (also known as Operating Margin). Operating Profits = Total Services Revenue – COS – total operating expenses.
1	**Gross Margin (%)**	The gross profit generated per dollar of service delivered. Gross Margin = Total Services Revenue – Cost of services delivered (COS), traditionally called "cost of goods sold" (COGS).
2	**Bill Rate**	Average billable rate achieved by class of consultant.
2	**Rate Realization**	The amount of revenue actually earned as a percentage of potential revenue represented by list prices.
2	**Labor Multiplier**	The average factor by which billable personnel can be charged over and above their fully loaded costs. (Fully Loaded costs = direct salary + direct fringe benefits + overhead + G&A + Margin). A Labor Multiplier of 1.0 indicates a breakeven point.
3	**Revenue per Practice**	Total service revenues incurred by specific consulting practice.
3	**Profit per Practice**	The profit generated by practice operations (also known as Practice Operating Margin). Practice Operating Profits = (Total Practice Revenue – COS – Total Practice operating expenses).
3	**Solution Revenue**	Total service revenues incurred from a specific solution.
3		Average margin experienced when delivering a specific solution.

Table 8.5 provides additional data on what these ten metrics can be used to manage. Figure 8.5 maps these ten metrics onto the metrics perspective graph.

TABLE 8.5 Zone 0 Metrics Perspectives

	Metric	Code	Sales	Delivery	Marketing	Dev.	Ops	Staff	Project	Business	Internal	External
1	Total Services Revenue	TR	Y	Y	Y	Y				Y	Y	
1	Operating Profit	OP										
1	Gross Margin (%)	GM	Y	Y	Y	Y	Y		Y	Y	Y	
2	Bill Rate	BR	Y	Y				Y	Y	Y	Y	
2	Rate Realization	RR	Y	Y				Y	Y	Y	Y	
2	Labor Multiplier	LM								Y	Y	
3	Revenue per Practice	RPP	Y	Y	Y	Y				Y	Y	
3	Profit per Practice	PPP	Y	Y	Y	Y				Y	Y	
3	Solution Revenue	SR	Y		Y				Y	Y	Y	
3	Solution Margin	SM	Y	Y		Y			Y	Y	Y	

FIGURE 8.5 Zone 0 Metrics Perspective Graph

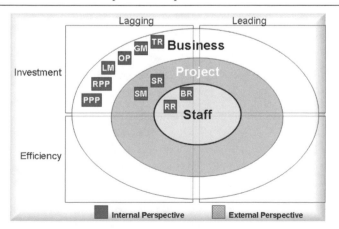

ZONE 0 DEFICIENCIES

Figure 8.5 illustrates the deficiencies of Zone 0 metrics. There is a natural tendency for the PS management team to fixate on Zone 0 metrics. This is understandable—if revenues and profits are falling, jobs are at stake. But a management team only tracking metrics in Zone 0 has a seriously flawed metric strategy. These ten metrics will not provide insights in the following areas:

Future economic value: Yes, you just had a good quarter! But what will future profits look like? Zone 0 metrics don't help here.

Operational efficiencies: Revenues and profits indicate whether you are managing the business well. However, they do not provide much insight into where operational challenges might exist. If margins were off, were sales costs too high? Did you simply scope the projects poorly? Zone 0 comes up empty when these questions are asked.

External perspective: Last but not least, the ten metrics in Zone 0 are all important to managers. They are not important to customers. Does a customer really care if margins and profits were down? No. If you are trying to determine how customers feel about you, Zone 0 does not help.

ZONE 0 TARGETS

The most frequent request I receive from management teams is to provide guidance for the following Zone 0 metrics:

Gross margin: How much margin should our PS business be generating?

Operating profit: What operating profit is reasonable and sustainable for a PS business?

Bill rate: Hey, are our bill rates too high (as our salespeople keep telling us)?

Rate realization: What rate should we be expecting from our consultants—65%, 75%, 100%?

I have found the specific targets for these four metrics vary widely from organization to organization, practice to practice, and industry to industry. Gross margins in PS range from 10 to 45%. Operating profits range from −20 to 20%. Realization rates range from 50 to 90%. Although the spectrums are wide, I do see some patterns.

First, actual gross margins are consistently lower than target gross margins. The most common target I see for gross margin is 40%, but the actual gross margins are much closer to 25%. Operating profit targets are typically set between 12 and 15%. Actual profits hover around 10%. I base these observations on the few companies that publicly report the gross margins and profits of their PS business and the various companies I have had the privilege to work with directly.

My experience leads me to this conclusion: *There are no universal targets that make sense for Zone 0 metrics.* Target margins and profits should be driven by the specific business model for your professional service organization, not by some mythical standard.

ZONE 1 METRICS

Zone 1 metrics provide important insights into the operational efficiencies of your PS business. However, these insights are lagging in nature—not predictive. If targets in Zone 1 are consistently below industry expectations, PS revenues and profits will always disappoint.

EXAMPLE METRICS

There are at least eight metrics that can be located in Zone 1. Table 8.6 defines these metrics.

ZONE 1 PRIORITIES

In the first column of Table 8.6, I have established the priority level for each of the eight metrics. These priorities are most likely the opposite of what most PS managers would assign to these metrics. Let me defend my prioritization:

> *Priority 1:* **Project per project, project overrun costs, cost of services delivered, and delivery labor costs.** All of these metrics inform the management team how much cost is actually involved in delivering its services. When project profitability decreases and project overruns increase, overall PS profitability (Zone 0 metric) will soon be impacted. If delivery labor costs are increasing, profitability will be impacted. These costs need to be monitored and aggressively managed. If they are not, the natural tendency is for project costs to become bloated and margins to erode.

TABLE 8.6 Zone 1 Metrics

	Metric	Definition	Calculation	Code
1	Delivery Labor Costs	The direct costs of billable services. Includes the labor costs of any managers that are more than 50% billable.	Delivery Labor Costs / Total Services Revenue	DLC
1	Project Overruns	The accuracy with which project costs are forecasted.	Total project costs incurred / total estimated project costs	POR
1	Profit per Project	The profit generated by a specific project. Project Profits = Total Project Revenue – COS – Sales Costs.		PP
1	Cost of Services Delivered	The fully loaded direct and indirect costs of billable services. Includes the expenses of any managers that are more than 50% billable. Costs of Services Delivered = Delivery labor costs + Delivery overhead costs.	Cost of Services Delivered / Total Services Revenue	COS
2	Delivery Overhead Costs	The fully loaded indirect costs of billable services. Includes the related expenses of any managers that are more than 50% billable. Delivery overhead costs = fringe benefits + travel + delivery – unit management costs + all other related costs with full-time consultants, hourly employees, or independents.	Delivery Overhead Costs / Total Services Revenue	DOC
2	Load Costs	Total business costs that are not directly related to the cost of delivering services		LC
3	Utilization Rate	Measures the organization's ability to maximize its billable resources.	Total number of hours billed / number of working hours in a year (varies by geography) × Number of billable employees	UR
3	Cash Flow	The amount of cash generated (or absorbed, if negative) by the organization.	Cash Flow from operations / Total Services Revenue	CF

Priority 2: **Load costs, delivery overhead costs.** These metrics are the next area management can track to identify potential improvement of efficiency. They provide insight into how much overhead the PS organization is carrying to support project delivery. It is difficult for even the healthiest project margins to cover unnecessary and inflated overhead costs.

Priority 3: **Utilization and cash flow.** That I placed utilization a third priority will be controversial. Every PS leader demands that consultant utilization be tracked and accounted for. I agree that utilization is an insightful metric. If consultants are only being utilized 50 to 60% of the time, the business is inefficient and overresourced. However, utilization is one of the most abused metrics available to the management staff. If you tell the PS staff you will be tracking utilization, they will be utilized—trust me. The question remains, though, just how beneficial the utilization is. Tracking project costs and overruns will provide more immediate and potentially more accurate insights into the efficiencies of your business.

Even if deals are being won and top-line revenue is growing, you may stink at actually delivering your service portfolio. These Zone 1 metrics help you discover how efficient your organization is.

Table 8.7 provides additional data on what these eight metrics can be used to manage. Figure 8.6 maps these metrics onto the metrics perspective graph.

TABLE 8.7 Zone 1 Metrics Perspectives

	Metric	Code	Sales	Delivery	Marketing	Dev.	Investment	Staff	Project	Business	Internal	External
1	Delivery Labor Costs	DLC			Y		Y			Y	Y	Y
1	Project Over-runs	POR			Y		Y		Y	Y	Y	Y
3	Utilization Rate	UR	Y	Y	Y			Y		Y	Y	
1	Profit per Project	PP		Y		Y			Y	Y	Y	
1	Cost of Services Delivered	COS		Y		Y			Y	Y	Y	
2	Delivery Over-head Costs	DOC		Y						Y	Y	
2	Load Costs	LC								Y	Y	
3	Cash Flow	CF								Y	Y	

FIGURE 8.6 Zone 1 Metrics Perspective Graph

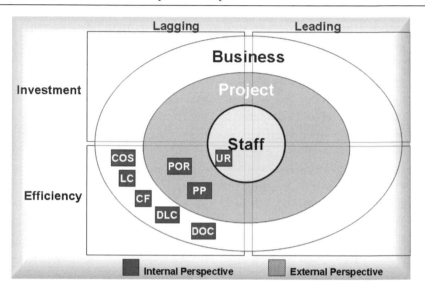

ZONE 1 DEFICIENCIES

Zone 1 metrics have two significant deficiencies. First, the metrics are lagging in nature. Soaring delivery costs or project overruns tell you there is a problem only after it has occurred. Second, these metrics are internally focused. As a PS manager, you care about utilization rates and delivery load costs. Your clients do not.

ZONE 1 TARGETS

When reviewing Zone 0 metrics, I suggested that best practice targets for many of these metrics are a slippery slope to stand on. However, there are some reasonable guidelines for two of the Zone 1 metrics:

Utilization: PS organizations have a tendency to target very high utilization rates. I believe this bias comes from the heritage of traditional professional services organizations such as law firms and accounting firms. In these environments, employees are often expected to bill over forty hours a week to client accounts. I believe PS activity within a product company is a different environment. I have yet to review such a PS organization that was sustaining 100% billable utilization. I do see PS organizations that report 100%+ utilization rates, but these rates track nonbillable activity such as pre-sales calls. , I believe billable utilization activity sits between 60 and 85%. If utilization is less than 60%, the PS organization cannot financially support itself. If it is greater than 85%, no time is left for ongoing staff development.

Project overruns: They occur. It is a fact of life when you are delivering complex technology-centered solutions. The order of magnitude is what's important. On an ongoing basis, project overruns should average 10 to 25%. If your project costs consistently exceed 25% of the initial estimate, your ability to estimate effort is seriously in question. If you are bidding projects at a fixed price, your ability to be profitable is clearly in jeopardy!

FROM LAGGING TO LEADING

Zone 1 metrics provide insight on the operational efficiency of the PS organization. Metrics such as project profitability, project overruns, and labor costs help determine how efficiently PS is delivering services. Weakness in these metrics will have direct and immediate impact on overall profitability. Improving these metrics leads to improvement in the Zone 0 metrics that every management team must account for: revenues, margins, and profitability. So Zone 1 metrics are important, though lagging in nature. Only after the project overrun report comes in do you know you have a problem. You need some leading metrics. What can you measure to get ahead of the profitability power curve?

ZONE 2 METRICS

The transition to leading metrics begins with Zone 2. Zone 2 metrics provide leading insights into the operational efficiency of your PS business. If Zone 2 metrics begin declining, operational efficiency will start suffering. If operational efficiency drops, reduced margins and profits are sure to follow.

EXAMPLE METRICS

There are at least ten metrics that can logically be placed in Zone 2. Table 8.8 defines them.

ZONE 2 PRIORITIES

In the first column of Table 8.8, I have established the priority levels for each of the metrics.

Priority 1: **Bid and Proposal Costs.** This metric is a little tricky. Even though it is a cost metric, and fundamentally reflects efficiency, it can demonstrate so much more. If you are winning more business but bid costs are going up, something is changing. Is your bid approach sloppy, are new competitors entering your space, or are you chasing business you simply should not be chasing? You need to review those bid costs now, before your revenues reflect the fact the sales folks were chasing the wrong business.

- **Channel Mix.** How efficiently are you using all of your sales channel options? Are the old partners getting any better at selling the new services? Does everything still get sold through the most expensive channel option we have: the direct sales staff? Act to improve the channel mix now, before you are forced to reduce direct sales staff later.

- **G&A.** Are these costs creeping up? I see this happen in service businesses. If G&A climbs as a percentage of total revenues, you are probably spending money to mask other fundamental issues in the business. Take a look at creeping G&A costs now, before the CFO requires budget cuts.

- **Project Completion Ratio.** Do you track project profitability for ongoing projects? Are the teams meeting commitments on time? This is the first metric I have mentioned that has an external perspective as well. Your customers care how you do here. Are you delivering on your commitments to them? Track project milestones now, before you realize chunks of revenue will be delayed next quarter.

Priority 2: **Research and Development Costs.** How much money does PS spend to manage intellectual property and improve delivery methodologies? If this number is becoming too large, profits suffer. If this number is too small, you struggle to increase the value you bring to customers. Track

TABLE 8.8 Zone 2 Metrics

	Metric	Definition	Calculation	Code
1	Bid & Proposal Cost	Total dollars spent on submitting a bid, including dollars spent on bid qualification, financial analysis, alliance and partner selection, feasibility analysis, proposal development, proposal submittal, and best and final offer (BAFO).	Total $ spent for submitting bids / total contract value of bids submitted	**BPC**
1	Channel Mix	Percentage of sales revenues that occur through each potential sales channel.		**CM**
1	General & Administrative Expenses (G&A)	The general expenses not captured in COS, Sales, Marketing, or R&D. G&A Expenses = Total expenses – Training costs + Management costs + other administrative costs.	G&A Expenses / Total Services Revenue	**G&A**
1	Project Completion Ratio	Measure the degree of completion against project milestones.	Number of milestones accomplished on schedule / total milestones targeted	**PCR**
2	Research & Development Costs	Degree of investment made to enhance the firm's tools, products, and methodologies. Total R&D costs = Infrastructure + Sales Tools + Delivery Tools.	R&D Costs / Total Services Revenue	**R&D**
2	Total Operating Expenses	The sum of all non-delivery operating expenses. Total operating expenses = G&A costs + Sales costs + Marketing costs + R&D costs.	Total Operating expenses / Total Services Revenue	**TOE**
2	Training Costs	The total cost of training. Training expenses include curriculum design and development, instruction costs, and facilities costs.	Training Expenses / Total Services Revenue	**TC**
2	Training Days	Average number of working days spent in training.	Number of employee working days spent training / total number of employee working days	**TD**
3	Alliances/ Partnering Costs	The amount of dollars spent on alliance and partner programs by line of business.	Alliance and partnering costs / Total Services Revenue	**APC**
3	Seminars and Collateral Material Costs	The amount of dollars spent on prospect and/or client seminars and marketing collateral (e.g. ,brochures).	Seminars &and collateral costs / Total Services Revenue	**COL**

how much money is invested in solution development and improvement now, before your possible solutions become stale and unmarketable.

- **Total Operating Expenses.** Many PS organizations are not disciplined in their tracking of sales costs vs. marketing costs, G&A, etc. To offset this common deficiency, I recommend that the management team track the total amount of money spent to support the business. If PS margins are flat and total operating expenses are growing, there is a problem. Understand total operating expenses now, before there are insufficient margin dollars to support them.
- **Training Costs and Training Days.** Like R&D costs, training cost is centered more on underinvestment. Catch severe declines in training investment now, before consultants embarrass your brand six months from now.

Priority 3:

- **Alliance and Partner Costs.** Partners are a critical component to the delivery of most "solutions." How much money are you investing in identifying, qualifying, and enabling your partners? Are you wasteful or underinvesting. Spend money certifying your delivery partners today, before they sink a critical engagement tomorrow.
- **Collateral Costs.** How much does PS spend on marketing materials? If they are the largest portion of your service marketing budget, you have a problem. Reduce marketing material costs now, before you wish you did.

These Zone 2 metrics provide quite a useful perspective on your business. No executive will be fired because R&D costs are too low or project completion ratios have slipped by 10%. But when a poorly differentiated services portfolio and poor project execution have created significant slippage in revenues and profits, a very unpleasant business review may be just four quarters down the road.

Table 8.9 provides additional data on how these ten metrics can be used to manage the services organization. Figure 8.7 maps these ten metrics onto the metrics perspective graph.

TABLE 8.9 Zone 2 Metrics Perspectives

Metric	Sales	Delivery	Marketing	Dev.	Ops	Leading	Lagging	Efficiency	Investment	Staff	Project	Business	Internal	External
Bid & Proposal Cost	Y	Y				Y		Y			Y	Y	Y	
Channel Mix	Y		Y			Y		Y				Y	Y	
General & Administrative Expenses (G&A)					Y	Y		Y				Y	Y	
Project Completion Ratio		Y				Y		Y	Y		Y	Y	Y	Y
Research & Development Costs				Y		Y		Y				Y	Y	
Total Operating Expenses					Y	Y		Y				Y	Y	
Training Costs					Y	Y		Y				Y	Y	
Training Days		Y			Y	Y		Y		Y		Y	Y	
Alliances/ Partnering Costs		Y	Y		Y	Y		Y				Y		
Seminars and Collateral Material Costs			Y			Y		Y				Y	Y	

FIGURE 8.7 Zone 2 Metrics Perspective Graph

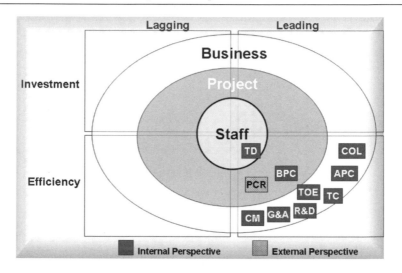

ZONE 3 METRICS

Finally, our long journey through PS business metrics comes to a close as we enter Zone 3. I believe the metrics in this zone provide the greatest insight into the future economic health of a PS business. Revenues and profits tell me if managers were paid their bonuses this quarter, but the metrics in this zone are early indicators of how bonuses will be paid four quarters from now.

If Zone 3 metrics begin declining, your PS business is in decline. It is only a matter of time before revenues and profits will suffer.

EXAMPLE METRICS

Table 8.10 lists ten metrics that provide a leading economic assessment of the PS business.

ZONE 3 PRIORITIES

In the first column of Table 8.10, I have documented the three priority levels for these ten metrics:

Priority 1: **Account Expansion.** This metric tracks how much additional business PS gets after the first engagement. If this dollar value is increasing per account, PS is doing a good job of delivering, establishing credibility, and identifying new opportunities. If this metric is declining, customers are *not* impressed with your services or staff. Typically, account expansion with existing customers should be easier than securing new accounts.

- **Backlog.** When your backlog slips, a decline in recognized revenues will not be far behind. Ideally, your quarter starts with at least 75% of the service work identified and booked. For most project-based services, a backlog below 50% of the target revenue for the quarter is a difficult hole to escape.

- **Hit Ratio.** This metric tells you how successful your sales proposals are. If your hit ratio is improving, your positioning and value proposition are likely improving as well. Also, your employees are getting more effective at selling your services. A declining hit ratio is an early indicator that a solution is growing stale or competitors are offering a more compelling value proposition.

- **New Client Ratio.** How much business is coming from new customers? This metric provides a mirror insight to account expansion. If all of your revenue is coming from the existing client base, you are not effectively selling or marketing the portfolio to new prospects.

Priority 2: **Customer Value.** Customer value, customer loyalty, and customer satisfaction are all related metrics. How do customers feel about the services you are delivering? A downward trend here provides an early warning signal.

- **Delivery Tools.** This metric is closely related to R&D spending. The difference is that here you want to measure how much has been invested in the tangible infrastructure that facilitates your delivery of services. If this percentage is flat or declining, you may be underinvesting in the tools that differentiate your services. This scrimping will not show up this quarter, but it can bite you later in the year.

- **Sales Yield.** How effective is your selling process? If sales yields are increasing, your sales skills are improving or your solution positioning is more compelling. Either way, the economic value of your PS business is increasing.

- **Solution Portfolio Maturity.** This metric measures your ability to deliver a particular service consistently. If service maturity is increasing, your ability to improve margins improves—a great indicator of the economic health of the business.

Priority 3: **Skills Gaps.** Do you have the skills you need to deliver your services? When you first start a PS business, this gap may be significant. The goal is to shrink it. If the gap is not improving or it is widening, you will eventually pay a very real price in margins and revenues.

- Turnover Rate. Last but not least is the question of your overall turnover rate in the PS business. A key consultant can leave today and the quarter is not lost. Your top ten consultants leave over the next six months, and revenues may be impacted. A spike in turnover rates can be an early warning sign that the business is not on track.

Once again, I believe Zone 3 metrics provide the greatest insight into the true health of your Professional Service organization. Ironically, these are the metrics that are least likely to show up on a monthly PS dashboard.

Table 8.11 provides additional data on what these ten metrics can be used to manage. Figure 8.8 maps these ten metrics into the metrics perspective graph.

TABLE 8.10 Zone 3 Metrics

	Metric	Definition	Calculation	Code
1	Account Expansion	The ability of a vendor to expand its account penetration and its volume of business within existing accounts.	Add on revenue/dollar value of original proposal	AE
1	Backlog	The total value of contract commitments yet to be executed. Total Backlog = Previous Fiscal Year's Commitments + Latest Fiscal Year's Sales - latest Fiscal Year's Revenue.	Total Backlog = Previous Fiscal Year's Commitments + Latest Fiscal Year's Scales – latest Fiscal Year's Revenue	BL
1	Hit Ratio	The competitive success rate of the company in the markets it chooses to compete in. Does not include single-sourced bids.	Revenue from proposals won / Possible revenue from proposals submitted	HR
1	New Client Ratio	Measures a vendor's ability to win new accounts and develop new business. New client ratio = New clients / Total clients.	Total dollar value of new client accounts / total dollar value of all client accounts	NCR
2	Customer Value	Measures how satisfied the customer is with the service delivered. Identifies how customers receive value from the service offering.	Perceived Business Benefit of service offerings – Cost of Service Offering. Benefit ultimately represent the sum total of expected cost savings and/or increased revenues.	CV

TABLE 8.10 Zone 3 Metrics (continued)

	Metric	Definition	Calculation	Code
2	Delivery Tools	The amount of R&D investment in Delivery Tools. Delivery Tools = automated methodology tools + project management + on-line skills inventory/resource + time scheduler + automated labor voucher + Real-time conferencing + Workgroup sharing + Knowledge data	Delivery Tools / Total Services Revenue	DT
2	Sales Yield	The sales productivity of the company. Target values or sales quota versus actuals are encouraged.	Sales dollar value / Number of direct or full-time equivalent sales people	SY
2	Solution Portfolio Maturity	The average maturity rating for target solutions	Average of: number of completed sales and delivery tools for a solution / total number of sales and delivery tools to be created	SPM
3	Skills Gaps	Measures the gap between the skills required to deliver target services and the skills available within the delivery staff		SG
3	Turnover Rate	A measure of attrition. An example of a Former Employee is a person who was on the personnel roster at the start of the previous fiscal year and was no longer on the personnel roster at the start of the current year.	Number of Former Employees (annualized) / Total number of employees (annualized)	TR

FIGURE 8.8 Zone 3 Metrics Perspective Graph

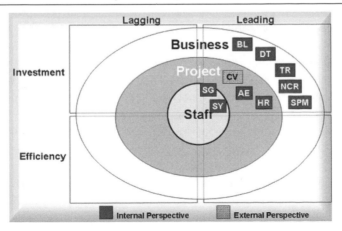

TABLE 8.11 Zone 3 Metrics Perspectives

Metric	Delivery	Marketing	Dev.	Ops	Leading	Lagging	Efficiency	Economic Value	Staff	Project	Business	Internal	External
Account Expansion	Y				Y			Y	Y	Y	Y		Y
Backlog	Y			Y	Y			Y			Y	Y	
Hit Ratio		Y			Y			Y	Y		Y	Y	
New Client Ratio		Y			Y			Y	Y		Y		Y
Customer Value	Y	Y	Y		Y			Y	Y	Y	Y		Y
Delivery Tools	Y		Y	Y	Y			Y			Y	Y	
Sales Yield		Y			Y			Y	Y		Y	Y	
Solution Portfolio Maturity		Y	Y		Y			Y			Y	Y	
Skills Gaps	Y		Y		Y			Y	Y		Y	Y	
Turnover Rate	Y	Y	Y	Y	Y			Y			Y	Y	

SUMMARY OF ZONES

Figure 8.9 provides a summary view of the four metrics zones we have just reviewed.

Understanding these zones, you can appreciate how you can realistically respond to data from specific metrics. When metrics in Zone 0 such as revenues and gross margins are poor, you should be concerned. However, these are not metrics you can fix on a dime. They represent the overall performance of the business. To find short-term fixes, you need to look into the Zone 1 metrics. If you improve utilization or load costs by reducing the work force, you will have an immediate impact on Zone 0 metrics. You need to be careful, however. Drastic short-term improvements can impact the long-term viability of the business. For insight on long-term viability, turn to the metrics in Zone 2 and Zone 3. By making improvements here, you may not see immediate improvements to Zone 1 metrics, but you will see improvement in the long term.

FIGURE 8.9 Summary of Metrics Zones

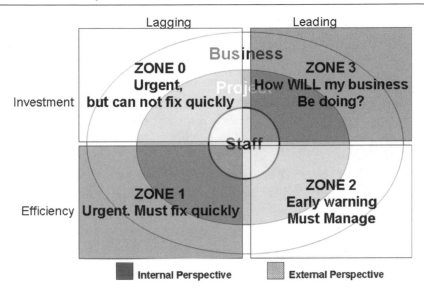

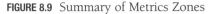

PRIORITIZING METRICS

Using the metric perspectives graph, you can effectively identify a metrics portfolio that minimizes blind spots. However, you still need to select which metrics to focus on. There are over fifty meaningful metrics that can be used to help evaluate a services business. Clearly, you cannot begin tracking all fifty metrics tomorrow. So how do you decide which metrics make the cut? I recommend a five-step process to help choose and implement a metrics portfolio:

Step 1: Inventory Potential Metrics: Identify all the metrics that could potentially be used to evaluate your services business.

Step 2: Apply Filters: There are four questions you can ask to help determine what metrics are important to your company:

1. By using this metric, will we improve the way we are doing business? If the metric will not result in direct action on your part, then it is suspect.

2. What metrics does the industry use? Is there a subset of all the potential metrics that are commonly used by competitors?

3. What metrics will impact strategic objectives? Are there any metrics that can directly track progress on a strategic objective? For example, the services organization may be tasked to develop new ac-

counts in new industries. A metric such as "new client ratio," which measures how much revenue is coming from brand-new clients, would be perfect to track this objective.

4. What metrics are important to key stakeholders? Are there specific metrics that critical stakeholders have requested? For example, does the CFO require a specific gross margin by service?

Step 3: Assess Blind Spots: Map the set of potential metrics into a metrics perspectives graph. Determine if there are any glaring blind spots. Do you have enough metrics in Zone 3 to provide leading insight into the health of the business?

Step 4: Assess Effort: Once you are satisfied you have a balanced metrics portfolio, estimate how much effort will be required to collect each metric on an ongoing basis.

Step 5: Design Rollout Plan: Now that you understand which metrics are most important for your organization and how much effort each metric will take to acquire, you can devise a rollout plan. I recommend a phased approach using the following guiding principles:

- Focus on low-hanging fruit: Start tracking the metrics that have impact and require minimal effort to acquire.
- From corporate intensive to geo intensive: If possible, start with metrics that management needs to collect. Then, push toward the metrics that are more labor intensive for the field organization.
- Implement leading metrics sooner than later: Don't wait to phase in leading metrics that seem like they'd be only "nice to have." The sooner you have metrics in Zone 3, the sooner you will be able to control your long-term destiny.
- Minimize blind spots: At every phase of rollout, strive to minimize bind spots!

Figure 8.10 captures this four-step prioritization process.

CUSTOMER VALUE PROGRAM

In *Building Professional Services*, I introduced the iron triangle of profitability for a professional services organization. That triangle is composed of the *revenue mix*, the ability to field *repeatable*, profitable solutions, and the depth of a *reference* database. A professional services organization cannot drive these

FIGURE 8.10 Prioritization Process

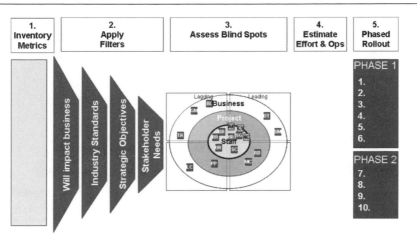

profitability levers if it does not know what customers think. Are customers satisfied with your solutions? Are customers impressed with your delivery staff? Where specifically do customers feel you bring value? And most important, will they serve as a positive reference?

To acquire this information, a services organization must implement a set of external facing metrics that are designed to extract this data directly from customers. Kathy Wilson, an industry expert in customer loyalty, and I call this a *customer value (CV) program.*[1] A successful CV program must be successful in three aspects:

1. *You must ask the right questions.* The right questions will enable you to collect data that can drive effective services positioning, consultant development, and future services development.

2. *You must ask at the right time.* At the end of engagements? During engagements? Timing is everything.

3. *You must ask in the right way.* In person? Over the phone? Through e-mail?

By getting these three attributes correct, a services organization can tap into a wealth of critical data. To my surprise, I find few service firms aggressively manage this process. Many firms conduct no ongoing customer reviews. Other firms issue a half-hearted customer-satisfaction survey.

---

1. Kathy Wilson has given me great insight into the areas of customer loyalty and satisfaction. For more information about her work, visit *www.thomaslah.com.*

FIGURE 8.11 Customer Value Program

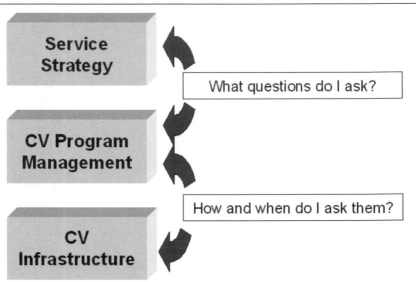

Figure 8.11 shows the three building blocks that should be in place to support an effective CV program. The infrastructure to support a CV program is becoming inexpensive and feature rich. Companies can build question databases and survey customers electronically. Responses can be sliced and diced multiple ways. The question remains, what firms will aggressively take advantage of this type of program?

EXECUTIVE SUMMARY

You can't manage what you don't measure—every senior manager will agree with this truism. Even though we all agree, we have a tough time living it. Metrics are a premium activity. It takes money and staff to generate data. PS organizations want to apply finite resources to the right activities. To address this reality, management teams need to decide on a tight set of metrics that will provide the most strategic insight into the business. Unfortunately, PS management teams have a tendency to focus on metrics that provide lagging information concerning the health of the Professional Services function.

To accomplish the objective of creating a tight set of metrics that provide the greatest amount of insight, managers can use the concept of metric perspectives to assess and prioritize what metrics they will use. By using this approach, managers can create a set of metrics that:

- Provide leading insight into the economic health of the PS organization
- Minimize potential blind spots into business deficiencies at the project, staff, or overall business levels

Chapter Nine

The Revenue Life Cycle

From Big "R" to Little "r"

CHAPTER OBJECTIVE

To link the key concepts of this book to the day-to-day activities of the professional services organization

KEY CONCEPTS

- The Revenue Life Cycle
- Required Skills Chart
- Available Skills Chart

IT ALL SOUNDS GOOD IN THEORY

This book is all about improving the performance of a professional services organization that is supporting the broader portfolio of company offerings. To optimize this type of professional services business, the management team must work through the nine strategy variables that I have defined in this text. By now, I hope you share my level of conviction. Still, some doubts might linger. Do we really need to define a business model? Why do we need to identify a target revenue mix? Why can't we simply focus on selling and delivering services engagements? Besides, no one has the time and energy to figure out all this stuff.

So there we have it—the gap between theory and reality. In theory, a proactive, sharp, strategically oriented management team would indeed be working on the types of things I have outlined. In reality, the management team is scrambling to close deals and meet the revenue objectives for the quarter. In theory, service leaders are actively pursuing markets strategic to overall company success. In reality, the services organization has to respond to the opportunities

177

thrown its way by a sales force that sells too far down the ladder of the customer's organization. In theory, the service organization has optimized its ability to scale delivery resources. In reality, local service managers scramble to get new hires approved after the customer has signed the statement of work (I call this "APO" hiring—hiring delivery staff after the signed P.O. arrives). But this book is not about a theoretical vacuum, but about improving your reality. So let's take the concepts introduced in this text and apply them to a topic important to every service manager: hitting revenue objectives!

BIG "R" AND LITTLE "R"

Two concepts that no service manager can hide from are revenues and profits. This is as real as it gets. If revenues and profits are trending the wrong way, there is explaining to do. If the negative trends continue, there are resumes to update. In fact, it is difficult to get executive management to understand anything about PS beyond service revenues and profits. How much did you spend on service marketing last quarter? How much will you invest in service sales this year? Who cares! Will you hit your revenue and profitability targets? Sure, the company's executive team will meet offsite to review product R&D budget, followed by a two-day meeting to review product sales compensation plans— but there is no time to discuss the partner strategy for services delivery. Such is the life of a service leader.

When most service managers think about revenue and profit objectives, they think in two levels: business and project.

At the business level, management must make sure the PS organization meets the overall revenue and profitability targets set for it by the executive staff. At the project level, service management is making sure that each specific engagement is on target to meet the financial objectives established when the engagement was initially scoped. Figure 9.1 shows the two revenue types: Big R and little r.

Figure 9.1 also demonstrates the relationship between Big R and little r. To meet the overall revenue and profitability objectives for the PS organization as defined in Big R on the left side of the figure, the revenue and profits of all those little r projects on the right side must be in line. If you have a Big R objective of delivering 8% profit to the company, all of your projects can't be merely breakeven. Big R is simply the sum of all its little r parts.

FIGURE 9.1 Big R and Little r

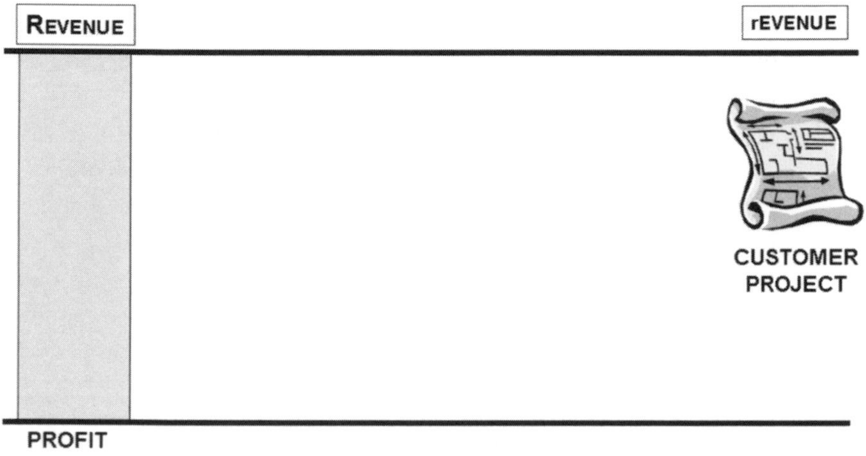

DOWNWARD DRAG

At the beginning of the book, I introduced three fundamental areas that can impede PS profitability:

1. Strategy: An unsustainable or incomplete service strategy
2. Structure: An immature infrastructure to support the service business
3. Culture: A product-centric environment that undervalues service activities

At the macro level, these are the hurdles that a management team must overcome for PS to succeed. But at the micro level of quarterly revenue, we need to focus on the daily realities of booking service engagements and delivering them at a profit. In other words, let's focus on how Big R gets connected to little r. At the end of the quarter, if total revenues and profits are south of expectations, we can probably find four basic faults:

• Pricing: Engagements are priced too low. Why? The product sales reps could be discounting services in order to sell product. Or the service organization has no experience delivering these types of services and the engagements require more effort than scoped. Regardless of the underlying causes, the engagements are priced too low to meet financial targets.

- <u>Mix:</u> Although the service organization has too many engagements that are low-margin activities, they cannot be priced higher because the market will not bear it. Adding up all of these low-margin engagements that comprise the service mix, not enough margin dollars are available to cover expenses and meet profit targets.

- <u>Sourcing:</u> Service deals are signed without the staff to deliver them. Higher priced subcontractors have to be used, reducing profitability. Or high-priced consultants are used to complete engagements that could be delivered by less costly resources.

- <u>Execution:</u> The delivery team simply mismanages or messes up a project that is priced fairly and sourced correctly, and the customer refuses to pay.

Figure 9.2 summarizes these four forces and the impact they have on project profitability. Of course, if project profits are down (little r), overall PS profits will be down (Big R).

Now, how do we improve the situation? How do we address these tactical drag points? By returning to strategy! We need to close the gap between the deals PS chases and the overall financial objectives of the PS organization. Too often PS organizations are off chasing anything that moves. If the customer wants services, we can help! But not every service deal is attractive. How can a service organization weed out the bad deals from the good deals? By explicitly connecting little r projects to Big R revenue objectives. Let me show you how.

FIGURE 9.2 Project Pressures

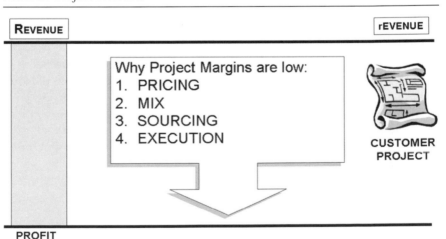

CONNECTING THE R'S

What projects should PS pursue? I think that without setting the nine strategy variables it is impossible to correctly answer that question. Without them, the best a management team can do is set blanket margin and/or profitability targets for the services organization. "Project margins can be no lower than 25%!" "Field organizations must contribute 10% to corporate PS." "Utilization rates must be 75% or greater." But this type of guidance is really no guidance. It provides little help to local service managers who need to determine which projects fit the company strategy. Which projects are aligned with company objectives? Which projects have lower risk? To answer these critical questions, a management team must connect project activity to overall service strategy. Four steps accomplish this connection:

Step 1: Plug in the Business Model: To begin the connection process, we start with the business model. Instead of simply defining revenue and profit objectives, the service organization needs to define its target business model. Why? For the full-blown rationale, refer to Chapter 4. For the purposes of this exercise, the service organization needs to define a target business model so it understands what gross margins are required to sustain the business.

Step 2: Plug in the Service Revenue Mix: Now that we know what gross margins this business needs to sustain, we need to map in a target portfolio of services. This portfolio should comprise services that sustain the types of margins we need. For example, if your business model requires an average of 30% gross margins, you cannot have 80% of your service revenues coming from highly competitive outsourcing services that only achieve 15% gross margins. The numbers will not add up at the end of the quarter. Either your business model needs to be adjusted to account for lower margins, or your service mix needs to be modified to secure better margins.

Step 3: Review Forecast: Now that you know what service mix makes sense to support your business, you need to begin tracking the pipeline for the desired service offerings. If demand is light for critical offerings, you need to consider activities that generate the targeted demand.

Step 4: Set Proposal Priorities: Now you understand which service opportunities get priority treatment. When opportunities are related to target service offerings, pursue them aggressively. When opportunities are not aligned with the target portfolio, consider them cautiously. This is not to say that bidding on service opportunities outside of the core portfolio is forbidden, only that every time you stray from the core, you introduce financial risk—and you must be aware of it.

FIGURE 9.3 The Revenue Life Cycle

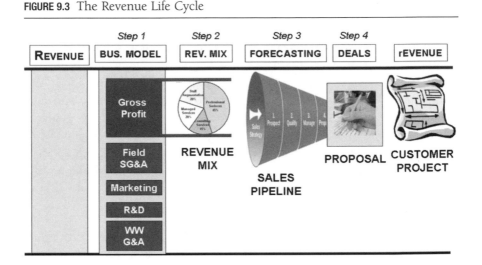

By completing these four steps, we have closed the gap between overall financial objectives and the specific service engagements that are being pursued. Figure 9.3 documents this linkage between Big R and little r. Without this linkage, your service organization might aggressively pursue almost any available service opportunity. Although this take-all-comers approach sounds good in theory, it is not. That approach dilutes your resources, your brand, and your ability to create differentiated intellectual property.

MANAGING THE CYCLE

To optimize the revenue life cycle, ten deliverables must be managed:

1. The Financial Plan: The profit and loss targets for the professional services business
2. The Target Business Model: The target business model for the professional services business (as defined in Chapter 4)
3. The Target Revenue Mix: The target portfolio of services (as defined in Chapter 5)
4. Market Opportunity Data: Market data assessing the size of potential service markets (as defined in Chapter 5)

Figure 9.4 Revenue Life Cycle Deliverables

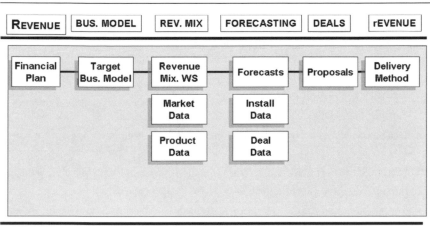

5. Product Forecast Data: Forecasts on product sales in specific target markets
6. Service Revenue Forecasts: The revenue forecasts for specific services
7. Install Data: Data on the existing customer install base (targeted to purchase the target services)
8. Deal Data: Project data from actual customer engagements
9. Proposal Templates: Sample proposals for target services
10. Delivery Methodologies: Engagement methodologies for delivering target services

Figure 9.4 shows where these ten deliverables fit in the process of connecting financial targets to service projects. These are the ten tangible items that close the potential gap between wildly optimistic revenue objectives and the deal you are pitching next week. By consistently improving the quality of these ten you improve the ability of the services organization to be profitable. You improve your ability to consistently hit your quarterly financial targets.

MISSING DATA

In this chapter I am connecting the outputs of service strategy to the daily activities of managing a service business. The ten deliverables I just itemized make it easier for service managers to connect revenue objectives to the specific service engagements they are pursuing. Considering these ten, we can see how immature most service strategies are. Ask a service to demonstrate these deliverables and you will find the following:

Financial plan: *Got it!*

Delivery methodologies: *Got some of them!*

Sample proposals: *Yep, have those too.*

Deal data: *Uh, yeah we have some project data around here. Not sure where it is.*

Install data: *Sorry, we don't track that for services. I have no idea who has purchased which services from us over the past three years.*

Target business model: *Parts of it are defined. We have target margins and target profits. Oh, and we have a G&A budget. No, we don't define how much we should be spending on services marketing, service sales, or services development.*

Target revenue mix: *Not defined. Next question.*

Service revenue forecasts: *Beyond a top-line revenue forecast, we don't ask our reps to forecast revenues for specific services. They have no idea.*

Besides, we don't provide bonuses for hitting specific service mixes. Hell, we are ecstatic if they sell any of our services.

Market data: *Never have seen it for service market opportunities. Should we be asking for that from marketing?*

Product data: *We don't look at the product forecasts closely. Should we?*

These sample responses represent the dark hole that currently exists between Big R and little r in most service organizations. Figure 9.5 shows that current state. The closer you get to the center of the diagram, the foggier the data becomes. Why is this acceptable?

If we were discussing the product mix of a company, this concern would be unfounded. We would not need to justify the linkage between deals closed and overall company financial targets. Product companies forecast product mixes ad nauseam. Product companies have a mixture of high-margin products and low-margin products. If sales of high-margin products are below forecast, the CFO knows there will be a problem with profitability. Also, product company executives do not tell their sales force to "sell whatever." The sales force is given a compensation plan and a bonus structure designed to maximize the product mix for overall company profitability.

FIGURE 9.5 Missing Data

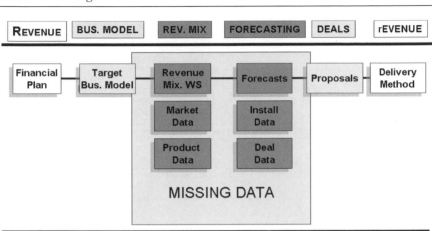

So why do these same companies approach the data required to manage the services mix so casually? Because service managers are under the impression that this missing or murky data is not a requirement for success. If this were ever true, it is no longer true. In a hypercompetitive, global economy where you are managing a human-capital-intensive business, this data can spell the difference between disappointment and success.

SUPPLY AND DEMAND

Another way to emphasize the importance of managing the revenue life cycle with more discipline is to consider the impact of supply and demand in a human-capital-intensive business. There are two aspects of matching supply and demand in a professional services business: matching volume and matching skills.

Matching Volume

Figure 9.6 shows the ebb and flow of services demand over time. The line labeled "target utilization" represents the capacity your service delivery staff has in terms of hours. Let's walk through the ups and downs of the graph:

FIGURE 9.6 Peaks and Valleys

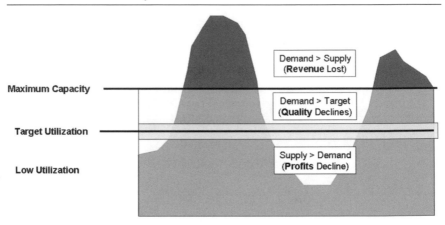

Demand increases: If demand for your services spikes upwards, your staff will most likely respond at first by working more hours but the quality of their output may suffer. If demand continues to spike, however, the staff will eventually run out of hours in the day and revenue opportunities will be lost unless subcontractors can be found or new consultants quickly hired.

Demand decreases: If demand for your services falls below projections, profitability will be sacrificed because you are paying for staff hours that are not generating income. Unless you can off-board staff quickly, profits could be ugly until you adjust to the downturn.

How quickly should a service organization be able to respond to fluctuations in demand? Let's say you have a forecast from your sales reps for $10M in service activity over the next three months. You have 150 consultants and contractors lined up to deliver that business. As the quarter proceeds, service deals start falling from the sky. How much more service business should you be able to accept and maintain profitability? Another $2M (a 20% increase)? Another $5M? Another $10M? At what point do you tap out the trained labor market and/or your ability to take on staff? If the growth rate data presented in Chapter 4 is any indication, PS will not be able to continuously support spikes greater than 50%.

What if the $10M forecast is unsupportable and demand drops by 30%. Some of the projected deals have not come through and some existing customers have decided to delay the start dates of follow-on phases. You now have 45 consultants too many. How much should you be expected to reduce your staff now that revenue projections have plunged? By 10 consultants? By all 45?

FIGURE 9.7 The Sourcing Zone

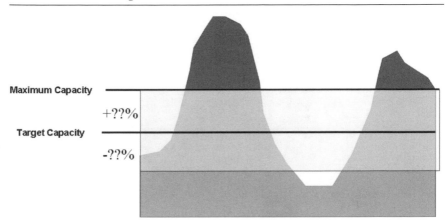

Figure 9.7 shows this dilemma. If a forecast is off, how quickly should a PS organization be able to respond and by how much? Plus or minus 40% of capacity? The answers are specific to the services you are offering and the labor markets you rely on. There are probably clear limitations you face, including labor laws and your ability to train new staff. These limitations in increasing and decreasing volume are real and inevitable and we need to plan for them. PS needs to establish boundaries so executive staff understands the ramifications of crappy forecasting. Month after month of "forecast surprises" makes it almost impossible for PS to hit profitability objectives.

Matching Skills

Unfortunately, a PS management team must do more than simply match volume. The managers must match specific skills to the specific services being sold. For example, let's say you offer a service called "Environment Assessment." This service assesses technical and process risks that exist in a customer's environment. By the way, this is one of your highest margin services. Your staff can provide an outstanding mix of skills to complete this assessment for install base customers, so you rarely face serious competition. To deliver the service, you supply a business analyst, a technical analyst, and a project manager. The service takes an average of 140 hours of effort from the project team. Figure 9.8 shows the mix of resources required to deliver one engagement.

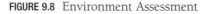

FIGURE 9.8 Environment Assessment

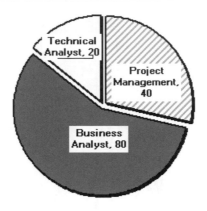

Over the next three months, you expect to deliver ten of these engagements. Table 9.1 records the resources required to deliver these ten engagements.

"Environment Assessment" is not the only service your organization delivers. To keep things simple, let's say there are only two other target services you promote: "Quick Install" and "Custom Development." You know the mix of resources required to deliver these services and the number of engagements you are expected to deliver. Multiplying the hours required to deliver each service by the forecast for each service, you can create a target service mix chart that looks like Figure 9.9. This summary pie chart documents how many hours of each skill set you need in order to deliver the forecast service mix.

Who will deliver this target service mix? On the other side of this matching equation are service delivery staff. As outlined in the chapter on scalability, these can be direct PS employees, support service employees, or outside partners. Figure 9.10 documents the skills and hours available from direct PS staff.

Documenting the same information for other labor sources, we can build our skills mix as shown in Figure 9.11.

TABLE 9.1 Environment Assessment

Resource	Hours Per Engagement	Number of Engagements	Total Hours Required
Project Manager	40	10	400
Business Analyst	80	10	800
Technical Analyst	20	10	200

FIGURE 9.9 Required Skills Mix

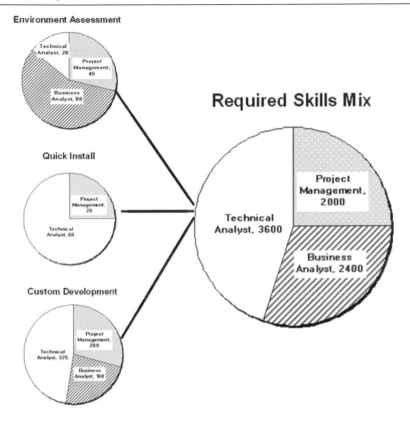

FIGURE 9.10 PS Staff Skills

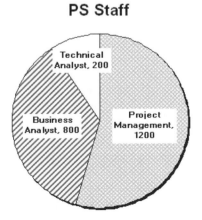

FIGURE 9.11 Available Skills Mix

At this point we have created a bottoms-up view of what skills we need to meet the service mix forecast (Required Skills Mix) and what skills we have available to us (Available Skills Mix). We want to merge these two views and assess the gap. Figure 9.12 shows this merger of the data. We want to determine if we have a gap between requirements and availability. We have moved beyond just matching the sheer volume of consulting hours required to source our forecast. We have validated that we have the required mix of skills to be successful.

PROFESSIONAL SERVICES IN THE 21ST CENTURY

Aren't the diagrams shown in this chapter great? Don't they provide awesome insights into your human-capital-intensive business? For instance, if you

FIGURE 9.12 Matching Supply and Demand

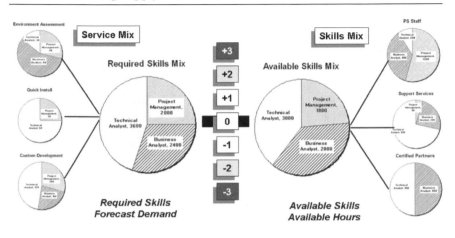

could accurately map required skills to available skills as shown in Figure 9.12 for your service organization, wouldn't you sleep better at night? Despite the potential, service organizations cannot draw Figure 9.12. Three things prevent them:

1. There is no defined portfolio of services.
2. Even if there is a target portfolio, there is no accurate service sales forecast.
3. Even if there is a forecast, there is no accurate assessment of skills available from the various delivery resources.

Perhaps, as an industry, we could deliver professional services profitably in the 80s and 90s without target portfolios, accurate forecasts, or decent skills tracking. If a gig came up, we threw people at it. If we ran out of people, we tapped a good partner to fill the gap. Work got done. Customers paid. Life went on. But the bar is being raised in the new century.

I opened this book by describing the trends that are driving companies to explore the potential of professional services. I do believe that the ability to deliver valuable professional services is one of the greatest potential sources of revenue and margin for traditionally product-centric companies. More important, the intimacy created by service capabilities protects traditional revenue streams. I want to close with a brutal assessment of our ability to capture that economic potential.

Companies cannot approach the business of building professional services with dated techniques. Customers have become savvy in the art of purchasing value-added services. They are demanding proven business results, not "trust me" time-and-material contracts. Competition for engagements is hyper.

Many many companies want to be solution providers. Traditional service providers such as EDS and Accenture are still around. Previous mainframe providers like Unisys and IBM are now full-service providers. New global competitors such as Legend Computers out of China could enter the markets and pressure pricing. The margin for error is becoming razor thin. The losses from a "bleeder" (unprofitable service engagement) are not so easily buried in the next customer engagement. This is no longer a business that tolerates sloppiness. Look at the declining gross margin of the long-time professional service firm Accenture. From 40% in 2001 to 31% in 2004![1] If this current rate of decline continues, Accenture would be facing 22% gross margins by 2007. To stop the erosion of margin, even tier-1 professional service providers must determine how they will deliver more value or reduce operating costs.

We are entering a new era in the discipline of managing professional services organizations. Companies are being forced to move beyond marketing the excellence of their services to truly delivering excellence. In this era, service leaders are being forced to manage the critical variables of their business. In this era, the firms that will dominate will move their service businesses from "organized chaos" to "disciplined control." In a recent book titled *Branded Customer Service*,[2] Janelle Barlow and Paul Stewart explain the importance of delivering a customer service experience that supports and propagates the brand equity of the company. I am in complete agreement with their strong belief that companies must learn to consistently align the service experience with the product experience. I also agree with them that this alignment will evolve as a defining source of differentiation for companies of all sizes. Yes, companies can continue to ignore the Scylla Fees that I have enumerated in this book. They can continue to manage their service businesses as technology-centered service businesses have been managed for the past twenty years. But it is unclear to me how such companies will be the solution providers of the future.

---

1. *Accenture 2004 Annual Report,* Income Statement Data Table, p. 31.

2. Janelle Barlow and Paul Stewart, *Branded Customer Service* (San Francisco: Berrett-Koehler Publishers, 2004).

Scylla Fees Summary

Reviewing the Cost of Success

In the Introduction, I defined the concept of Scylla Fees. These are critical trade-offs a management team must make to move its professional services business forward. A company must pay these fees—they are non-negotiable—if the company intends to create a global, scalable, sustainable, and, most important, profitable professional services business. This appendix provides a summary table of the eleven Scylla Fees that were defined throughout the book. The Table A.1 identifies where each Scylla Fee was defined in the text. The table also provides symptoms a company may be experiencing that indicate the time for payment is at hand. Finally, the table itemizes frameworks that can assist a management team through the process of addressing a specific Scylla Fee.

TABLE A.1 Scylla Fees

	Scylla Fee	Introduced	Symptoms	Applicable Frameworks
1	The strategy for the professional services business unit should be formally and explicitly defined.	Ch 2: Service Strategy Context	PS consistently misses financial objectives. PS focuses on tactical objectives such as quarterly profitability. Constantly shifting priorities are given to the service organization. Severe friction occurs between product and service organizations.	Nine Variables of a Service Strategy
2	For a professional services strategy to be viable and sustainable, nine critical variables need to be set.	Ch 3: Three Pillars of a Service Strategy	Inconsistent financial performance from the PS organization: some quarters are good, some quarters are bad. PS struggles to accurately predict financial performance.	Service Strategy Map Strategy Variable Alignment Strategy Variable Maturity Strategy Variable Stress Ratings Strategy Data Maturity
3	The management team must prioritize which of these four objectives are the most important for the professional services organization: Increasing professional services revenues Improving professional services margin Improving customer satisfaction Increasing overall company market share	Ch 4: Mastering Financial Objectives	Severe friction occurs between product and service organizations. Executive staff of the company does not agree on the priorities of the PS function. PS consistently misses financial objectives.	The PS Charter Graph

TABLE A.1 Scylla Fees (continued)

	Scylla Fee	Introduced	Symptoms	Applicable Frameworks
4	A viable service business model must include ongoing investment for services development, services marketing, and service sales.	Ch 4: Mastering Financial Objectives	PS consistently misses financial objectives. PS has difficulty scaling capabilities. PS has difficulty generating demand for service offerings PS delivery staff are overworked and overstressed.	The PS Business Model Table PS Business Model Parameters
5	Because professional services is a human-capital-intensive business, a management team must set realistic growth rates.	Ch 4: Mastering Financial Objectives	PS consistently misses revenue growth objectives.	PS Business Model Table Three Year PS Business Plan PS Growth Rates
6	The target markets professional services is asked to pursue must support the financial expectations set for professional services.	Ch 5: Mastering the Services Portfolio	It is unclear what markets PS is targeting with its service offerings. Opportunities in target markets do not match financial objectives.	Target Market Map Table: Aligning Markets to Revenue Objectives
7	The services organization and the marketing organization must have a common market taxonomy.	Ch 5: Mastering the Services Portfolio	It is unclear what markets PS is targeting with its service offerings. PS has limited data regarding target markets.	Target Market Map Service Types Table Forecast Quality Graph Forecast Data Streams
8	Target services must be validated against the actual needs of the target markets.	Ch 5: Mastering the Services Portfolio	Demand for PS offerings is anemic. Sales force is unable to articulate the value of PS offerings. PS offerings are heavily discounted.	Forecast Quality Graph Forecast Data Streams

TABLE A.1 Scylla Fees (continued)

	Scylla Fee	Introduced	Symptoms	Applicable Frameworks
9	The ability for existing channels to sell the new service portfolio must be honestly assessed.	Ch 5: Mastering the Services Portfolio	Sales forecast for PS offerings remains weak. Attach rate of services sales with product sales is poor.	Channel Options Table Channel Mix Graph Marketing Mix Graph
10	Channel mix must be understood.	Ch 5: Mastering the Services Portfolio	The company cannot identify market opportunities that meet PS revenue objectives.	Marketing Mix Graph
11	The skills required to deliver the target service portfolio must be understood in order to profitably scale a PS business.	Ch 6: Mastering Scalability	PS is constantly scrambling to identify qualified delivery resources for sold engagements. PS utilization is poor—PS profitability is poor. PS has limited visibility into the future skills requirements.	PS Positions Map Skills Table Scalability Mix Graph

The Positioning Pentagon

Service Differentiation

APPENDIX OBJECTIVE

Service positioning is a component of effective demand generation. It is one of the five P's of service marketing that I outlined in Chapter 5. Over the past three years, I have had the opportunity to review the service positioning of many product companies. Regardless of company size, product companies position their services pretty consistently: *"We have really smart people, who are a joy to work with, and, if you engage us, we will save you money."*

This me-too, generic positioning is extremely ineffective in motivating potential customers to engage your professional services organization instead of the host of others knocking on the door. When I point this deficiency out, product companies agree their service positioning has always been an afterthought. However, they are not sure how to fix their approach. Positioning and differentiating services is a mushy, gray experience for product companies, which are accustomed to positioning tangible products. This appendix introduces a clear process a company's management team can follow to create effective service positioning that motivates clients to purchase the company's services.

KEY TOOLS

- Proposal Strike Zone
- Service Attribute Triangle

THE POSITIONING CHALLENGE

Every services marketing director has the same fundamental challenge:

> **How do we position our services so that customers will buy them from us and not from somebody else?** ■

The service marketplace is crowded. Customers can choose to receive consulting services from their product vendors; large national system-integration firms; or small, specialized boutique firms. Why should a customer sign a service contract with your company? Service marketing managers within product companies have a stock answer to this critical question: "Because nobody knows our products like we do." I do not believe this answer is compelling enough in today's hypercompetitive marketplace. You need to say more. You need to truly differentiate your service portfolio. But how? Where to start? And how do you know the positioning is on the right track? This appendix presents a simple model to help answer these positioning questions. By the end of this appendix, you should have a solid sense of how mature your current service positioning truly is.

PRODUCTS VS. SERVICES

Before we take the plunge into positioning, we need to acknowledge a simple fact: services are different from products. A common—and huge—mistake made by marketing managers within a product company is to approach service positioning the same way they approach product positioning. Yes, product and service positioning absolutely need to align and complement each other. However, these are two different animals. In the book *Marketing Professional Services,*[1] Philip Kotler has written on the differences between products and services. Let me summarize some of the key attributes that separate services from products:

Tangibility: Products can be seen and touched. Services cannot.

Separability: Products can be physically separated from the person that manufactures them, sells them, and installs them. A service offering and the person delivering the service are inseparable.

---

1. Philip Kotler, Thomas Hayes, and Paul Bloom, *Marketing Professional Services* (New York: Prentice Hall Press, 2002).

Inventory: A product can be manufactured at one time, stored, and sold at a latter date. A service offering cannot be manufactured in advance and stored for later purchase.

Demonstration: Product capabilities typically can be demonstrated. The results of a service offering can sometimes be demonstrated, but the actual service experience is impossible to demonstrate. The customer must purchase the service and have faith that the ensuing experience will be positive.

Pricing: Products lend themselves to fixed, line-item pricing. Services lend themselves to variable pricing that is driven by the complexity and risk of the solution, the quality of the delivery team, and other factors.

Production: Products are capital intensive and lend themselves to efficient mass production. Services are human-capital intensive and require longer lead times to enable delivery. Also, it is likely that each delivery of the service will have customized components.

Channels: When feasible, low-touch channels are the most cost effective for driving product sales. Services are more effectively sold through high-touch channels.

Warranty: Products come with warranties that reduce customer risk. Services often have no warranties associated with them, which dramatically increases customer risk.

Table B.1 summarizes the differences between products and services. The table underscores the fact that positioning a service and positioning a product are very different activities. Acknowledging that service positioning is a unique challenge, where can we start?

TABLE B.1 Products vs. Services

Attribute	Product	Service
Tangible?	YES	NO
Separable?	YES	NO
Inventory?	YES	NO
Demo?	YES	NO
Pricing?	FIXED	VARIABLE
Production?	MASS	CUSTOM
Preferred Channel?	LOW TOUCH	HIGH TOUCH
Warranty?	YES	NO

WHY YOU WIN

The objective of service positioning is very simple: motivate *potential* customers to become *actual* customers. How does this happen?

Reference

The Information Technology Services Marketing Association (ITSMA) conducted a very interesting survey in 2004. ITSMA asked over two hundred senior managers a series of questions concerning their selection of service providers. One question ITSMA asked was why a manager even considered a particular service provider. Was it due to slick marketing materials? An aggressive sales representative? A witty commercial? The answer should not surprise you, but it might. Figure B.1 provides a summary of the responses. As the graph shows, the number one reason a company is even considered to provide professional services: personal reference. In *Building Professional Services*, I defined the "iron triangle" of success for a professional services organization. The triangle was composed of revenue, references, and repeatability. The ITSMA survey reinforces the validity of that triangle. If a service organization does not have strong references, it may not even get invited to the party.

Relationship

According to the ITSMA survey, the second most important factor for senior managers when considering a service provider is relationship. Once again, services are a very "personal" product. You cannot separate the product delivered from the consultant delivering it. A manager willing to let the service consultants loose wants and needs to have a personal relationship with someone from the service firm. It could be the service sales rep. It could be the product sales rep. It could be the CEO. Without a relationship, the manager's leap of faith gets a lot longer.

Response

Relationship and reference get a service provider in the door, but winning the business is based on the service provider's ability to prove it can actually deliver the promised results. Figure B.2 shows the results from another question ITSMA asked in the 2004 survey: "What one factor is most important in choosing a service provider?" If the service provider has been used before and performed well, life is good. If this is a new account for the service provider, the service provider needs to demonstrate it can actually deliver the results.

For more information on this survey and other research conducted by ITSMA, I encourage you to visit *www.itsma.com.*

FIGURE B.1 ITSMA, *How Customers Select Service Providers Survey,* 2004.

How do you typically first learn about vendors and their services?

Recommendation/reference from a colleague	34.8
Used them before, had past experience working with them	16.7
Worldwide Web	16.2
Article	12.4
Analyst firm recommendation such as Gartner, Meta, Forrester	11.0
Preferred vendor list	10.5
Research	8.6
Phone call: sales representative from the service firm	7.6
Overall reputation/image of the vendor	6.7
Advertisement	6.2
Response to RFP	5.2
User Group/Trade show	4.8
Seminar or workshop	4.3
Direct contact	4.3
Direct Mail	2.9
Consultant recommendation	2.4
Email: sales representative from the service firm	1.9
Other	2.4

0   10   20   30   40
% of Respondents (N=210)

Note: Multiple responses allowed.
Source: ITSMA, *How Customers Choose*, 2004

FIGURE B.2 Most Important Factor in Service Provider Selection

Which one factor is really most important to your decision?

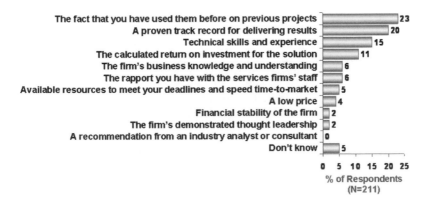

The fact that you have used them before on previous projects	23
A proven track record for delivering results	20
Technical skills and experience	15
The calculated return on investment for the solution	11
The firm's business knowledge and understanding	6
The rapport you have with the services firms' staff	6
Available resources to meet your deadlines and speed time-to-market	5
A low price	4
Financial stability of the firm	2
The firm's demonstrated thought leadership	2
A recommendation from an industry analyst or consultant	0
Don't know	5

0   5   10   15   20   25
% of Respondents
(N=211)

Source: ITSMA, *How Customers Choose*, 2004

WHY YOU LOSE

Superior relationships, solid references, and successful prior engagements dramatically improve your ability to close service business. Apparently marketing and positioning have very little to do with the final choice! Although positioning carries little influence during the endgame, effective positioning is critical to starting the game. The reasons you lose service business are not the exact opposite of why you win that business.

How many times has your company pitched a perfect potential customer—only to see that customer refuse to act. You know the potential customer would benefit from your service, but it does not bring you in. Why?

Pretium Partners[2] is a firm that focuses on training product sales representatives to sell services. During training, Pretium emphasizes how critical it is to overcome three hurdles if you expect to close a service deal: risk, indifference, and price. Pretium instructs the trainees that if they do not address these areas, their potential service deal will die.

Risk

The most common reason a potential service customer does not become an actual service customer centers on risk. Why is a senior manager looking for relationship, references, and a quality response before signing on the dotted line? Because all of these help minimize the risk of selecting your firm. If this is a new solution with a new customer, you must get creative. If you do not reduce the perceived risk to an acceptable level, the customer will remain indifferent.

Reward

The second most common reason a customer does not try a service you know would help him or her centers on how tangible the potential rewards are. Yes, it seems so damn obvious to you how the customer would benefit from your services. If you cannot articulate and substantiate the potential value of your services, however, the customer will remain indifferent.

Figure B.3 summarizes this concept of risk and reward overcoming indifference. When motivating a customer to engage your company, your service positioning must move the customer into the proposal strike zone. Positioning

---

2. For more information on the work of Pretium Partners, please visit its Web site at *www.pretiumpartners.com*

FIGURE B.3 Proposal Strike Zone

that minimizes perceived risks and maximizes perceived rewards helps accomplish this.

So what do we know now?

- Customers typically use prior relationships and strong references to drive their final decision on which service provider to use.
- A customer will not actively consider specific service providers unless it sees a use for the service in the first place.
- Getting the customer receptive to your service requires that you effectively articulate the benefits of that service and reduce any fears the customer may have of executing the service.

We will use this knowledge to drive our service positioning. Any positioning work we do must address these realities.

OVERVIEW OF THE POSITIONING PENTAGON

Based on what we now understand about the service-selection process, there are at least five elements that influence service positioning:

1. *Service Attributes:* Every product or service is positioned around *something*. That something could be anything from cost savings to how cool the customer will be if it uses your cutting-edge firm. The *something*

you choose to position around is called the service attribute. I will define service attributes in more detail, but for now, let's simply acknowledge that to effectively position your service offering, you must understand what you want to position around.

2. *Competitors' Positioning:* To differentiate your positioning, you should understand how your competitor's is positioned. If you do not understand what your competition is focusing on, it is very difficult to claim your positioning is differentiated.

3. *Current Positioning:* Very few of us are starting this positioning exercise with a brand-new startup and a blank canvas. Your company and its products already stand for something. What is that something?

4. *Benefits:* What are the benefits of the service offering you want to position? Benefits can be much more than simply cost savings. Service benefits can include reduced risk, higher customer satisfaction, or reduced time to market.

5. *Customer Validation:* Even though you have defined a set of benefits your service can deliver, can you demonstrate that the benefits are actually delivered? Do your customers actually receive the benefits you promote?

These five elements are summarized in Figure B.4. Each point in the pentagon influences the positioning of your service offerings. The clearer your understanding of each variable, the more effective your service positioning will be.

FIGURE B.4: The Positioning Pentagon

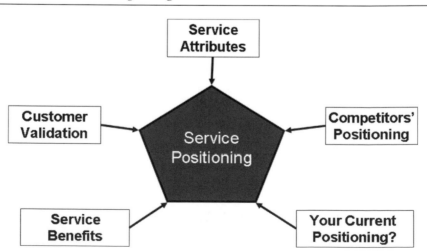

SERVICE ATTRIBUTES

Before we use the positioning pentagon, I need to better define the concept of service attributes. In *Marketing Professional Services*, Philip Kotler inventories a list of items a service firm can choose to differentiate around. Example items include location, price, and industry knowledge. Each one of Kotler's items is a potential attribute of your service positioning. Kotler emphasizes how subtle service attributes can be. Because services are a personal experience in which product delivered and the deliveree cannot be separated, simple items like the dress code of your consultants become potential service attributes. Table B.2 provides a list of items that could be used to differentiate and position a service offering.

Attribute Categories

The challenge with service attributes is to choose which ones to focus on. To facilitate this selection process, I strongly recommend you group all of the potential service attributes into the three main categories identified in Table B.3.

TABLE B.2 Example Service Attributes

Service Attribute	Comments
$50,000	We can fix your problem for $50,000. We are so confident, we will bid this service for a fixed fee.
$250 an hour	Our consultants are top notch. Our lowest rate is $250 an hour.
.9995	By using our service, you will improve uptime of your computer servers to .9995.
2 weeks	We can remove this headache in two weeks.
Since 1925	Our firm isn't going anywhere.
Columbus, OH	Hey, we are close to everything.
Mountain View, CA	We have our finger on the pulse of Silicon Valley.
Polo shirts	We are casual and creative.

TABLE B.3 Main Attribute Categories

Category	Rationale
Expertise	When you position your service around the attribute of "expertise," you are promoting the benefits that come with superior knowledge. By buying your unique expertise, the customer is hoping to reduce risks, improve performance, and decrease implementation time. You believe the customer will recognize you have either unique or superior expertise that provides business benefit.

TABLE B.3 Main Attribute Categories (Continued)

Category	Rationale
Experience	When you position your service around "experience," you are promoting items such as quality care and customer satisfaction. The concept of "relationship" fits here. You believe customers will purchase your service because they feel comfortable doing business with your company.
Expense	When you position your service around "expense," you are promoting the cost savings the customer will receive by purchasing the service from you as opposed to someone else.

Table B.4 plots several potential service attributes into these three main categories.

Qualifying Attributes

Even by simplifying potential service attributes into three main categories, there is still the challenge of determining what category (or categories) you should position around. This is not an easy decision. However, when reviewing potential service attributes you might focus on, consider the characteristics of a strong attribute as defined by Kotler:

- *Important:* The attribute that is important to your target customers. If your customers do not care that all of your project managers are PMI certified, then don't make that a positioning point.
- *Distinctive:* The attribute that is unique to your company. For service organizations within product companies, this often centers on their unique access to internal technical information.
- *Superior:* The attribute that your company delivers better than your competitors.
- *Tangible:* The attribute that can be quantified in some way. How does this attribute of yours result in real dollar savings or faster delivery for the client?
- *Affordable:* Your target audience can afford your services.
- *Profitable:* This attribute is not cost prohibitive for the customer. In other words, the benefit to your customer of taking advantage of this differentiator does not exceed its cost to maintain it.
- *Believable:* The attribute is aligned with the product brand positioning. If your product is positioned as the low-cost choice, why would you try to build an elite and expensive consulting staff?

TABLE B.4 Specific Attributes Spread in Categories

EXPERTISE	EXPERIENCE	EXPENSE
Specific product knowledge	Customer orientation	Low cost
Breadth and depth of technical expertise	Geographic location (Columbus, OH)	Premium cost ($250/hr)
Industry knowledge	Stability of company (since 1925)	ROI or TCO
Technical superiority of solution	Quality of work (.9995)	Time to market
Innovation	Breadth of product line	Time savings

With a working understanding of what service attributes are and what makes them useful, we can move onto the actual process of creating effective service positioning.

THE POSITIONING PROCESS

The Starting Point

The starting point of any positioning process is to have something to position around. This is where most service marketing managers hit the wall. You have a brand-new service offering that the PS team wants to take out the door. At this point, you have the following items:

1. Service Name: a working title for the service. Not necessarily very sexy at this point, but you have to give it a name so people can refer to it without reaching for a descriptive title.
2. Service Description: A paragraph or two that describes what the service is.
3. Service Benefits: The benefits that a customer will get from the service. At this point these benefits can be located on a spectrum going from documented and validated across to hopeful speculation. It is likely that they are educated speculation at this point.

Note: These three items *do not* constitute service positioning. If you can enunciate these three items, means you have a service that now needs to be positioned into the marketplace. This is where the real fun begins.

Step 1: Important Service Attributes

The first step in effective service positioning is to understand what is important to your customers! This understanding comes from determining which service attributes are important to your potential customers.

Let's work through an example. Say you want to offer a new service to consolidate computer storage infrastructure. Storage consolidation saves money—the obvious benefit of such a service. There are several ways you might position and differentiate your consolidation offering. Referring back to Table B.4, you could choose to position around a multitude of attributes. Table B.5 provides an example of all the ways you could position your storage consolidation service.

Here is the puzzle at hand: Which attributes should you position the storage consolidation service around? Expertise-based attributes? Experience? Expense? The answer should be driven by which attributes are important to potential service customers. If you sell high-end storage products to Fortune 500 companies with mission-critical data needs, expense might not be the overriding concern. Yes, these customers want to save money by consolidating their storage environment, but not at the expense of data availability. Perhaps "expertise" or "experience" are more critical attributes to these customers.

The point is simple: Find out which attributes matter to *your potential customers*. Once you understand this, you can continue the positioning process.

Shotgun Positioning

Before leaving this step, I must address the most common error I see in service positioning: *shotgun positioning*. This occurs when the service marketing manager really has no idea which service attributes are most important to target customers. To compensate for this lack, the marketing manager "covers all the bases" by positioning around multiple attributes. There are a number of problems caused by this approach. First of all, you confuse your customers. What are you really good at? Secondly, it is difficult to differentiate yourself from competitors if you are promising to provide everything they do—only more of it. Finally, and most important, every service attribute you add to your

TABLE B.5 Positioning Storage Consolidation

[EXPERTISE	EXPERIENCE	EXPENSE
Specific product knowledge *Our consultants understand our storage products better than anyone else.*	**Customer orientation** *We will meet all of your expectations and make sure we consolidate in a way that maximizes employee productivity.*	**Low cost** *No one can consolidate your storage environment for less money than we can.*
Breadth and depth of technical expertise *Our consultants understand our products and more industry products than anyone else.*	**Geographic location** *We are the only consolidation firms to have local consultants in 56 major cities throughout the world.*	**Premium cost ($250/hr)** *Because our consultants know more about storage consolidation than anyone on the planet, they cost $250/hr.*
Industry knowledge *Our consultants understand the unique storage consolidation challenges of your business.*	**Stability of company (since 1990)** *We have been consolidating storage environments since 1990—In fact, we invented the term "storage consolidation."*	**ROI or TCO** *Our storage consolidation process will reduce your storage costs by no less than 32%— guaranteed.*
Technical superiority of solution *We have figured out a new way to consolidate storage that is faster, cheaper, lower risk.*	**Quality of work (.9995)** *Our processes and methodologies guarantee minimal risk of data loss.*	**Time to market** *Less money on storage means more money for other things— like engineers that build your products.*
Innovation *On a monthly basis, we are improving our storage consolidation process by developing new processes, scripts, etc.*	**Breadth of product line** *Our company offers the most comprehensive line of products and services designed specifically for storage consolidation for both large and small enterprises.*	**Time savings** *By using our consultants you can start now and be saving money sooner.*

positioning adds effort. Why? Because it takes effort to convince customers that your claim to that attribute is warranted. Because you must validate your service attributes with customer testimonials, project data, etc., the more things you say you can do, the more things you have to prove you can do. Mike Moser has a great picture of this reality. In *United We Brand*,[3] he presents

---

3. Mike Moser, *United We Brand* (Boston, MA: Harvard Business Press, 2003), p. 59, Figure 3-2.

a "positioning bull's-eye diagram." Basically, Mr. Moser argues that the more a company drifts from its core positioning, the more marketing effort is required to make that positioning stick. In our terms, for every service attribute you add to your positioning, the further you move away from the positioning bull's-eye. The further you move from the bull's-eye, the more your message gets diluted. Think laser—not shotgun.

Step 2: Competitors' Positioning

The next step in effective service positioning is to understand how your competitors are positioning their services. The more you know of this, the easier it becomes to differentiate your offerings.

You can review competitive positioning on an attribute level or a category level.

Attribute Review

If you know which service attributes are important to your customers, you can do some market research to find out how customers rate your competitors on those attributes.

Using our storage consolidation example, let's say you polled customers to discover the top two attributes they were looking for:

1   Best ROI (after paying for hardware and services)
2. Highest quality implementation (lowest risk of data loss)

Knowing this, you could work to determine how your competitors are rated by customers on those two attributes. These ratings can be placed on a service attribute chart as shown in Figure B.5.

Category Review

A second way to map competitors' positioning is to rate them on the three main service attribute categories:

- Expertise
- Experience
- Expense

FIGURE B.5 Service Attribute Chart

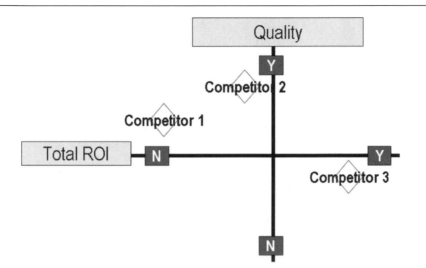

Using a simple ranking system in which 0 means the competitor has no credibility on this attribute and 2 means the competitor is viewed as an industry leader on this attribute, you can create an industry positioning map as shown in Figure B.6.

FIGURE B.6 Industry Positioning Map

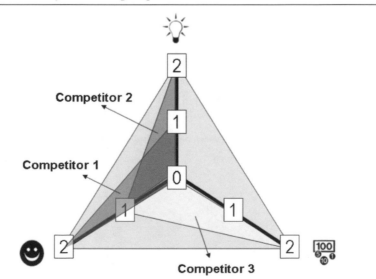

Estimated Effort

Both attribute analysis and category analysis provide wonderful insight into how your competitors are positioning their services with customers. Of course, most management teams are sighing at this point. "Yeah, great insight—but who has the time or money to complete this type of analysis?" I believe your company already has this data. I believe your marketing and sales staff already have a very good sense of how customers perceive your competitors on key attributes. However, no one has created the maps. And no one is having simple conversations with customers to validate the maps.

Step 3: Your Current Position

The next activity in effective service positioning is to appreciate how your company is currently positioned. How do customers rate your company on the important service attributes? You should now update the attribute maps and industry maps with your current positioning in the marketplace. Before launching a new marketing campaign, you must know where you're starting from! Figures B.7 and B.8 show how your current company positioning can be added to the analysis.

FIGURE B.7 Updated Attribute Map

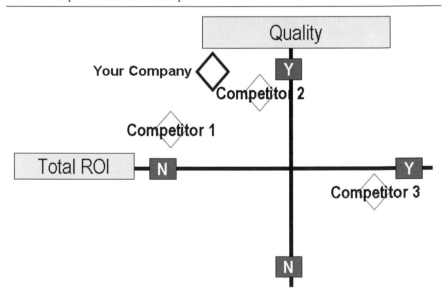

FIGURE B.8 Updated Industry Map

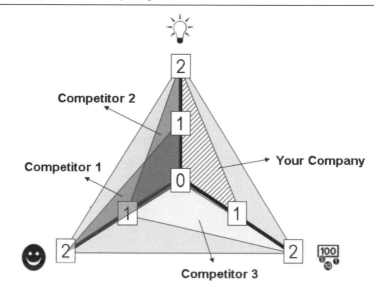

Step 4: Target Service Attributes

Now we know the following critical information regarding storage consolidation:

- What is important to your customers concerning storage-consolidation services
- How your competitors currently rate on those important items (attributes)
- How your company currently rates on those important items

At this point, we are truly armed and dangerous. We are in position to create effective service positioning. We can now select the specific service attributes that our marketing will promote. In Table B.3, we identified fifteen potential service attributes on which we could have positioned our storage consolidation service. Many marketers would have chosen all fifteen, written up a *long* data sheet, and called it a day. But we did our positioning homework. Based on that homework, we plan to market the following key attributes of our storage consolidation services:

1. Quality of work: Our processes and methodologies guarantee minimal risk of data loss.
2. ROI or TCO: Our storage-consolidation process will reduce your storage costs by no less than 32%—guaranteed.

These attributes address items that are important to customers and are pretty well aligned with how customers currently view our company. At this point, we should be feeling great about our laser-focused positioning. However, we have not yet taken the most important positioning step of all.

Step 5: Validation

Even the most extensive market research conducted by an outstanding marketing team can miss the mark. Sometimes, customers tell you they care about one thing when really they care about something else. Sometimes customers find value in your service in ways that were never anticipated. Anticipating this possibility and managing for it, we must *validate* the positioning. Are customers getting the benefits we said they would? Do they value the benefits we deliver? This is an ongoing process of questioning that should be conducted throughout the lifetime of a service offering. By the way, the more you can back up your service benefit claims, the stronger your positioning becomes. You move from selling promises to quoting facts.

Let me say that again. Don't sell promises—sell facts.

Not a Linear Process

The reason I created a model titled "the positioning pentagon" and not "the five steps of positioning" is to recognize that a linear positioning process—going step by step—is not always possible. You may go to market having only completed two or three of the five steps. That is why the picture is a pentagon. All five points influence the center. The more you know about the five points, the stronger the positioning will be. The less you know, the weaker. The objective of a service marketing manager should be to continue to mature the positioning pentagon for all key service offerings. It is a never-ending exercise in continuing improvement. If you thought you simply launched and were done, you were wrong.

POSITIONING, BRANDING, AND MARKETING

When managers start talking marketing, the world quickly turns gray. Right before your eyes, concepts and issues that seemed crisp and clear fade and grow fuzzy.

- *"We need to differentiate our positioning!"*
- *"How is our brand positioned?"*
- *"Brand is everything!"*
- *"What type of brand equity do we have?"*
- *"Our marketing has got to be on target."*
- *"Is our brand differentiated in our target markets?"*

Welcome to marketing speak—where a simple word like "positioning" can have multiple meanings based on context. To keep things simple, I want to clearly define the concepts of "positioning," "branding," and "marketing."

Positioning describes how you differentiate your service offerings from the service offerings of providers your company is competing against. Positioning involves trying to answer these key questions:

1. Which service attributes are most important to our customers?
2. How are competitors perceived on those attributes?
3. How are we perceived on those attributes?
4. What specific attributes will we position on?

Branding supports and aligns with your company positioning. A brand is your company logo, your company tagline, and much more. I don't want to define branding in great detail. However, your brand should become an icon that communicates your positioning.

Marketing comprises all the activities you pursue to communicate your positioning. Marketing includes partner training, advertising, customer presentations, etc. Marketing is effective if customers and partners understand and believe your positioning.

Perhaps one of the most strategic activities a services marketing team can engage in is a review of the company's positioning, branding, and marketing. Does our branding align with the service attributes we are positioning around? Do our marketing messages align with our brand and target attributes?

POSITIONING EVALUATION

To close this appendix on positioning, I want to give you a simple tool you can use to evaluate how mature your service positioning currently is. Go to your company's Web site. Click on the button that says "Our Services" or

"Professional Services." Now, I want you to start reading the text. As you read, I want you to start filling in Table B.6. Every time you recognize a service attribute, place it into one of the three rows of Expertise, Experience, or Expense in the Attribute column. Then complete the other columns in the table if you can.

> **Benefits**: Does the copy on the Web site state any clear benefits for this attribute? For example, if your site states, "We have the most creative Web designers in the world," is there an explanation of why this is a good thing? Even if the Web site does not state the benefits, do you know them? If so, pencil them in.
>
> **Validation**: Are proposed benefits validated on the Web site? Are real customer quotes provided that reinforce the proposed benefits? Are example dollar savings listed? Even if the Web site does not provide validation, do you know of supportive data? If so, pencil it in.
>
> **Brand aligned**: This is subjective. Do you feel the service attribute listed aligns with how your company brand is perceived in the marketplace? If yes, write yes. If no, write no.

So, what are we looking for?

If your completed table lists multiple service attributes scattered throughout all three categories, or if you could not pencil in hard benefits or hard validation for positioned attributes, or if none of the attributes are aligned with your company brand, *you have a service positioning problem.*

TABLE B.6 Positioning Evaluation Table

Category	Attribute (used in positioning)	Benefits	Validation	Brand Aligned
Expertise				
Experience				
Expense				

To make this process more concrete, let's work through an example. Figure B.9 provides service positioning being used by a fictitious product company named "Big Iron."

After reading the positioning on Big Iron's Web site, I completed the evaluation documented in Table B.7. The table makes several points obvious. First of all, Big Iron is trying to position on *everything*. We are smart, great to work with, and save you money. Can the company defend all that? Also, the table shows a lack of crisp correlation. Attributes such as "best-practice methodologies" and "42 countries" are included, but no clear benefits are attached to them. Benefits such as flexibility, cost savings, customer loyalty, and time to market are listed with no clear correlation to service attributes. Also, a little validation would not hurt. Can Big Iron list a customer testimonial that reinforces one of the attributes? In summary, the positioning is too broad, unaligned, and unsubstantiated in any meaningful way.

FIGURE B.9 Sample Positioning

SERVICE POSITIONING for BIG IRON
The success of your enterprise depends on your ability to manage change. You are constantly being challenged to cut costs and creatively solve tough business problems. As a result, flexibility has become critical.

Our PS team possesses extensive industry-specific experience designing, delivering, and managing solutions tailored to the unique needs of business in areas that include manufacturing, higher education, government, and telecom. Using our proven methodologies and expertise, we can help you improve business flexibility—as you align business strategies to market new services, build customer loyalty, boost revenues, increase profitability, and contain operational costs.

Professional Services at Big Iron brings you the following key benefits:
- A proven, best-practices-based methodology for analyzing, building, and implementing
- 20+ years of manufacturing experience
- One-stop shopping for complete end-to-end solutions
- Strategic partnerships with best-in-class ISVs, integrators, and consultants
- Offices in 42 countries
- A uniquely collaborative approach that fosters efficient knowledge transfer

One of our most innovative solutions involves vehicle-quality problems. These problems can eat into profits and be a source of low customer satisfaction. Our quality solution responds to quality issues with advanced technology that allows direct transfer of vehicle data for rapid analysis.

TABLE B.7 Big Iron Positioning Evaluation Table

Category	Attribute (used in positioning)	Benefits	Validation	Brand Aligned
Expertise	Deep industry expertise in manufacturing		20+ years in manufacturing	YES
	Best-practice methodologies		YES	
		Flexibility, cost savings, customer loyalty, time to market		
Experience	One-stop shopping			
	Strategic partnerships			
	Offices in 42 countries			
	Collaborative approach	Efficient knowledge transfer		YES
Expense	Unique quality solution	Saves money, also improves customer satisfaction		NO

CLOSING COMMENTS

This concludes our walk on the wild side of service positioning. This is an area begging for more discussion. Effective service positioning is rare in today's services-based economy. Why is that? Service positioning, unlike product positioning, is in its infancy. My goal is that the positioning pentagon can be used to help quantify the current deficiencies in service positioning. I leave the rest of the positioning effort to the true marketing gurus.

The Pricing Pentagon

Pricing is another component of the Five P's of services marketing I discussed in Chapter 5. In some ways, pricing seems like a mundane topic that is grossly out of place in a book focused on services strategy and next-generation management techniques. Because product companies are often badly misguided in their attempts to price service offerings, however, the topic requires some attention.

Every product company wants to migrate to value-based pricing for their offerings, but a majority of product companies wallow in brute-force cost-based pricing. And of course, if you are not very good at estimating the costs to deliver services, cost-based pricing can be an unprofitable approach. This appendix is designed to introduce a clear process a management team can follow to create effective service pricing that maximizes profitability and that is understandable to the sales force.

KEY TOOLS

- Pricing Pentagon
- Pricing Range
- Pricing Models
- Pricing Scenarios

THE PRICING CHALLENGE

After facing the challenge of effectively positioning a service, the equally challenging task of pricing that service still awaits the services marketing manager.

I have seen very little written on how to face this challenge. Pricing services being offered by a product-centric company can be particularly dicey. Often, because the product line has center stage, service pricing and profits are an afterthought.

The service organization is pressured to keep service pricing "competitive." The product sales force does not want services to become cost prohibitive. The product sales force prefers to offer low-cost (sometimes free) services that can be thrown in to cement a sales deal. Also, product sales folks like fixed pricing, which can be given a part number and become a line item on a purchase order. Cheap fixed prices for service offerings—that is the order of the day at a product company. This chapter introduces a framework to guide the services marketing manager through this hostile environment to create service pricing that makes sense.

OVERVIEW OF THE PRICING PENTAGON

So what influences the price of a service? In Appendix B, I introduced five factors that influence service positioning. There are also five elements that influence service pricing: costs, financial objectives, competitors' prices, customer's price point, and value.

Costs

It is impossible to pursue a pricing strategy without understanding the cost line. What are the costs you will incur to deliver the solution or service to the customer? Costs could include:

- **Hardware:** Hard infrastructure required to support the service
- **Software:** Custom or off-the-shelf software required to support the service
- **Outside services:** Consulting services required from other companies to implement and integrate the service
- **Staff time:** Effort required by service staff to implement the solution

Regardless of your pricing strategy, the objective is to determine your cost component as accurately as possible. The better you understand costs, the greater chance you have of pricing services profitably.

Financial Objectives

What revenues and profits does the company expect to receive from the service offering? Refer back to the revenues dimension discussion in Chapter 4 and the revenue life cycle discussed in Chapter 9. This is where having a business model for the services organization becomes very helpful. Having a target business model helps guide what margins and growth are required from a service offering to support the overall services business model. Without a target business model, a company's financial objectives for a service offering must be debated on a case-by-case basis and can end up all over the place.

Competitors' Prices

If the service you are offering is available from other companies (and more than likely it is), it is helpful to understand what those companies are charging. As always, it is risky to determine appropriate pricing in a market vacuum.

Customer's Price Point

What is the customer willing to pay for the service? This seems such a simple and obvious question, yet it is not an easy one to answer. The salient point is that the more you understand about the customer's price sensitivity, the better your target pricing will be.

Value

Where customers find value in your service should clearly influence how you position that service. Value also influences pricing. Do you have a clear sense of what value the customer places on the purchase of the service? When discussing the topic of pricing professional services, Philip Kotler introduces the following equation:[1]

> **Value = Benefits − Costs ■**

---

1. Philip Kotler, *Marketing Professional Services*, page 281.

The trick to profitable services pricing is to accurately assess the benefits the customer receives from the service and the total costs incurred to deliver that service. The more tangible you can make the benefits and the more accurately you can estimate the costs, the clearer the value of the service becomes. No great insight so far: Most service marketing managers have a clear understanding of this equation, but how many marketing managers are actually using this truthful equation to help guide their pricing decisions? Not enough, in my observations, and that needs to change.

These five elements are summarized in Figure C.1. Each point in the pentagon influences the pricing of your service offerings. The logic is simple: The better you understand each variable, the more effective and profitable your services pricing will be.

THE VIABLE PRICING RANGE

A viable pricing range represents two extremes:

- The most a customer would be willing to pay for a service
- The least compensation you would be willing to accept for the service

FIGURE C.1 The Pricing Pentagon

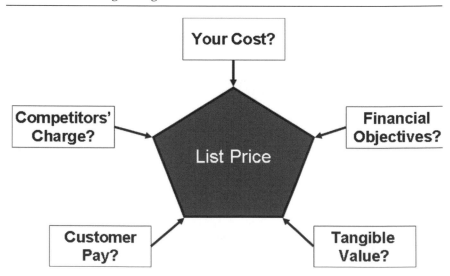

FIGURE C.2 Viable Pricing Range

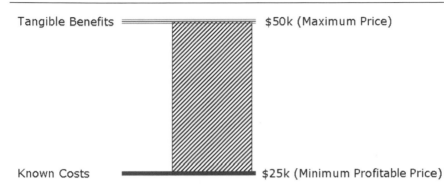

Tangible Benefits ═══════════ $50k (Maximum Price)

Known Costs ━━━━━━━━━ $25k (Minimum Profitable Price)

The top and the bottom of a viable pricing range are determined by two of the five variables found in the pricing pentagon: cost and value. The top of the range is determined by how much value the service actually brings to a customer. Not many customers will pay you more than they perceive the benefits to be worth. The bottom of the range is determined by how much it costs you to deliver the service. Figure C.2 shows the viable pricing range for a service offering that delivers $50,000 in benefits to the customer and costs $25,000 to deliver.

Figure C.2 makes it obvious to me why pricing services at a product company is so difficult. As mentioned earlier, product sales reps like inexpensive fixed pricing. How many service organizations have a clear sense of what it costs to deliver some of their more complex services and solutions? Next, how many service organizations can articulate the true value of their service? Without these two lines firmly in place, the service organization can be very handicapped when trying to determine pricing. But all is not lost—in the next section I present three pricing models that the service organization can pursue, even if each of the five variables of the pricing pentagon is not known.

PRICING MODELS

There are three distinct approaches you can take to create pricing for your service offerings:

- Cost-based pricing
- Value-based pricing
- Market-based pricing

We will review each approach as it relates to the pricing pentagon.

Cost-based Pricing

Cost-based pricing is the most straightforward approach to pricing a service. It involves two simple steps:

1. Determine the costs required to deliver the services.
2. Add on your target margin to meet financial objectives.

Figure C.3 shows the two variables of the pricing pentagon you must understand to create cost-based pricing that meets your financial objectives. Figure C.4 shows how these data points map onto the viable pricing range.

Cost-based pricing requires the least effort of the three approaches. That is the good news. There is some downside, however. First of all, to meet your financial objectives, this approach banks on your cost estimations being accurate. If the services involved are complex and new to your organization there is a decent chance the cost estimations will not be accurate. Second, there is the issue of the market. What if your customers are not willing to pay the *cost-plus* price you have come up with? Yes, in theory, you can meet your financial objectives—but that assumes you can get some customers to purchase the service at the target price.

FIGURE C.3 Cost-based Pricing and the Pricing Pentagon

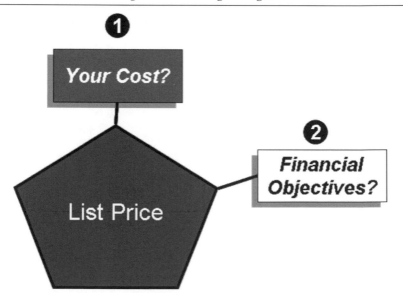

FIGURE C.4 Cost-based Pricing on the Pricing Range

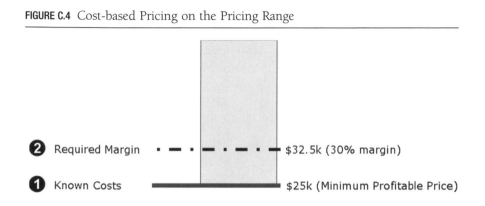

② Required Margin · ▬ · ▬ · ▬ · ▬ · ▬ · $32.5k (30% margin)

① Known Costs ▬▬▬▬▬▬▬▬▬ $25k (Minimum Profitable Price)

Value-based Pricing

If managers get together to talk about pricing services, the phrase "value-based pricing" will inevitably come up early in the conversation. Because *everyone* knows that value-based pricing means *high margins*. And everyone knows that value-based pricing is the most straightforward approach to pricing a service. However, to pursue value-based pricing, the marketing manager must now understand three variables of the pricing pentagon. Value-based pricing involves three key steps:

1. Determine the actual value the customer receives from the service.
2. Determine the cost of delivering the service.
3. Pick a price between the value line and the cost line that meets financial objectives.

Figure C.5 shows the three pieces of the pricing pentagon you must understand to create value-based pricing that meets your financial objectives. Figure C.6 shows how these data points map onto the viable pricing range.

This approach to pricing clearly takes more effort than cost-based pricing. For now you must somehow quantify, in real dollars, how the customer benefits from the service. This is the bad news. The good news occurs after you do that work. By doing the homework on value you can draw a clear value line on the pricing range. By having that line drawn you now have the potential to set your pricing anywhere between costs and value. This means you can price significantly above the cost line (i.e., high margin) and still have a potentially viable price. This is why managers like value-based pricing: It can equate to high margins. Using the example shown in Figure C.6, this means the marketing manager has the potential to price the service anywhere from $32,500 to $50,000. In cost-based pricing, the marketing manager is forced to stay closer to the $32,500 because the value line is unknown.

Value-based pricing means pricing flexibility. It also removes some of the risk associated with cost-based pricing. By determining the value line, the manager reduces the risk the price of the service will be completely out of line. However, we have not removed all the risk. The final approach to pricing works to further minimize market risks.

FIGURE C.5 Value-based Pricing and the Pricing Pentagon

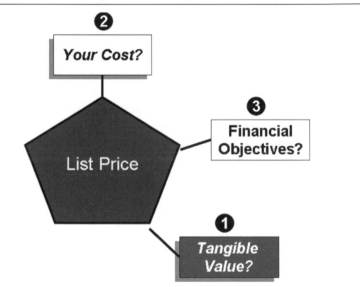

FIGURE C.6 Value-based Pricing on the Pricing Range

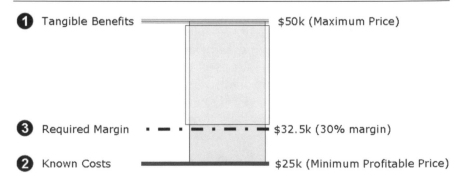

Market-based Pricing

The final approach to service pricing is one advocated by none other than Peter Drucker. In the book *Managing in a Time of Great Change*, Mr. Drucker slams both cost-based and value-based pricing. In itemizing his five deadly business sins, Drucker lists "premium pricing" as sin number one and "cost-driven pricing" as sin number three. His recommendation to companies is to use market-based pricing. In other words, first determine what customers are willing to pay. By understanding this target price, a company can then work backward to determine what costs are allowable. Drucker's point is simple: *"Customers do not see it as their job to ensure companies a profit. The only sound way to price is to start out with what the market is willing to pay—and thus, it must be assumed, what the competition will charge—and design to that price specification."* [2]

Following Drucker's advice, value-based pricing involves three key steps:

1. Determine what the customer is willing to pay for the service.
2. Subtract the target profit margin required to meet financial objectives.
3. Arrive at the target cost for the service offering.

Figure C.7 shows the three pieces of the pricing pentagon you must understand to create market-based pricing that will meet your financial objectives. Figure C.8 shows how these data points map onto the viable pricing range.

This approach to pricing requires the greatest amount of effort and discipline, which is why few service organizations follow it. However, there is huge upside to market-based pricing. First of all, by researching what customers are willing to pay for a service, the marketing manager minimizes the risk of releasing a service at a price that is unacceptable to customers. In other words, this approach minimizes "market risk." Second, this approach provides the greatest chance to generate the most profits. By understanding the customer price point and assuring you can deliver the service profitably at that price point, you should generate a profit on every engagement. With cost-based pricing, you may face unforeseen price pressure from customers that requires you to discount the service below cost. The same can be true in value-based pricing. In market-based pricing, your price target already reflects what customers are willing to pay.

---

2. Peter F. Drucker, *Managing in a Time of Great Change* (New York: Penguin Group, 1995), p. 47.

FIGURE C.7 Market-based Pricing and the Pricing Pentagon

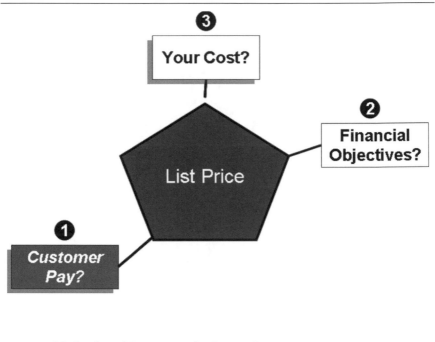

FIGURE C.8 Market-based Pricing on the Pricing Range

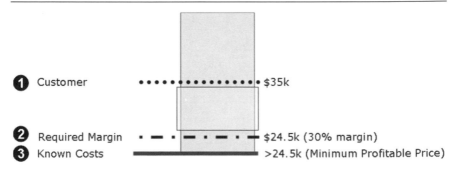

Table C.1 compares the three pricing strategies on three dimensions:

> **Effort:** How much is required to pursue one pricing strategy in relation to the other strategies?
>
> **Potential profits:** How much does one pricing strategy have the potential to generate in relation to the other approaches?
>
> **Market risk:** How much does each approach introduce?

TABLE C.1 Pricing Strategy Comparisons

	Effort	Potential Profits	Market Risk
Cost Based	LOW	LOW	HIGH
Value Based	MEDIUM	MEDIUM	MEDIUM
Market Based	HIGH	HIGH	LOW

As Table C.1 demonstrates, there are no free lunches. Each approach has strengths and weaknesses. Cost-based pricing is the low-effort approach but it results in minimal required profits—its pricing does not exploit the true value of a service. Also, cost-based pricing creates the greatest market risk. Your service may simply be overpriced and deliver little value. Value-based pricing takes more effort but increases profit potential because it exploits the value line by matching price to value. Value-based pricing also has less market risk than cost-based pricing. Market-based pricing requires the most effort but rewards you with the greatest potential for owning the market.

COMMENTS ON COMPETITIVE PRICING

Conspicuously absent in the three pricing strategies is consideration of competitors' pricing. Competitors' pricing is one of the five pricing-pentagon variables influencing your pricing. Although I haven't discussed it yet, what competitors charge will influence your final pricing decisions. However, a competitor's price does not influence which *method* you use to initially price the service. How competitors impact pricing will be shown in the next section.

PRICING SCENARIOS

Let's look at some real-world scenarios. I will review three pricing difficulties that service sales reps often find themselves in. I will map each scenario onto the viable pricing range diagram and discuss what your options are in responding to the sales difficulty.

Scenario #1: Customer Unwilling to Pay

Challenge. The amount the customer is willing to pay for the service does not meet your financial objectives.

Viable Pricing Range. Figure C.9 shows the scenario on the viable pricing range. The customer is willing to pay between $20 and $30k for your service. However, it costs you $25k to deliver the service and to meet your target margin you must charge at least $32.5k.

Options. To response to this impasse and still get the business, the company has four options:

1. *Lower the price and the expected profits.* This option is the path of least resistance. It means taking less profit for delivering the same service by offering it for closer to $25k.

2. *Lower the price and costs.* This means accepting the customer's price point and lowering the cost line to maintain your target profit. This takes effort and ingenuity.

3. *Keep the price and draw the value line.* Perhaps the customer's price point is low because you have not clearly drawn the value line. If you can demonstrate there are $50k in benefits from getting the service, the customer may be more willing to pay the target $32.5k.

FIGURE C.9 Customer Unwilling to Pay Target Price

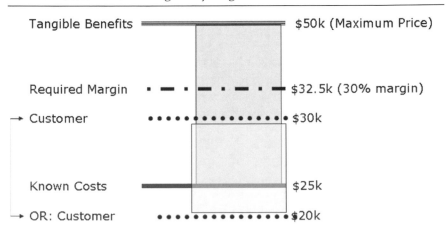

TABLE C.2 Options When Customer Unwilling to Pay

	RISK	EFFORT
1. Lower price and profits	LOW	LOW
2. Lower price and costs	MODERATE	MODERATE
3. Keep price, document benefits	MODERATE	HIGH
4. Take % of value	HIGH	HIGH

4. *Take a percentage of the value delivered.* Change the conversation. Offer to be paid a percentage of any savings the customer realizes as a result of your service. If the service really saves the customer $100k, offer to be paid 50 cents of every dollar the customer saves.

Table C.2 summarizes the effort and risk involved in pursuing each option. As you can see, the path of least resistance is to roll over. To go back in and educate the customer on the true value of the service (i.e., solution selling) takes effort and clearly involves risk—the customer may go with a less pricey provider.

Scenario #2: Value Below Cost

Challenge. The value of the service is below what it costs to deliver the service

Viable Pricing Range. Figure C.10 shows this scenario on the viable pricing range. The service costs $25k to deliver. To achieve target margins, you would like to charge $32.5k for the service. However, there is one small snag: The service only delivers $15k in benefits.

FIGURE C.10 Value Below Cost

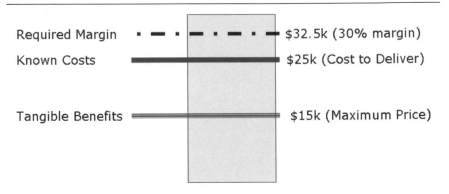

Options. This is an ugly but common scenario. The defendable value the customer receives from the service is below what it actually costs to deliver the service. There are two simple responses to this dilemma:

1. *Raise the tangible value line.* Are there benefits to this service that have not been itemized and quantified? Hope that you did not design a service that truly costs more to provide than the benefits it delivers are worth. What are the benefits the customer does not see or that you have not documented?

2. *Lower the costs.* Reduce the costs required to deliver the service. This could involve removing service items the customer sees no value in.

Table C.3 summarizes the effort and risk of pursuing each option. Why do I spend time on this scenario? Because many service organizations are unwilling to be intellectually honest when faced with this scenario. When a customer declares it will not pay the list price for a service, the company convinces itself that it is actually facing the previous scenario in which the customer is simply unwilling to pay for a great service. The company never admits that the service, as scoped, does not provide enough value to justify the price tag.

Scenario #3: Competitor Price Dropping

Challenge. Even when the value is clearly documented, competitors are dropping their prices to win the business.

Viable Pricing Range. Figure C.11 shows this scenario on the viable pricing range. The service delivers $50k in documented benefits. You charge $35k for the service which costs you $25k to deliver. New competitors enter the market

TABLE C.3 Value Below Cost

	RISK	EFFORT
1. Increase perceived value	HIGH	MODERATE
2. Lower price and costs	MODERATE	MODERATE

and start offering the service at $20k—below your actual cost to deliver the service.

Options. To respond to this impasse and still get the business, the company has three options:

1. *Lower the costs and price.* This option requires that you rework your delivery strategy and determine if you can profitably meet your competitors' low price points.

2. *Stay Firm.* Perhaps the customer is not looking for the lowest cost provider. If the service is executed well, there are $50k in benefits. Make the discussion about execution!

3. *Take a percentage of the value delivered.* Change the conversation. If you are convinced the service delivers the $50k in benefits, offer to be paid a percentage of the difference.

FIGURE C.11 Competitors Lowering Price

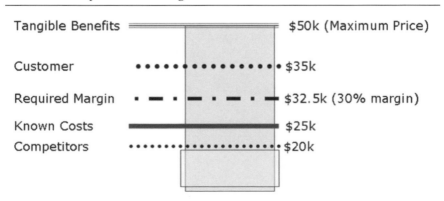

TABLE C.4 Competitors Lowering Price

	RISK	EFFORT
1. Lower price and profits	MODERATE	MODERATE
2. Keep price, reiterate benefits	HIGH	LOW
3. Take % of value	HIGH	HIGH

Table C.4 summarizes the effort and risk of pursuing each option. There are no easy outs when responding to severely competitive pricing. In this scenario, simply matching prices is not a long-term response because you lose money on each deal. Revisit the cost and value lines to determine if and how they can be moved. If the lines cannot be moved, you may need to exit the market.

FEEDING THE PRICING PENTAGON

Pricing services can be a painful exercise, especially when data from key components of the pricing pentagon are missing. The more complete the pricing pentagon data is, the easier the pricing process becomes. How many services are being priced with only one or two of the variables clearly understood? Is it any wonder service pricing can be so hard to defend to both customers and product sales reps?

There are ways to feed the pricing pentagon. Figure C.12 maps company activities that provide critical data for the pricing pentagon and Table C.5 comments on each of these activities.

FIGURE C.12 Feeding the Pricing Pentagon

TABLE C.5 Feeding the Pricing Pentagon

Pricing Pentagon Variable	Activity	Comments
COSTS	Time reporting	Without accurate time reporting, it is impossible to accurately estimate the cost of delivering a service.
	Project review	Project review should capture billable time, nonbillable time, travel costs, subcontractor costs, and hardware/software purchases.
FINANCIAL OBJECTIVES	Project review	Project review should document realized profit compared to target profit and actual expenses compared to estimated expenses.
TANGIBLE VALUE	Project review	Project review should document any tangible and intangible benefits the customer received by purchasing the service.
CUSTOMER PAY?	Customer interviews	When designing effective interviews, consider what questions you can ask to elicit how the customer benefited from the service, when you will ask the questions, and how you will ask them.
COMPETITOR'S CHARGE?	Market-rate analysis	What are the going rates for the skills your consultants have?
	Competitive analysis	What are competitors charging for similar services? How well have they drawn the value line for customers?

CLOSING COMMENTS

When I work with technology companies, I am amazed at their services pricing process. It often involves setting a fixed price for a service because "that is what the sales force can sell it for." I am assured that the fixed price agreed to has "lots of margin built in." Yet, when I ask for cost data to substantiate the claim of high margins, I am told that data "is really hard to get." When I ask the actual dollar value of the benefits the customer receives by purchasing the service, I am told "that data is *really, really* hard to get." Services pricing needs to become less art and more science. A company would never base the list price of a new product solely on the input of the direct sales force. The company would query customers, check the pricing of potential competitors, and validate profitability targets. Why should services pricing be so, so different?

Service Leadership

Hiring for Success

OBJECTIVE

To introduce a process executive managers can use to evaluate applicants to lead the professional services organization

KEY TOOLS

- Job Profile: VP of Professional Services

LOW SUCCESS RATES

There are few leadership positions within product companies that are more maligned than the executives who lead professional services. Whether their title is senior vice president of professional services, vice president of solutions, or director of services, they typically have a short tenure ahead of them. Why?

A RECRUITER'S PERSPECTIVE

I asked Joanne Giudicelli, who has conducted hundreds of executive searches in Silicon Valley, why the VP of PS is such a hard position to fill. To answer that question, she started by explaining how she conducts any executive search. She evaluates the potential success of an executive on three fronts: hard skills, soft skills, and fit. For hard skills, Ms. Giudicelli is looking at the traditional attributes of education and experience. Has the candidate ever done this before? For soft skills, she is evaluating the executive's ability to build relationships, create vision, and lead staff. Finally, she is evaluating how the candidate will fit into a company's environment. Is the candidate demanding and unforgiving while the company environment is nurturing? Does the candidate relish collaboration while the environment is competitive?

This approach is clearly as much art as science. And art takes time. How does Ms. Giudicelli evaluate the very mushy areas of soft skills and fit? She has lunch with the candidate. She processes. She collects feedback from others. She processes. She has dinner with the candidate. She processes. She interviews executives at the hiring company. She processes. And much of that processing is occurring at a very intuitive level. In fact, she spends at least 80% of the recruiting process evaluating soft skills and fit. In comparison, hard skills can usually be assessed and validated relatively quickly.

FAILURE POINTS

Building on Ms. Giudicelli's perspective, I believe executives who lead the professional services function fail for one of three reasons:

- *Wrong experience:* The executives do not have experience building value-added services at a product company. They may be successful support services executives. Now they are being asked to build professional services. Everything from the financial metrics to the business processes are different. Or they may come from independent consulting firms. Now, for the first time in their careers, they must operate within the environment and culture of a product company.

- *Unclear expectations:* The executives do not successfully align the financial and market objectives of the services function with the expectations of senior management. Ms. Giudicelli's concept of "fit" plays here. If the new VP of PS cannot effectively communicate and align with the existing management team, expectations will never be defined effectively.

- *Lack of execution:* The executive misses key objectives, specifically, revenue or profitability targets.

Because PS within a product company is a relatively new phenomenon, I believe it is very easy to set a candidate up for failure. How can this situation be improved?

THE INTERVIEW CHAIR

Picture a conference room. In fifteen minutes, you will be interviewing a candidate to lead the professional services organization. Think of the chair the candidate will sit in. Is it strong and supportive? Or is it weak and wobbly? You would not offer a prime candidate a chair that was about to collapse. How embarrassing. By not preparing for the interview, though, that is exactly what you are doing. You are seating the candidate in a chair that cannot possibly support the candidate through the interviewing process.

Continuing the chair analogy, there are four legs that support the interview process:

1. **Position definition:** Have senior managers clearly defined what they want from the professional services function? Is this function about enabling product sales or generating new revenue? What is the charter? What is the target financial model?
2. **Knowledge:** What knowledge and experiences should a qualified candidate have? In other words, what hard skills are required to be successful?
3. **Skills:** What characteristics and attributes will help the candidate succeed? In other words, what soft skills are required?
4. **Fit:** What type of environment is the candidate being hired into? Static? Dynamic? Growing? Nurturing? Competitive? Will the candidate fit into the company environment?

Figure D.1 shows the four legs that support the interviewing chair. The more a management team discusses and defines each leg, the more effective the interviewing process. If one of these legs is missing, the interview process collapses.

FIGURE D.1 The Interview Chair

Having read this book, a management team should be better equipped to address the areas of "position" and "knowledge." This book should help a management team define a services strategy. Even without the VP of professional services in place, a senior management team can review the business objectives of its services strategy and begin defining what the company wants out of the professional services function. What charter makes sense? What revenue and margin objectives are required to make the business attractive enough to incubate?

By reviewing the nine parameters of a services strategy, the management team can refine its view of the knowledge required to lead professional services.

Clearly defining the legs of "position" and "knowledge" gives the chair increased stability. The legs of "skills" and "fit" will take more work, more discussion. How they are defined will vary from company to company. The important point is that the management team should take time to discuss and define these legs. A two-legged chair is still not functional.

At this point, you may be sighing.

> *This approach is unrealistic!*
>
> *You expect us to define the position, understand the knowledge and skills required to have the position, and debate what type of candidate would best fit into our company?*
>
> *Who has time for all this discussion?*
>
> *Isn't that why we are hiring someone? To figure out all of this professional services stuff!*

If that's you, you're right! Defining these four legs will take some effort. However, think of the alternative. *Not* defining these legs creates a shaky interview process. A shaky interview process increases the probability of filling the position with the wrong candidate. And that scenario, as the next section reviews, is a costly one.

COSTLY MISTAKES

As Lee Iacocca writes, "The most important thing any manager can do is hire the right new people.[1]

---

1. Lee Iacocca with William Novak, *Iacocca: An Autobiography* (New York: Bantam Books, Inc., 1984).

Few executives would argue with Mr. Iacocca on this point. Hiring the wrong leader for a function costs the company time and money. A failed executive can cost over $700,000 to remove and replace.[2] This number does not even include damage the executive may have caused to customer relationships, employee morale, and brand equity.

The leader hired to build the services function represents even greater potential exposure to a product company. This executive will definitely be communicating with the largest and most important customers of the company. This leader will be responsible for crafting and delivering some of the most complex business solutions the company will ever propose to customers. And finally, if this leader fails, the confidence of employees can be shaken. The sales forces of most product companies are skeptical of new service initiatives—they have been burned before. If the services executive goes down in flames, the level of doubt and mistrust increases. I am aware of one multibillion dollar product company that is on its fourth attempt to launch a new professional services organization. You can imagine the cultural crater the current VP of services is starting from.

EFFECTIVE EVALUATION

I hope, at this point, that we can agree that an effective interviewing process is critical to finding the right leader for professional services. I contend that finding that right leader requires that a hiring company spend time defining the areas of position, knowledge, skills, and fit. Now, how does a management team actually conduct effective interviews? For that answer, I turn to another industry expert.

Jim Kennedy is an author and the president of Management Team Consultants. His firm teaches organizations how to dramatically improve the interviewing process. In his book *Getting Behind the Resume,*[3] he stresses that interviewers must understand six key areas about the position they are hiring for:

1. *Essential functions:* What are the basic responsibilities and day-to-day requirements of the position?
2. *Organizational culture:* What type of services organization is the candidate walking into? Is it a start-up situation, requiring the candidate

2. Jenny C. McCune, "Sorry, Wrong Executive," *Management Review,* October 1999.
3. Jim Kennedy, *Getting Behind the Resume* (Paramus, NJ: Prentice Hall, 1987).

to build a new management team from the ground up? Or is this a well-established team that simply needs tuning? Are business requirements dynamic and changing daily or relatively static and stable? What values, beliefs, and attitudes exist in the organization?

3. *Required education:* What educational level is required for the candidate to be considered?

4. *Required experience:* What previous experience is required of the candidate?

5. *Required knowledge:* What specific knowledge is required for the candidate to be effective and successful in the role? For example, does the candidate need to understand sales forecasting techniques? Market segmentation analysis?

6. *Predictive performance factors:* What general competencies must the candidate have to succeed? Competencies can be segmented into three distinct categories: intellectual, interpersonal, and motivational.

These six areas represent the same four themes articulated earlier: position (essential functions), knowledge (education, experience, knowledge), skills (predictive performance factors), and fit (organizational culture).

Mr. Kennedy refers to all of this data as a "job profile." In documenting these six areas for the position, the interviewer has assembled a complete job profile. With a mature job profile, a meaningful interview can be conducted. Kennedy goes on to provide techniques to draw out relevant data from candidates and assess that data for evaluation against the job profile.[4]

I want to use this approach to construct a baseline job profile for the vice president of professional services. My job profile focuses on documenting the hard skill areas of education, experience, and required knowledge. By discussing and documenting information for all six of Jim's categories, I believe a hiring company can dramatically improve its ability to evaluate candidates that want to lead their professional services organization.

REQUIRED KNOWLEDGE FOR THE VP OF PS

Throughout the text, I have argued that the success of a services organization at a product company is dependent on clearing three distinct hurdles:

---

4. *For more information on Mr. Kennedy's interviewing tactics, visit www.interviewedge.com.*

- *Strategy:* Creating a *viable* services strategy, which is aligned with overall corporate objectives, has executive support, and is achievable
- *Structure:* Updating the product-centric infrastructure of the company to support a services business
- *Culture:* Influencing the product-centric culture to support the success of services

In the area of strategy, this book identifies nine key variables that an executive must manage in order to create a viable services strategy. I introduced Table D.1 in Chapter 3.

In the area of *structure*, there are at least nine variables a services leader must manage. The variables itemized in Table D.2 were first introduced in *Building Professional Services: The Sirens' Song.*

TABLE D.1 Nine Variables of a Services Strategy

	Strategy Variables	Comments
Business Objectives	1. Charter	What is the new services organization being chartered to achieve? Enable product sales? Acquire new revenue streams?
	2. Financial Business Model	What is the target business model for this unit? What are the gross margin targets? Target operating profits?
	3. Financial Objectives	What are the revenue, profitability, and growth targets for the function?
Market Objectives	4. Target Markets	What markets will services target? Install base? New vertical industries?
	5. Service Offerings (pricing, positioning)	What services will be offered? Education, managed, professional, outsourced?
	6. Target Channels	What channels will be used to sell the new service offerings? Direct sales force? VARs? Distributors? Telesales?
Competencies	7. Core Competencies	What competencies will the services organization build internally?
	8. Partnered Competencies	What required competencies will the services organization use partners to deliver?
	9. Scalability Model	How will services scale both core and partnered competencies?

TABLE D.2 Nine Variables of Services Structure

	Structure Variables	Comments
Organizational Design	1. Key Functions	What are the key functions of the services organization?
	2. Organizational Structure	What functions will be centralized?
	3. Organizational Interfaces	What are the key internal and external interfaces?
Roles & Responsibilities	4. Roles & Responsibilities	What are the key roles required to support a services organization? What are the responsibilities of each role?
Processes	5. Sales Processes	What are key processes required to manage the process of selling professional services?
	6. Delivery Processes	What are key processes required to manage the delivery of service offerings?
	7. IP Management Processes	What processes are used to capture and leverage the intellectual assets of the services organization?
Metrics	8. Lagging Metrics	What metrics will be used to assess the current health of the services business?
	9. Leading Metrics	Beyond revenue and margins, what metrics will be used to determine if the health of the business is improving?

Finally, in the area of culture, the candidate must understand what aspects of a product-centric culture are the most difficult to overcome for a services organization. Table D.3 highlights four areas of conflict that can be severe although other stress points do exist.

Assembling the areas of strategy, structure, and culture, we can create a powerful list of required knowledge for the job profile to help evaluate potential candidates. When assessing an area of knowledge, a simple four-point scale is used:

0: Candidate has displayed *no knowledge* of the topic

1: Candidate has demonstrated *limited knowledge* of the topic

2: Candidate has a *thorough knowledge* of the topic

3: Candidate could be considered an *expert* on the topic

A sample job profile follows. Obviously, not all areas listed on the profile can be probed in one interview. An effective tactic is to have multiple interviewers

TABLE D.3 Four Variables of Modifying a Product-Centric Culture

	Culture Variables	Comments
Role Conflicts	1. Pre-sales and Delivery consultants	How will the company consultants work as part of the sales process, and what is billable?
	2. Service and Product Sales Representatives	How will account strategies be coordinated by product reps and service reps?
Strategy Conflicts	3. Channel Mix	How will the channel strategy for the company be modified to support both product and service sales?
	4. Strategic Partners	When strategic partners are selected, how will the benefits to both product sales and service sales be evaluated?

divide topics among themselves. This way, each interviewer can probe and validate specific competencies. I hope that having a job profile that captures key concepts a qualified candidate should understand will shield product companies from the costly missteps that often occur when they attempt to hire that next VP of Professional Services.

Job Profile: Vice President, Professional Services

Area	Details	Evaluation Objectives
Essential Functions	This is a senior management position, reporting directly to the CEO. Responsible for the global Professional Services organization. Overriding responsibility is to create a profitable Professional Services organization that is focused on servicing the company's product install base. Additional objectives include: • Improving customer satisfaction • Improving service margins Duties include: • Defining a profitable services portfolio • Working directly with large named customer accounts to assess needs and propose services • Working with channel partners to resell service offerings • Managing the Professional Services P&L	To make sure the candidate understands the scope, objectives, and responsibilities of the position.

Job Profile: Vice President, Professional Services (continued)

Area	Details	Evaluation Objectives
Organizational Culture	The company currently has an established support services organization with revenues exceeding $30M (8% of total company revenues) and over 200 employees worldwide. This is the company's second attempt to establish a profitable Professional Services organization. The first attempt occurred two years ago. Currently, there are 30 employees in PS, delivering time- and materials-based consulting services. The services organization is viewed as a key source of future revenue growth. However, the direct sales force has been resistant to selling any services beyond warranty contracts.	To make sure the candidate understands the current maturity level of the services organization and the internal environment within which it operates.

Job Profile: Vice President, Professional Services—Specifics

Area	Details	Evaluation Objectives
Education and Requirements	• Undergraduate degree required • MBA preferred	To assess if the candidate has the educational background required to succeed in the position.
Experience Requirements	• 10+ years of consulting and consulting management experience • 8+ years of P&L management experience • Prior experience in services sales, services delivery, and services management • Demonstrated ability to grow a business unit	To assess if the candidate has the previous experience required to succeed in the position.
Predictive Performance Factors	• Intellectual	Does the candidate possess the required intellectual attributes to succeed in the position? Example intellectual attributes include: decision-making style, analytical ability, and use of intuition.

Job Profile: Vice President, Professional Services—Specifics (continued)

Area	Details	Evaluation Objectives
	• Interpersonal	Does the candidate possess the required interpersonal skills to succeed in the position? Example interpersonal skills include: a team player, outgoing, and persuasive.
	• Motivational	Is the candidate motivated by factors that can potentially be satisfied by the position? Example motivational factors include: goals, interests, commitments, and values.

Strategy Knowledge

Area	Topic	Rating	Comments
Business Objectives	Services Charter	0 1 2 3	
	Services Business Model	0 1 2 3	
	Financial Objectives	0 1 2 3	
Market Objectives	Target Markets	0 1 2 3	
	Service Offerings	0 1 2 3	
	Channel Strategies	0 1 2 3	
Competencies	Core Competencies	0 1 2 3	
	Partnered Competencies	0 1 2 3	

Structure Knowledge (continued)

Topic	Rating	Comments
PS Functions	0 1 2 3	
Organizational Structure	0 1 2 3	
Organizational Interfaces	0 1 2 3	
Roles & Responsibilities	0 1 2 3	
Sales Processes	0 1 2 3	
Delivery Processes	0 1 2 3	
IP Management Processes	0 1 2 3	
Leading Metrics	0 1 2 3	
Lagging Metrics	0 1 2 3	

Cultural Knowledge

Topic	Rating	Comments
Pre-sales vs. Billable Activities	0 1 2 3	
Account Management	0 1 2 3	
Setting Channel Mix	0 1 2 3	
Signing Strategic Partners	0 1 2 3	

SUMMARY

When I showed this job profile to Jim Kennedy, he had two concerns: too long, too detailed. How would one interviewer be able to evaluate a candidate on all these topics? I want to acknowledge this concern. The job profile should not be taken verbatim into the interviewing process. Consider the profile a template that your company should prune to focus on the areas you are most concerned with.

In reality, building professional services at a product company is a relatively new phenomenon. This means that there are very few senior managers that have had direct experience leading the function. There are still fewer that have been successful at it. The dearth of qualified candidates will require product companies to consider leaders that have never been in the role before. The two most likely candidate profiles will be support-service executives and independent consulting partners. Support-service executives are individuals who have successfully led large support-service organizations, but they will not have responsibility for building a professional services portfolio. These candidates understand the product company environment, but they will not have an understanding of the strategy and structure required to build professional services. Partners from independent consulting firms should have a good handle on the structure required to support professional services, but they will have to learn how to align a service strategy with a product strategy. And they will need to adapt to the harsh environment of a product-centric culture.

Knowing that the candidate pool is thin, product executives can use a well-thought-out, documented job profile to help identify the most qualified candidate. A well-documented job profile provides the information critical for an effective interview:

- What do we want this leader to achieve?
- What does this leader need to know and understand to be effective?
- What personal skills are required to succeed in this role?
- What about our company environment could influence success?

When these questions are discussed *before* the interviewing begins, candidates can truly be qualified. If the answers to these questions are a mystery, you will be asking your job candidates to have a seat in a creaky old chair—a chair that may well collapse before the interview is over. How embarrassing.

Bibliography

Barlow, Janelle, *Branded Customer Service: The New Competitive Advantage* (San Francisco, CA: Berrett-Koehler, 2004).

Christensen, Clayton, *The Innovator's Dilemma* (New York, NY: Harper Business, 1997).

Friedman, Lawrence G., and Furey, Timothy R., *The Channel Advantage* (Woburn, MA: Butterworth Heinemann, 1999).

Gerstner, Louis V. Jr., *Who Says Elephants Can't Dance?* (New York, NY: HarperCollins, 2002).

Kaplan, Robert S., and Norton, David P., *The Balanced Scorecard* (Cambridge, MA: Harvard Business School Press, 1996).

Kotler, Philip, *Marketing Professional Services* (Upper Saddle River, NJ: Prentice Hall Press, 2002).

Lovelock, Christopher, *Product Plus* (New York, NY: McGraw-Hill, 1994).

Maister, David H., *Managing the Professional Services Firm* (New York, NY: Simon and Schuster, 1993).

Mintzberg, Henry, *The Rise and Fall of Strategic Planning* (New York, NY: The Free Press, 1994).

Moore, Geoffrey, *Living on the Fault Line* (New York, NY: HarperCollins, 2002).

Moser, Mike, *United We Brand* (Boston, MA: Harvard Business School Press, 2003).

Porter, Michael E., *Competitive Strategy* (New York, NY: The Free Press, 1980).

Index